Praise for Surviving the Grief Cave

"An important and beautifully written book of hope. I felt like I walked alongside Bob on his journey through the depths of grief to a life renewed and love reclaimed."

— Rick Moss, PhD, Author of *Drops of Wisdom: Guidance on the Path of Awakening*

"The impact of this book will stay with you for a long while. McGuire writes with great vulnerability about the dark edge of loss, and then describes the heart's great challenge to open and expand past the pain. Through the telling of his story he shows us what it means to begin again. A beautiful teaching."

— Paula D'Arcy, author of *Waking up to This Day* and *Winter of the Heart*

"Bob McGuire has written a compelling, inspiring and emotionally honest story. He shows us how the grieving process can break our hearts open and expand our capacity to be more loving."

— Fred Jealous, Founder, Breakthrough Men's Community

"The power of McGuire's pen is employed in such a way that readers will emerge hopeful—and, perhaps, less grief-stricken than they were when they began this book."

— D. Donovan, Senior Reviewer, Midwest Book Review

SURVIVING
THE GRIEF CAVE

ONE MAN'S JOURNEY THROUGH DEEP SORROW
TO NEW LIFE, LOVE AND FAITH

BOB MCGUIRE

RLM
Publishing

Surviving the Grief Cave
One Man's Journey Through Deep Sorrow to New Life, Love and Faith

© 2025 Robert McGuire
RLM Publishing
RLMPublishing.com

Publisher's Cataloging-in-Publication

Names:	McGuire, Bob, 1956-
Title:	Surviving the grief cave : one man's journey through deep sorrow to new life, love and faith / Bob McGuire.
Description:	Palos Verdes Peninsula, CA : RLM Publishing, [2025]
Identifiers:	ISBN: 979-8988944102 (paperback) | 979-8988944119 (hardcover) | 979-8988944126 (eBook) | LCCN: 2024917827
Subjects:	LCSH: McGuire, Bob, 1956- | Spouses of cancer patients--Biography. | Widowers--Personal narratives. | Grief--Religious aspects--Christianity. | Bereavement--Psychological aspects. | Loss (Psychology)--Religious aspects--Christianity. | Spouses--Death--Psychological aspects. | Camino de Santiago de Compostela. | Christian pilgrims and pilgrimages--Spain--Santiago de Compostela. | Drug addicts--Family relationships. | Drug addiction--Treatment. | Healing. | Mental healing. | Resilience (Personality trait) | Consolation. | Peace of mind. | Christian life. | LCGFT: Autobiographies. | Self-help publications. | BISAC: FAMILY & RELATIONSHIPS / Death, Grief, Bereavement. | BODY, MIND & SPIRIT / Healing / Prayer & Spiritual. | RELIGION / Christian Living / Death, Grief, Bereavement.
Classification:	LCC: BF575.G7 M34 2025 | DDC: 155.9/37--dc23

Editing: Jeff Braucher
Cover & Book Design: Diane Rigoli

DISCLAIMER:
Surviving the Grief Cave depicts actual events in my life as truthfully as my memory and journal entries allow. I have likewise to the best of my ability tried to re-create conversations and dialog. In some cases, to respect privacy and anonymity, I have changed the names of individuals. This book reflects my unique life experience and is not intended as counseling, advice, or any recommended course of action for the reader.

DEDICATION

This book is dedicated to all those who have been crushed by the loss of a loved one and are struggling to find their way forward. To those who feel lost, alone, afraid, and trapped inside a dark cave of grief and are trying to find their way through. I know. I've been there.

To those loving souls who helped me navigate the cave and work my way into a new life with my Higher Power, who I refer to as God, Jesus, and Holy Spirit. To my dear friends, family, and fellow pilgrims who gave me the encouragement and support I needed to keep going.

To Lauren, who opened her heart and made new love possible.

To my parents, who gave me a solid foundation for life. Especially my dad who encouraged me to write from the heart, but not to "wear it on my sleeve."

And to those who left this earth too soon, especially Annie, Stephen, and Kevin.

My desire for this book is to give the reader a foothold—a sense of hope that a new life is possible, whatever the circumstances. Everyone's journey is unique and personal, but the grief cave doesn't have to last forever. It can, in fact, become the very pathway to a new life.

In gratitude, grace, and love.

CONTENTS

PART 1: THE CAVE 1

1. Thursday, April 18, 2013 3
2. The Longest Night 13
3. Brain Tumor 19
4. Stephen Robert 23
5. Surgery and Diagnosis 31
6. Gain and Loss 41
7. The Unthinkable 49
8. Lourdes 59
9. This Can't Be 65
10. Free Fall 73
11. My Upside-Down World 79
12. The Grief Cave 87
13. A Season? 99
14. A Glimpse Outside 105
15. Three Sinkholes 113
16. The Dating World 123
17. The Call to the Camino 135

PART 2: THE CAMINO 141

18. Clear the Runway 143
19. Arrival 153
20. The Road Begins 159
21. Back to School 171
22. Shut Down 183
23. Roller Coaster 193
24. The Real Destination 205

25. No More Good-byes 213

26. The Final Approach 219

27. The One Who Walks Alongside 227

28. The New Shore. 233

29. The End and The Beginning. 241

PART 3: MY NEW LIFE 247

30. Surprise 249

31. Who Are You?. 257

32. Who Am I? 267

33. The Hidden Revealed 277

34. Jump! 285

35. Transitions 289

36. New Life 301

37. The Circle 307

Notes from the Author 313

Resources. 315

About the Author. 317

PART 1

THE CAVE

"*I don't want to know what time it is. I don't want to know what day it is or where I am. None of that matters.*"

—Jon Krakauer, Into the Wild

CHAPTER 1

THURSDAY, APRIL 18, 2013

I drove west along Highway 68, the scenic Monterey-Salinas stretch of road, homeward bound after a typical workday. The rush hour traffic had mostly passed, so the road had a calm, open feel. I listened to the latest Bay Area sports scores and updates on my car radio as I rolled past green hills and tree-lined curves.

Relaxed and content, my mind wandered through the events of my workday and started to plan my Friday and the restful weekend ahead. But I also wondered why my wife, Annie, had not answered the phone when I had called a few moments earlier. Odd. She could be out for a walk around our neighborhood, but even so, she always kept her cell phone with her.

We had talked two hours earlier, about 5:30 p.m., just as she arrived home from her postwork visit to the health club. I told her of my plans to meet up with some work colleagues and would be home afterward. After thirty-two years of marriage, I still looked forward to our end-of-day time together.

I turned onto our street and past the rows of new single-family homes, all lined up next to each other. The new housing development, with approximately four hundred homes located near the Pacific Coast Highway in the city of Seaside, had been completed ten years earlier, and we were fortunate enough to buy one of the smaller single-story models.

As I pulled up to our house and into our driveway, I noticed an orange glow from the early evening sunlight on the white roll-up garage door. I pushed the button clipped to the visor and waited as the large door opened. The orange glow spilled into the garage like a guiding light as I inched my car inside and parked.

I gathered my empty lunch bag and jacket from the passenger seat and climbed out of the car. The garage door clanked and rattled closed as it slowly eclipsed the fading sunlight into total darkness. I watched as it slammed shut against the concrete garage floor, then turned and entered the house through the laundry room door.

"Hello! Is anyone home?" I asked, half joking as I pushed away my rising anxiety.

Instead of her typical, playful response, no reply came. No response at all.

The muscles in my neck stiffened. My breath shortened. My heart pumped faster.

Something was wrong. Normally, the humming sounds of our washer-dryer would be churning away on Thursday, a weekly ritual we created many years earlier to minimize weekend chores to maximize fun and relaxation. But they sat silent and still. A scattering of dirty clothes lay on the laundry room floor. Every muscle in my body tightened and my stomach twisted. My breath stayed in my mouth. My mind shifted to that place when a sudden noise startles me in the middle of the night.

As I stepped over the dirty clothes and tried to dismiss my internal alarm bells, I announced another greeting with as much cheer as I could muster. "Hello! I'm home!"

The only sound came from the living room TV, tuned to the local news. I stepped further into the house—and then I saw her. Annie stood stiff as a statue at the kitchen counter, facing across the room toward the TV, with her face in a trancelike state. A trapdoor instantly snapped open under my feet and dropped me into the unknown.

My heart stopped. My breathing stopped. My mind froze.

Her face—her food-smeared face—looked blank and lost. Void. Vacant. Dazed. She stood next to the sink, staring blankly into nothingness. In a violent, surreal instant, every alarm inside me erupted.

I shifted into crisis-response mode. I rushed to her side and held her tightly against me, desperate to find out what happened. Had she fallen? Hit her head? Knocked into a semiconscious state somehow?

"Annie! What happened?" I shouted. "What's wrong? What happened!? Annie! Are you OK?" She didn't turn her head to look at me. She didn't acknowledge me at all. She didn't respond to me, like I wasn't even there. She just stared straight ahead, in another world.

She slowly nodded her head back and forth with an empty stare and murmured, "OK...OK..." My heart pounded in panic as my mind raced to figure out what to do. My stomach twisted. I could barely breathe.

Through my narrowed vision, I saw her hands move in slow motion on the countertop. I saw our multivitamins, knocked out of their jars, randomly scattered over the glossy white tile along with smeared food from her spilled dinner. She moved the pills aimlessly, as if she were trying to arrange them somehow.

"Annie, can you move? Can you walk? Do you hear me? Annie!"

She stayed stuck in a motionless stupor. "OK...OK..."

My body moved out of gut instinct. I grabbed her around the waist and started to pull her away from the kitchen counter. She resisted, so I pulled harder. I nearly vomited. I had to get her to the hospital.

I shifted into authority mode. "Annie! Listen to me! We have to move, now! We have to get to the hospital. We have to go. Now!"

"OK...OK..." she muttered.

Every step was a struggle. Her 5 feet, 6 inches, and 130 pounds felt like my 6 feet, 200 pounds. Her stiff body resisted every move. I wrapped my arms around her and pushed, prodded, and pulled her toward the front door of the house.

"Good, Annie. You're doing good. Let's get to your car in the driveway and get to the hospital. Let's go. Let's go. Keep moving. Next step. Come on. Good."

My heart pounded and my mind spun out of control as we inched our way toward the front door. Fifty feet away, then forty feet, then thirty, then twenty. When we got ten feet away, Annie pulled to the right, toward the front bathroom.

"Annie, no. We don't have time. We need to leave. We have to get to the car." She pulled harder toward the bathroom. I relented. "OK, but hurry!"

I guided her into the bathroom and onto the toilet seat, and then stepped back to give her space. My body vibrated from head to toe as I waited for her to finish, and then helped her up.

"Annie, we have to get to the car. Don't worry about the mess. We have to go now!"

We stopped at the bathroom sink to clean off her hands. I held her body in my left arm, and I turned on the water with my right hand. The sound of water flowing into the sink gave a contradictory sense of normalcy.

For a brief second I looked into the mirror directly in front of us. I saw both of our faces, side by side. Annie's clear, sparkling, and expressive brown eyes had been replaced with blank, expressionless eyes that stared beyond the mirror into nothingness. Her full-of-life personality —the spark that made her who she was—had completely vanished. She looked lost and empty. Her clean, animated, and smiling face had been replaced with a deadpan mask with dried red pasta sauce smeared across it. White residue from a half-chewed vitamin pill stained her lips. Her neat and clean, shoulder-length auburn hair sat ruffled on top of her head, with bits of food stuck to it. Everything about her had been stripped away.

My normally open, casual expression and clear blue eyes were squished together in a wrinkled contortion of total fear and raw panic. I had to force myself to speak to her in a raised tone of voice, which felt so out of character. But I had to push her.

"Annie! We have to go—now!"

We finally made our way out the front door, onto the driveway, and to the passenger side door of her blue SUV. I wrestled her into the passenger seat, managed to strap her in, and began the panicked, seven-mile trip to the hospital.

I narrated the whole way there, just to try to calm myself down: "It's going to be OK, Annie. It's going to be OK. The traffic isn't bad. We're making good time. We're halfway there. Two more exits. It's going to be OK. Don't worry, Annie. OK, our exit is right there. I'm going to turn right. Almost there. Hang in there. OK, there's the sign for the Emergency Room. OK, almost there. We made it! We're here."

I pulled the car up at the ER curb and ran around the car to open the passenger-side door. I unbuckled her seatbelt and helped her out of the car. I put my arm around her and pulled her one step at a time into the

ER. We stepped through the doors, and I blurted out words to a nurse at the reception counter. "My wife. She can't talk…she doesn't recognize me, and…"

My voice cracked and tears burned my eyes. I tried to articulate words, but they wouldn't come out. Fear, sorrow, and dread strangled my throat shut. I could barely breathe. My knees buckled. At the same time, a sense of relief washed over me that we got to the ER safely.

The nurse immediately signaled a code to the emergency medical staff, who instantly surrounded us. They pulled Annie from my grasp and lifted her onto a gurney. I watched through tears as nurses attended to her and wheeled the gurney into an exam area. I followed right behind as I tried to hold myself together.

I stood back, breathless and shell-shocked in the corner of the exam room, behind the bent-over backs of three or four doctors and nurses who connected her with tubes and wires as they shouted questions and commands at Annie's unresponsive body. Nausea and dizziness filled me. I glanced up at the round clock on the wall. 8:15 p.m.

The medical team started peppering me with questions: "Is she allergic to any medications? Does she have a history of heart trouble in her family? Family stroke history? Is she on any medication? Is she diabetic? Does she have high blood pressure or other health problems? Who is her primary doctor?"

My "no" answers, followed by "Dr. Campbell," only emphasized the sheer insanity of her condition. She was a 100 percent healthy woman in great physical shape.

I blurted out every piece of information I could in short bursts: "She had been at the health club earlier this evening…she was on her way home when I spoke to her via phone…it was about 5:15 p.m…I found her this way about 7:45…she has no medical problems or issues…she has regular medical checkups…she does not have high blood pressure…she is not diabetic…she is not on medication…her family medical history is good…"

Despite her excellent health history, every medical indicator now showed abnormal: Her heartbeat raced with arrhythmia, her blood pressure and blood sugar skyrocketed. She had lost control of her bowels. Each time I caught a glimpse of her between the tubes and doctor's backs, and saw her still catatonic and unresponsive, a surge of tears would rise up and choke my ability to breathe.

Every test they gave Annie ended in a sickening failure:

"Can you tell us your name?" No response.

"What day is today?" Nothing.

"Can you show your teeth in a smile?" Nothing.

"Do you know where you are?" Nothing.

The on-call neurologist entered the exam room and started some of his own testing procedures. Each test ended without any response. When he ordered a CAT scan, I watched as two nurses wheeled Annie's gurney out of the exam room. I sat there alone, in shock, and waited. Every muscle in my body trembled. My logical brain screamed in confusion and despair as it tried in vain to make any sense out of what was happening.

A short time later they wheeled Annie back into the exam room. Nothing had changed with her condition. Slowly, the swarm of medical staff subsided. When the last nurse exited the room and closed the sliding door, an abrupt silence filled the little room. The two of us were alone. I sat alongside her. I held her limp hand in my restless hands. It was warm, but she didn't squeeze back. I couldn't talk. She just lay there, motionless, eyes open but staring blankly into nothing.

A few minutes later, the neurologist reentered the exam room with the results of the CT scan. A serious and studious man, well over six feet tall, thin, dark haired, and around forty years old. He stood and explained the test results in a calm, direct, and deliberate manner. The scan showed a damaged area on the left frontal side of the brain known as the temporal lobe.

"The damage," he explained, "appears to be the result of a stroke caused by interrupted blood flow to the brain. A blood clot may be present, but I'm not 100 percent sure. I need to run more tests, including an MRI scan so I can get a better look. But the initial signs indicate a stroke has occurred."

A stroke? Annie? At fifty-seven years old? The pressure on my head and stomach ratcheted up and squeezed me into an ever-tighter ball of nerves and anxiety.

He went on to describe a medication called TPA, used on stroke victims in the first few hours of the stroke event. The medication breaks up blood clots and restores normal blood flow. "We can administer

TPA, but it can also cause excessive bleeding and could have fatal results if administered outside the optimum time period." He sat down
and looked at me closely, face to face. "I think we are too late to administer the drug," he said. "At this point it presents more risk than benefit.
The damage to the brain appears to have already happened. It's possible
the drug could help, but I don't think it's worth the risk. But a decision
is needed. Now."

I strained to hear and grasp the meaning of the doctor's words.
Fatal results? Excessive bleeding? Stroke? Brain damage? Already done?

Guilt tortured me as the seconds ticked away. *Why wasn't I home
when this happened? I could have got her to the hospital on time if I had
come home earlier. If I had just come home right after work instead of getting together with some work buddies, we wouldn't be in this position!*

My mind could not think, trapped in a fog of confusion, guilt, and
disbelief. I asked him to repeat the information multiple times. Each
gentle explanation he gave drove the devastating words down from my
head into my heart like a sledgehammer.

Finally, in exhausted desperation, I asked, "What would you do if
you were in my shoes?"

He looked at me with kind eyes and calmly responded, "At this
point in time I wouldn't advise it. If it was two or three hours earlier,
yes. But now, no."

"Then no," I said.

He nodded, put his hand on my shoulder, and said, "For now, tonight, there is nothing else we can do except to make her as comfortable
as possible. Her vital signs have stabilized, so we'll check her into the
hospital, keep her under close observation, and start the next set of tests
tomorrow morning."

After those words, everything shifted gears to a crawl. The exam room
suddenly turned quiet and empty, except for the rhythmic *beep…beep…
beep…* of a monitoring device next to Annie, who just lay there, breathing but unconscious.

A lone nurse entered the room, checked on Annie, and asked me:
"Would you like me to bag up her clothes to take home?" I looked at the
pile of soiled clothes that had been cut off her with scissors and shook
my head.

My mind fought off an internal interrogation:

Where are we? — The Emergency Room.

What? Are you kidding me? — No.

Why? What the hell happened? — Initial test shows Annie had a stroke.

What? What the hell does that mean? — I don't know.

Will Annie be OK? She'll be OK, right? — I don't know.

What do you mean you don't know? — I don't know.

What the hell is really happening here? — I DON'T KNOW!

A nurse started the process to check Annie into a hospital room. She asked me questions and gave me paperwork to sign. I couldn't read the words on the form but signed it anyway.

Another doctor came in the exam room and gave me a general update and asked if I had any questions. I didn't know what to say or think. I just looked at Annie. The doctor put his hand on my shoulder, looked at me, and said, "I know this is difficult. Try to hang in there. We are doing everything we can for your wife. She is in good hands now."

I looked at her again. *Annie, where are you?*

I walked alongside the nurse who pushed the portable hospital bed into an elevator, which opened into a quiet hospital ward. Soft light illuminated the entire floor, which created a strange calmness. I took a seat in a small waiting area outside the room assigned to Annie as the nurse got her settled and connected to the monitoring equipment. All patients in other rooms were asleep as nurses attended to their duties quietly. I sat in stunned silence.

A charge nurse approached and gently greeted me. She asked me if Annie had an Advance Healthcare Directive. I thought for a few seconds and then stopped in shock: We had signed them with an attorney just days earlier and didn't even have our own copies yet.

After the nurse got Annie settled, I stepped into her room. Annie was there, but only physically. She lay in the same prone position, eyes closed. She appeared to be in a coma, deep in the grip of the violent force that crushed her. I pulled the chair next to the bed and just sat there. I felt numb. Exhausted. Adrift. Nauseous. Afraid. Hopeless.

The nurse came back in the room. "You can stay here for the night if you want to. I can get you a pillow and blanket. But if you live close by, it might be best to try to get some sleep at home in your own bed. But it's up to you. Your wife is in good hands."

After a while I decided to go home and try to regroup. Before I left, I looked deeply into Annie's face, which somehow conveyed a look of peaceful serenity despite the torture happening inside her. I laid my hands on her head and prayed: "Dear God, help. Help Annie. Help me. Help us. Whatever this is, heal Annie. Heal her, Lord. Please, God, heal Annie."

I kissed her on the forehead and whispered I would be back in a few hours, clinging to a dim hope she somehow heard me. I walked in a lost fog out of the room and down the long, empty, softly lit hallways toward the front of the hospital. The sound of the central water fountain guided my unsure steps. When I exited the hospital doors, the desolate and cold outside air jolted me. I felt a sudden sense of being alone. I had arrived hours earlier with Annie but now left without her. I made my way to the car and climbed inside. I took deep breaths, trying to calm myself.

I had to call someone. I had to talk to someone. But who? After 1:00 a.m.? Our twenty-eight-year-old son, Stephen, who lived in southern California? No. What about Bill, Annie's older brother? I fumbled through the contacts on my phone and found his. I pressed the call button. He answered.

"Hey…Bob…" he mumbled, half asleep. "What's up? Is everything OK?"

I tried to tell him what happened, but barely got any words out between sobs. He listened and then said, "Hang in there, Bob. It's going to be OK. Annie is one tough cookie—believe me, I know. And she's going to be OK." His words gave me the tiny sliver of strength I needed to drive home and face what awaited me there.

I didn't know it then, but we had just been catapulted into our three-year battle with brain cancer.

*"Even the darkest night will end
and the sun will rise."*

—Victor Hugo

CHAPTER 2

THE LONGEST NIGHT

In a state of shock and exhaustion, I slowly maneuvered the car through the deserted hospital parking lot and out onto the dark and empty Highway 1. The world around me had suddenly turned strange and forbidden. No cars, no people, no life. With a knotted stomach, pounding head, blurred vision, and racked body, I pulled into our driveway around 1:30 a.m. to face the scene where this nightmare started.

Less than six hours earlier I had pulled into the same driveway, inside a life that had been blown to pieces. That life disappeared in an instant and would never be the same. Besides Annie's brother, no one knew anything. Our family, neighbors, and friends all slept peacefully unaware, within their normal lives.

The moment I opened the front door and stepped inside, I felt a strange and ominous energy. The only sound came from the TV, still on in the lifeless house. Instead of a familiar and welcoming friend, the house now felt like a stranger who held a hidden secret. It knew something I didn't know. It saw something I didn't see. It had been the last one to see Annie in her normal life. It witnessed what happened. But stayed silent. All I could do was look for clues.

The living room looked the same and undisturbed. The family pictures sat straight and normal on the walls and coffee table. The colorful crucifix with an image of Jesus with outstretched arms occupied its usual place on the wall. The scenic vineyard landscape print sat centered over the wooden fireplace mantel, along with tiles from California missions. The light brown carpet looked clean as usual. I picked up the remote control from the tan sectional couch and clicked off the TV. Deafening silence now surrounded me. I saw the three lined-up wooden barstools undisturbed along the bar-height, white tiled kitchen countertop.

I moved to the kitchen where I saw her six hours earlier. I took a deep breath and stepped gingerly onto the dark brown, wood-paneled floor, as if it were thin ice. What the hell happened here?

I saw an empty Lean Cuisine frozen food box on the kitchen counter, along with the thin plastic covering that must have been pulled off after she removed it from the microwave. The vitamins and low-dose aspirin lay scattered across the kitchen counter, where Annie had poured them out for some unknown reason.

But where was the actual food and plastic dinner tray? I looked in the garbage bin under the sink. Not there. In the microwave oven? No. In the refrigerator? In the dishwasher? In the wooden kitchen cabinets somewhere? Not there. I walked over to double-check the living room, but still no plastic dinner tray.

I walked back to the kitchen and looked closer at the brown, wooden dining room table—one of our first purchases as a married couple in 1980, from a furniture store in Santa Rosa, California. It looked normal. All four chairs sat in their positions around the table, each with a padded cushion. My eye caught something underneath the table, through the chair legs. I pulled out a chair from the table, got down on my hands and knees, and saw it.

There sat the cooked dinner, spilled out across the floor, along with Annie's wire-rim reading glasses, smeared with food. I saw a dinner fork on the floor next to some scattered dinner napkins. Then I noticed a red blood stain, which must have been left behind from her violent fall to the floor.

As I absorbed the scene of suffering where Annie had been struck down, I broke down on the wooden kitchen floor, unable to hold back any remaining sorrow and anguish. Tears of despair and anger flowed out. My lungs let out a primal scream. I pounded the floor until my fists ached.

Eventually I pulled myself together and took a deep breath. I took photos of the mess with my phone before I worked through it in slow motion, piece by piece, item by item. As I removed each morsel of food, each smear of blood, I relived what must have happened to Annie. My stomach churned as I realized I had fallen into a dark pit of anguish.

Everything hurt—my head, my stomach, my heart, my muscles. My brain pounded itself over and over against a brick wall as it tried to make any sense out of it.

After I cleaned up the kitchen, I turned my attention to the front bathroom. I knew Annie would be horrified to see the mess left behind, so I focused on getting it clean again. When I got to the pedestal sink and looked into the mirror, the memory of the reflected empty look on Annie's face haunted me.

I snapped out of my daze and went to work returning it back to normal. But nothing was normal. Everything had been turned upside down.

I made my way down the hallway, lined with more family photos. They all showed happy faces and happy times that chronicled our thirty-two years together. One of my favorites showed Annie and me with our six-year-old adopted son, Stephen, on a visit to an ocean-themed amusement park. The photo showed us riding a life-size, fiberglass but realistic-looking, black-and-white killer whale as it appeared to jump in midair. The expressions on our faces always made me smile—looks of fake terror and real laughter.

I stepped into the silent bedroom, exhausted but nowhere near sleep. I climbed into bed sometime after 2:30 a.m. and felt the crush of aloneness, like part of me was missing. I reached across the bed and turned Annie's nightstand lamp on low, thinking that would somehow comfort me, but it just made her absence worse. I turned it off. The glow from the candle that burned in the tall clear glass jar on the bathroom sink counter had the same effect—it emphasized the fact she wasn't here. I tossed and turned in torment.

Kidnapped. It was as if Annie had been kidnapped. The suddenness. The shock. The devastation. With zero warning, she had been suddenly snatched and taken away from me.

I thought of her in the hospital bed, only a few miles away. But where was she, really? What happened? *My God, this can't be. She can't be gone. This can't be happening.*

I looked at the glowing red numbers on the digital clock—3:20 a.m.—as my mind spun out of control in a nonstop loop of fears:

Will she ever be able to talk again?
Will she be able to recognize me?
Will she even know who she is?
Will she be able to function normally again?
Why the hell wasn't I here when it happened?
I looked at the clock again. 4:40.
What will our life be like now?
What's going to happen?
Again. 5:00.

At some point the torturous thoughts paused for a few minutes of unconsciousness. I looked at the clock again—5:51. I pulled off the covers and forced my body out of bed. Technically, a new day had arrived, but it was just a continuation of the nightmare that wouldn't end. An empty numbness filled me, along with a dull, throbbing pain. I forced myself into the shower, put on some clothes, and put something in my stomach.

I had to get back to the hospital. Overwhelming dread squeezed the breath out of me. What would Annie's condition be? I felt seasick. Lost. But I had to get back. I had to see her.

"There is peace even in the storm."

—Vincent van Gogh

CHAPTER 3

BRAIN TUMOR

6:30 a.m., Friday morning. Cold and damp air slapped my face as I stepped out of the house in a daze. I could see my neighbors' homes and driveways through the gray, foggy mist. They were probably just waking up, or still sound asleep—completely unaware. On any normal Friday, Annie and I would be getting ready for work and looking forward to the weekend. But not today. Less than twelve hours had passed, but all sense of time had stopped inside this nightmare dimension.

I drove to the hospital in a stunned state of shock at how suddenly life had changed. Cars and trucks surrounded me as the morning rush hour traffic commenced on Highway 1 like it does every day, but everything looked alien and strange. *How can these people go about their day as if everything is the same? As if nothing's happened? Don't they know what happened to us? What's wrong with them?*

I gave zero thought to the radio, my job, the weather, the sports report, or the daily news. Nothing mattered, except to get to the hospital and see Annie—no matter what awaited me.

I arrived and parked in the mostly empty parking lot. The thought of seeing Annie in a near vegetative state was too painful, so I didn't think. I just moved my body mechanically. Entering through the glass front doors at around 6:45, I took a few steps toward the main lobby, smelled coffee from the cafeteria, and saw a few signs of life. I walked down the long, quiet hallways to Annie's room. My heart pounded with nervous anticipation. I wanted so badly to see her, but fear gripped me. I didn't know what to expect and braced myself for the worst.

The patient ward sat silent and still in the early dawn light that filtered through the windows. As I approached the door to her room, I took a deep breath. I gently pushed the door open and could see the foot of Annie's bed. I stepped into the dimly lit room and approached the side of her bed. I saw her lying in the same position she was in when I left her hours earlier. My heart pounded in my throat.

After a few seconds, as if she sensed my presence, she turned her head toward me and made eye contact. The expression on her face was one of simultaneous recognition, relief, pain, and confusion. "Bob, what happened?" she said. "Where am I? What am I doing here? My head is throbbing. I feel so sick. And why are you crying?"

Pure relief and joy erupted inside me as tears flowed out. Every dark emotion inside me—every fear that tormented me—instantly vanished. I could breathe again. Annie was back!

From that very moment, my entire approach was set in stone: Whatever we have to do, we will do. Whatever medical procedures we have to go through, we will go through. We can do this together, whatever it is. Bring on whatever, and we will deal with it together. God is here with us, and Annie is here with me. Nothing else mattered.

I pulled up a chair next to her and explained everything that happened over the last twelve hours. I told her every gory detail, every painful step. She didn't remember a thing. Nothing sounded familiar. It was all a complete blank to her. The last moments she remembered were of her stopping at the mailbox, parking the car in the driveway, and walking into the house.

At 9:30 the neurologist who had examined Annie in the emergency room the night before arrived. A look of shock covered his face when he heard her speak. She stumbled over some words, but she spoke and enunciated clearly. "Hi, Doctor. I don't feel good. I threw up earlier this morning. My head hurts."

"This is so unusual," he said as he examined Annie. "Stoke victims don't recover their speech this fast. We need to look at an MRI, which will give us a clearer picture of what's going on."

Or maybe just maybe, I thought, *God had intervened and healed her already.*

After the MRI a few hours later, the neurologist returned. "The results of the MRI are clear," he said. "You didn't have a stroke. You have a brain tumor in the front-left temporal section of your brain. What happened to you last night was not the effect of a stroke, but a grand mal seizure caused by the tumor. The next thing is to find out what type of tumor it is and take it from there."

A brain tumor. A brain tumor? Impossible.

How? What?

Annie?

What does that mean? This makes zero sense.

How could this be? Her family has no history of cancer.

My first mental image of a brain tumor was something physical, like an object or growth—maybe the size of a grape or a walnut. Somehow, some "thing" got inside her brain, and it can be removed. And that will be the end of it.

When I asked the doctor to explain the exact nature of the tumor, he said, "There's no clear answer to that question right now. Not until the actual tissue is examined will we know for sure. The only way we can get the tissue is to perform surgery. The tumor appears to be a 'low grade' tumor, meaning a nonaggressive type. But that's just speculation until a tissue sample is examined. Until then, we need to manage the symptoms with medication to prevent another seizure."

Annie lay there in the hospital bed as her weary eyes looked at the doctor and listened. She didn't say anything. She just listened. I looked at her, and she looked at me. No tears. No drama. I took her hand and squeezed. "OK. We'll deal with this," I said. "One step at a time."

I turned to the doctor and asked, "What's next?" The neurologist explained he would prescribe anti-seizure and anti-swelling medications and begin the process to schedule the actual brain surgery.

None of his words registered or made any sense. But it didn't matter. We were in this altered universe together and would get through it, no matter what.

"*The child must know that he is a miracle, that since the beginning of the world there hasn't been, and until the end of the world there will not be, another child like him.*"

—Pablo Casals

CHAPTER 4

STEPHEN ROBERT

I had so many people to contact, but none more important than our twenty-eight-year-old son, Stephen, who lived seven hours away by car in southern California. Four years earlier he had entered a three-month drug rehab program in Costa Mesa and then stayed in the area. Although he portrayed himself as a rough and tough guy, I knew the impact of his mother's brain tumor would buckle his 5-foot-8, 220-pound frame. Beneath his thick and tattooed exterior, the love for his mother ran deep to a soft interior he seldom showed.

Stephen Robert. Our miracle child. Our only child. After several years of struggle with infertility related to endometriosis, we nearly gave up on becoming parents—a prospect I couldn't bear to face. As one of five siblings, raised in a bustling and Catholic home, I always expected to be a father of at least two or three children.

After deciding to investigate adoption, we became aware of a private adoption case through Michelle, a childhood and lifelong best friend of Annie's. We applied, were selected by the birth mother, and carried home a three-day-old baby boy from the hospital in early August 1985.

Due to the uncertainties of the adoption process, we kept everything quiet except for a few close friends and family. But when Stephen came home with us, I sent out a letter to announce his arrival:

Dear family and friends who are in a state of shock due to this "sudden arrival"—this is the story of Stephen Robert:

It all started when we weren't making any progress for over two years, so we decided to start the process of fertility testing and looking into adoption. Everything was slow and discouraging until a friend told us about a private adoption. We applied and were selected by the birth mom.

The waiting process was difficult, knowing that the birth mother could change her mind at any time, not to mention a hundred other "what-ifs." All we could do was hope and pray, which we did; but not only us, we asked for prayers all over the place.

The due date was August 2, 1985. That day came and went, as did the 3rd and the 4th. But then came August 5, 1985, Monday morning, at work. Words cannot describe the feeling when I picked up the phone and heard Annie screaming and laughing about a 10-pound baby boy!! Our "prayer child" made it, officially, on August 4.

Stephen Robert is a pure gift. It's amazing, but we didn't do anything to "get" him. He was dropped on our laps, a gift.

So, forgive us for the suddenness and for not telling everyone what was going on, but we had to do it that way. And, endless thanks for all the prayers and breath-holding. He never would have made it without you.

With love to all,

The McGuire Family—Bob, Annie and Stephen

Every parent says their child is the most beautiful child in the world, and that was certainly the case with Stephen. We marveled at his growth from infant to baby to child. With each passing year, his light grew brighter, his personality blossomed, and he gave us more joy than we thought possible. His handsome face, olive skin, brown hair, sparkling brown eyes, and beautiful spirit lit up our lives. His funny sense of humor, laughter, and zest for life made our lives complete. As Annie would say, "We are three little peas in a pod."

Then, without warning, everything changed. Between the ages of thirteen and fourteen, Stephen metamorphosed into someone we didn't even recognize. He didn't just withdraw like many teenagers; he became angry and reckless. Distant and dark. He no longer spoke to us. We watched helplessly as we witnessed our beautiful child change from happy to sullen, then from sullen to angry, then angry to destructive.

Desperate for help, I called a friend who worked as a counselor at an adoption agency.

"Do you feel like he's become abducted by aliens?" she asked me.

"Yes, exactly," I replied.

"This is not unusual. It isn't always the case, but this can happen with adopted children as they get older. They struggle with who they are and have difficulty expressing it."

She offered some counseling services and resources, which Stephen resisted with all his might. He was the horse we pushed and shoved to the water, only to have him rear up and kick us.

With each passing teenage year, Stephen's anger got deeper and deeper. His face grew stern and tight. He closed up and wouldn't let us in. Everything became a battle. Internet pornography. Hours on the phone with girls. Neglected schoolwork. Fights at school. Suspensions from school. Dismissal from the football team due to alcohol use. Wrecked cars. Theft. Juvenile hall. Drug use. Courts. Police. Lawyers.

Our marriage and family started to break apart under the pressure of the ever-ratcheting stress. Annie and I argued daily over how to handle it and couldn't agree. Our home turned from a happy refuge into a place of utter chaos. We became outcasts in our circles. Friends who had known us for years distanced themselves. Parents of Stephen's childhood friends avoided us. We had become the parents of "the bad kid."

The more I considered the train wreck our family had become, the more my anger burned toward God. *Why is this happening? Why couldn't we have a normal family life like everyone else? Why couldn't we get pregnant in the first place? We raised him in a loving Christian home. We prayed together, attended church together, and honored You in our family. We taught him the difference between right and wrong, and instilled in him the never-failing love You have for him.*

I felt like a complete fool and failure as a parent. I felt betrayed by God. We did all the right things. How could this happen? Proverbs 22:6, the scripture verse I had taken to heart as a parent, now mocked me: "Direct your children onto the right path, and when they are older, they will not leave it."

Despite everything, Stephen managed to make it through his senior year and graduate from high school. Then he decided to attend Butte Junior College outside of Chico in northern California and left the house in the fall of 2003. After more than five years of utter turmoil, we just wanted some peace. We wanted our life back.

But the respite didn't last long. Soon, phone calls began coming in from police, hospitals, and angry landlords. On and on it went, month after month, year after year. Finally, one day in 2008, he came home from college and delivered the bombshell: "Mom and Dad, I'm an addict. I need help."

When Stephen announced the word *addict* to us, somehow it made sense. It registered. Everything we had battled over the years now had a name: addiction. We just didn't see it until he spoke it. We knew the symptoms all too well—chaos, confusion, insanity, anger, destruction, pain, guilt, shame, and on and on and on—the giant vacuum cleaner that sucks everything and everyone into it.

Addiction. Addict. How do we even begin to deal with this?

We immediately connected with a drug-alcohol addiction treatment program affiliated with the local hospital. Stephen checked into the program, and Annie and I participated in the Family Program designed for parents, spouses, and family members of addicts. We would handle this and get through it as a family.

The first few meetings we attended were a total blur. Annie sobbed and I couldn't talk. We had to face the fact that our son was an addict. We were introduced to Step One of a 12-Step Recovery Program: "We admitted we were powerless over the addict, that our lives had become unmanageable."

The word *unmanageable* didn't begin to describe our lives. Chaos continued to throw us in every direction. We grasped at anything to hang on, but Stephen's addiction problems just got worse. From alcohol to OxyContin to heroin, the dark pit of addiction got deeper and deeper. It started to destroy all three of us in different ways: Annie tried to control his behavior through any means she could think of, but nothing worked. I tried to fix Stephen's addiction and help him, but my enabling just threw gasoline on the fire. Stephen's life energy slowly drained out as he relapsed over and over.

The strain slashed at our marriage and our souls like a thousand razor cuts. A thousand little deaths. We argued and fought over how to handle it and what to do. Addiction drove an ever-widening wedge between us.

Annie arrived home one day with a look on her face I had never seen before: a combination of anger, sadness, exasperation, and panic. Instead of greeting her with a hug, I kept my distance. "On my way back from the store," she said, "I had to pull over. I sat and screamed at the top of my lungs and pounded the steering wheel until I couldn't anymore. What the *hell* is happening? What are we going to do?"

We were referred to a family therapist named Gregor who specialized in addiction. We attended more meetings and met more parents in the same boat. Soon, we heard about an in-patient rehab program in southern California where he would live 24/7 for three months—surrounded with recovery resources—and then merge into an out-patient program. Maybe this was the answer. Maybe this would help him live a life of recovery. On a clear September morning in 2009, with shattered nerves, broken hearts, and high hopes, we dropped him off at the San Jose Airport and watched him disappear into the terminal to board his plane.

The southern California rehab program helped for a while, but soon Stephen relapsed and started over. Then he relapsed again and we helped him find a new program. The extreme depth of the addiction hole he had fallen into began to dawn on us. How on earth would he ever climb out? What would happen to him? To us?

But something else started to happen as Annie and I attended to our own recovery. At first, we attended Al-Anon meetings, a 12-Step program for family members of alcoholics. We met parents like ourselves and gained tremendous comfort and strength from one another. Then, Annie worked with a small group of other moms to establish a Nar-Anon meeting in the Monterey area to address the issues unique to families of drug addicts.

I learned about the three C's of addiction: I didn't Cause it, I can't Control it, and I can't Cure it. I started to focus on myself, not Stephen—the exact opposite of what my parental DNA told me to do. I learned the only person I have control over is myself. I learned to let go of my death grip on the rope tied to Stephen, the wild horse who dragged me through the rocks and dirt. I learned to step out of the middle between Stephen and the wrecking ball of consequences and let it crash into him, not me. Pure torture. The hardest thing for me to do as a dad was to allow Stephen to experience the pain that addiction caused instead of rescuing him from it.

But as we slowly started to let go and release Stephen to his Higher Power, something amazing happened—our relationship as husband and wife started to heal. Rather than battling against each other, we worked in the same direction. We had a common path to follow. Sometimes it was one step forward and two steps backward, but we finally moved together.

*"When we meet real tragedy in life, we can react in two ways—
either by losing hope and falling into self-destructive habits,
or by using the challenge to find our inner strength."*

—DALAI LAMA

CHAPTER 5

SURGERY AND DIAGNOSIS

I sat alongside Annie as she slept in her hospital bed. Stunned silence filled the room over the news of a brain tumor. I still pictured the tumor as an object that just needed to be removed, and that would be the end of it. Then it dawned on me that maybe this tumor would be the catalyst needed to motivate Stephen to get clean and live a life of recovery. Maybe we could finally reunite as a family and work through this together.

I called and told him what happened to his mom. After the initial shock of the news passed, Stephen said, "Dad, I promise I'll be there with you and Mom for the surgery. I'll be there. I promise." Hope surged inside me after hearing those words, especially the "promise" word. Since his childhood, Stephen knew its meaning, and saw it as an oath.

The days leading up to the surgery were filled with an outpouring of love from family and friends. Cards, flowers, visits, meals, groceries, and offers to help in any way came from all directions.

But the closer the day of surgery came, the magnitude of it loomed in my mind. *This is brain surgery, not knee surgery. What is going to happen? Will Annie be able to talk afterward? Should I record her voice now so she can say something vital to me or Stephen? What about her thinking and cognitive skills? Will she recognize me after surgery? Will she ever be the same?*

Over several consultations with the brain surgeon and neurologist, they assured us the surgery would remove the tumor only where it was safe to do so. Adjoining areas of the brain would not be impacted. Still, many unknowns remained, and recovery would take some time.

One night, a few days away from surgery, we lay in bed wide awake, thoughts spinning in all directions. In the dark stillness, Annie turned to me and said, "Bob, if anything happens and I don't make it through this, I want you to live your life. I want you to find someone and be happy. I want you to live your life."

"Please don't say that," I said. "You're going to make it through this. You're going to be OK."

The next day she made phone calls to her eighty-eight-year-old mother, Germaine, who lived at a nearby assisted-living facility, her brother Bill, and a few of her closest friends. She wanted to tell them things she might not be able to say after surgery. "I love you," she said to her mom. "You mean so much to me. Thank you for who you are, and everything you've done for me."

I too made phone calls to family and close friends. On one of the calls, a friend told me a story of a young man with a brain tumor. The man's church community got together and prayed for God to deliver a miracle. The surgery was scheduled, but the presurgery MRI revealed the tumor no longer existed. God had delivered a miracle. The man had been healed, and the surgery was canceled.

A glimmer of hope flickered in my heart as I read Bible passages like John 14:13: "And I will do whatever you ask in my name, so that the Father may be glorified in the Son." And one from Mark 11:24: "Therefore I tell you, whatever you ask for in prayer, believe that you have received it, and it will be yours." I prayed that God would remove the tumor, and just like the case of the young man, that the presurgery MRI would be clear.

The moment Stephen arrived at the house, my heart jumped with a mixture of anxiety, hope, and joy. He made the seven-hour drive, and the timing couldn't have been better. It was Mother's Day weekend, normally one of the most difficult days of the year for Annie. For more than fifteen years, that day had been filled with sorrow, heartbreak, or some addiction-related crisis.

But not this one. This Mother's Day was a rare gift. Stephen took his mother out on a special date. They did their favorite things together: Ate hamburgers, went shopping, and then caught a movie and had popcorn. They spent the whole day together. When they arrived home,

I saw the joy in Stephen's face that I hadn't seen since his childhood "wonder" years. His brown eyes twinkled on his square face under brown hair that was mostly covered by the new baseball hat they had just bought.

He knew how much this meant to his mom, and he came through. He bounced around the house like a confident boxer entering the ring. "Mom is going to kick this thing's ass," he said. Annie just smiled with a look of contentment that showed how much she cherished each moment of their time together. She was at peace and ready to take the next step.

When the day of the surgery arrived, we left the house at 5:45 a.m. Few words were spoken on the drive. Annie focused on one thing: get through the surgery and to the other side. I prayed for the presurgery MRI miracle. Everyone we knew prayed for Annie's healing. God could do it. I believed it was possible.

We checked into the hospital and were escorted to the pre-op room, where patients, doctors, and nurses prepared for surgery. We were brought into a small curtained-off area with a few chairs and an exam table. Sleepy-eyed but alert, Stephen arrived a few minutes later and sat with us. Annie had a look of determination and calmness on her face. If she felt fear, she didn't show it. My nerves were on edge, but Annie's attitude calmed me down. One by one, several doctors and nurses entered our little space to perform presurgery checks. Then the surgeon entered.

"So how are you doing this morning?" he asked as he looked closely at Annie.

"I'm fine. I'm ready," Annie said.

After several minutes of explanation of what would happen in surgery, the surgeon asked, "Do you have any questions?"

"No," Annie replied. "Let's get this thing done!"

Annie was taken away for the presurgery MRI and removal of hair on her left scalp. I prayed again for the MRI miracle. *Please, God, You can do this. Please take away this tumor.*

Thirty minutes later a nurse wheeled Annie back into the pre-op room. I held my breath. The surgeon came in a few minutes later and announced that the surgery team awaited her arrival in the operating room. No change in diagnosis. No miracle. The MRI showed the tumor still intact.

Deep inside, I heard a loud CRACK as my faith recoiled from reality.

After a few minutes the nurse wheeled her away, through some doors and out of sight. It would be several hours before I knew anything. Stephen and I stepped outside the hospital into the morning air. I had to force my thoughts away from anything related to brain surgery and what was happening to Annie at this very moment. Everything was in the hands of the doctors, the nurses, and God. All we could do was wait.

Soon, Stephen said he was going to visit a friend and would be back later. I walked back into the hospital and waited. The hours crawled slowly past.

10:00 a.m.

I thought of that magic moment in 2012—when Annie stood on top of the world. Friends and family had gathered to celebrate her graduation from a master's degree program in psychology, a huge step toward her dream of becoming a marriage and family therapist. Gregor, the therapist who guided and encouraged Annie along the way, presented her diploma. She beamed with purpose and joy. She had gone to night school for two years while working a full-time job and graduated with a perfect 4.0 GPA. Her motivation propelled her like a human rocket.

I thought of how it all started, when Annie returned from her first therapy visit with Gregor, when she was on the verge of a nervous breakdown from the addiction chaos in our family.

"I told him about the nightmare we're going through with Stephen," she said. "I told him every detail: the constant worry, the craziness, the wrecked cars, all the lies about money we've sent him that ended up being used on drugs, the calls from the police and the hospital emergency room, and not knowing from one moment to the next what would happen to him. What would become of our son? Would he even survive?

"When I finished, Gregor looked at me and said: 'You need to face something: You're an addict.'

"'What? Me? An addict?'

"'Yes, you're addicted to your son.'

"He went on to explain that I have zero control over Stephen. I have to learn to let go of him, to release him, and focus on my own recovery. The complete opposite of what I've—what we've—been doing."

From that point on, our recovery started to gain traction. One thing led to another, and eventually, she redirected the entire focus of her life.

Her mission was simple: to help others endure the nightmare that she herself had endured—the drug addiction of a loved one. She heard the call and responded. Therapist work was the fulfillment of a dream— one that lay dormant for more than thirty years, since her college graduation in 1979 with a bachelor's degree in social welfare and corrections.

12:00 p.m.

I had never seen someone so excited to leave a full-paying job to start volunteer work until Annie began her internship program at a local recovery center. Her dream, her calling, her ministry—she performed face-to-face therapy with addicts and their families. The internship required her to log 3,000 hours of supervised experience as a therapist, which could take years to complete. But it didn't matter. This was what she was born to do.

She was so enthusiastic that she pasted a label on the back of her employee ID badge with the word *BREATHE*—just to remind herself.

1:00 p.m.

When April 18 arrived, she had already logged close to 1,500 hours— almost halfway. A wave a nausea hit me. *Dear God, You can't let this thing stop her now. She is doing so much good for so many people. She is making such a difference in people's lives. She's doing what You've called her to do.*

Sometime after 2:00 p.m., the surgeon came into the waiting room where I paced with a few other people waiting for their own postsurgery reports. He sat down next to me and matter-of-factly said, "Surgery went well. I was able to get 75 to 80 percent of the tumor removed safely. We will have to wait a few days for the initial pathology report to get more information. It will tell us if the tumor is malignant or benign and will enable us to determine how we proceed."

I felt relieved and confused—relief that the surgery was over; confusion over what he'd said. *What? Why wasn't the entire tumor removed? He said he removed 75 percent, not 100 percent. That means the tumor is still there. Damn it! Malignant or benign? What? There's a possibility that it's malignant?*

I shoved all of it out of my mind as I made my way to her bedside in the Intensive Care Unit a few minutes later. She was nearly unrecognizable behind the multiple tubes, wires, and bulging white turban of head bandages that partially covered her closed left eye. I took a nervous deep breath and sat down in a chair next to the bed. Stephen entered the room a little later and sat with me. Then two nurses entered the room to check Annie's vital signs and overall condition.

One of the nurses addressed Annie in a clear and firm voice: "Hello, Annie. My name is Jill and I need to ask you a few questions and run a few tests, OK? Can you open your eyes for me?"

Annie slowly opened her eyes and tried to orient herself. "Hi there!" the nurse said. "You're OK, Annie. You are in the Intensive Care Unit, and your surgery is over. Everything is OK. We're just going to ask you a few questions and run a few tests."

The nurse asked me to stand up and place myself directly in Annie's field of vision. "Do you recognize this person? Who is this?" the nurse asked Annie.

Annie paused and then spoke in a soft and gravelly voice: "Bob."

Then Stephen stood in her line of sight. The nurse asked Annie, "What about this person? Who is this?"

"Stephen."

"Very good! Excellent!"

After a few more tests to ensure she could chew and swallow, they gave approval for Annie to eat dinner, and then left the room. Annie's eyes opened and closed as she continued the slow climb out of the deep postsurgery hole.

Over the next two days in the ICU, Annie gained more awareness and strength. She could talk, but only in short and fragmented sentences. With the help of a physical therapist on her left side and Stephen on her right, she used a walker to take her first steps around the ICU hallway.

Annie continued to make good progress and was transferred out of ICU to a standard hospital room on Day 3. The ICU staff congratulated her as the nurse guided her wheelchair, loaded up with flowers, candy, and cards. She smiled through her bandaged head and thanked everyone.

The next day, Sunday, May 19, I sat with her in the hospital room when the surgeon walked into the room at 2:00 p.m. At the mere sight of him, my heart pounded and my breath shortened.

"How are you feeling?" he asked Annie.

"Good," Annie replied.

"The initial pathology results are in," he said straightforwardly. "The tumor is a nonbenign type of cancer known as an astrocytoma. The name refers to the star-shaped cells that…" I couldn't hear anything else. Words didn't register. All I heard was "nonbenign"—meaning malignant. My breath stopped. My heart stopped. I sat stunned. Paralyzed. I wanted to tell him to shut up and stop talking, but I couldn't speak. I didn't want to hear or believe a word he said. This cannot be real. Annie sat in bed quietly and looked down toward her feet.

CRACK.

Then he said, "Do you want to know the average amount of time someone has to live with one of these types of tumors?"

"No!" I fired back. "No! We don't want to hear it!" I wanted to scream at him to get out, but I didn't. I couldn't. I just tried to hold myself together.

He kept going: "It will grow back. Over time it could change to a more malignant form. It's an infiltrating tumor which cannot be removed without removing some of the brain itself. It can't be cured. It can only be treated. Ultimately, it wins."

Time stopped. Sound stopped. I couldn't see. The room closed in. Nothing existed.

After a few minutes of other unintelligible garble, the room started to come back into focus. I saw the doctor leave. Less than a minute later, Stephen walked into the room. He knew something was wrong by the look on my face. Annie sat quietly and looked straight ahead. She didn't cry out or weep. She didn't scream. She just sat quietly.

I stumbled over the words, but I told him what the doctor had said. Stephen's thick, strong body buckled. He put his hand up to his mouth and started to cough. "I need some air," he said and quickly left the room. I followed behind, leaving Annie in the room alone. My knees and body struggled to walk under the force that shoved me toward the ground. Once outside in the hospital parking lot, I stopped him, and we grabbed onto each other. We heaved and sobbed into each other's shoulders in a hug of agony. For the next ten minutes, we cried, walked, and tried to talk. Then he said he wanted to be alone. I slowly walked back into the hospital in a daze, at a complete loss.

The brutal reality of a malignant brain tumor was impossible to process. Everything changed at that moment. The world changed. My naïve belief that the tumor would be gone or benign had been destroyed. I felt like a complete fool. How could I believe in such a fantasy? There was no mercy, no miracle, no relief—just the cold and suffocating crush of reality.

We were caught in a swirling whirlpool, slowly circling around the edge of an ever-increasing vortex—drawn down into a black, overpowering, and unknown darkness below.

My anger turned from the surgeon to God. *DAMN IT, GOD! Where are You? Where the hell are You? She gave everything to follow Your call in her life, and now this?*

Annie had given everything to pursue her dream of becoming a therapist to help addicts and their families. She was so happy, so fulfilled. She had found her life's calling. She gave all of herself to start a whole new life—a life of service to others. And yet, here she was, struck down, barely able to speak or function. I couldn't bear to witness the death of Annie's dream.

When I reentered the room, Annie still sat quietly in bed. Her sad eyes were red and wet from tears. I looked at her, sat down next to her on the bed, and hugged her. I didn't know what to say. We sat in silence as we tried to come to grips with the news and what it meant.

Soon Stephen stepped back into the room. His face showed a combination of sadness, anger, and determination. "I'm going back to southern California now," he said. He walked over to Annie's hospital bed and hugged and kissed his mom good-bye. "I love you, Mom," he said.

"I love...you too..." Annie said. "Be...careful...I love you."

He hugged me and said, "I love you, Dad," and then left. I stood in disbelief as I watched Stephen leave the room. *How could he leave now? How could he leave his mom at this very moment? Why can't he stay a little longer? We are all together as a family. We are in this together! You can't leave!*

As confusion and despair pulled me downward, my attention snapped back to Annie.

Wait a minute. Annie's not gone, or in a coma. She's here with me and needs me now more than ever. This is not over. It's just starting. And we are in this together. We can fight this thing. We will fight this thing, and we'll do whatever we have to do. Modern medicine is awesome. There's got to be a solution. There's got to be some treatment out there that will work. This is not a death sentence—regardless of what the surgeon said.

I gently took Annie by the shoulders, looked at her, and said, "We're going to figure this out. We're going to take this one day at a time and get through it. You're going to be OK. We are in this together. Don't worry. We're going to get through this. I promise."

Within two days we returned home loaded down with medications, postsurgery instructions, and follow-up doctor appointments. Among the first was the neuro-oncologist, the brain cancer doctor. A week later we sat in his office as he explained the pathology results of the actual tumor tissue taken from Annie's brain. "The exact type of brain cancer you have is called Oligodendroglioma, or Oligo for short," he said. "If you're going to have a malignant brain tumor, this is the kind to have. It's famously slow and is considered low grade. Patients can live a long time with this type of cancer. I'm aware of one case where the patient lived seventeen years. This is *not* the aggressive type of brain cancer that amounts to game over. This is manageable."

A sense of relief came over me, and it almost sounded like good news. Annie had a look of concentration on her face as she tried to follow the conversation.

When I asked him the "why" and "how" questions of brain tumors, he said, "There's no good answer for this. We don't see evidence that they're caused by cell phones or electrical waves. We don't know what causes them. But it's probably been inside Annie for years. The brain kept compensating and working around it until the tumor became too much."

I held Annie to my side as we slowly walked to the car, encouraged by the words "manageable," "famously slow," and "seventeen years."

"We can do this," I said. "We can do this."

*"I will love the light for it shows me
the way, yet I will endure the darkness
because it shows me the stars."*

—Og Mandino

CHAPTER 6

GAIN AND LOSS

One week later I sat and watched the brain surgeon remove forty-eight staples from Annie's shaved scalp, starting just above her left ear, then curved backward and up her head to left side of her temple hairline, like a sideways question mark.

"The incision has healed perfectly," the doctor said. "Now it's a matter of time until you recover your speech, your cognitive abilities, your balance, etc., so you can return to as normal a life as possible. Your daily care will now be handled through the oncologist, who will manage the treatment needed to fight the tumor."

"How…much…time?" Annie asked as she searched to find each word. "When do…can…I return…with work?"

"It takes time for the brain to recover from the trauma of surgery. It can take up to a year or more. You can't force it or rush it," the doctor said. Annie sat still and silent.

On the drive home I stopped at a red light and looked over at Annie. She burst into tears. "A…year?" she choked out through sobs. "A year? All I want…to do…is return…to work…to help."

For the next year, the single goal became how to fight the tumor and recover enough of her faculties to return to the therapist work she loved. We focused on anything—any activity, resource, medical treatment, or surgery—that would allow her to return to any semblance of the life she wanted so desperately to live.

At first we stayed connected with Stephen through phone calls, but then his cell phone number would inexplicably change and we had to wait to hear from him. Weeks would go by without any contact. We found the strength we needed to cope with the unknown by focusing on our own recovery through Nar-Anon friends and meetings.

Despite every obstacle thrown in her path, Annie's determination didn't waver. She crawled, inch by inch, through that first year. Chemotherapy knocked her down each month, but she would get back up and press ahead. Every inch of regained ground—speech, word-finding, clear vision, walks around the neighborhood, physical exercise, cognitive skills like reading and comprehension—created momentum and cause for celebration. Bit by bit, she climbed out of the hole.

Her determination even led her to pick up her Yamaha acoustic guitar, which she had played since her teenage years. A fellow guitar-playing friend came over to the house and sat with her on the couch and reintroduced Annie to chords, melodies, and finger placements. A smile of recognition covered her face each time she managed to create a familiar key, like an old touchstone.

But as Annie slowly regained her life, my mother's life slowly faded. At ninety years old, she lay bedbound in the living room of her southern California home, tended to lovingly by Paz, her full-time caregiver. Mom's health had steadily declined over the past five years after she suffered a fall at the house, where she lived alone. She had lost her strength to stand and would spend the rest of her life confined to a wheelchair or bed.

Mom rarely if ever lost her strength. Frances Marie Lawson, one of four southern belle sisters, was born in Mansfield, Louisiana, in 1923 and raised in rural east Texas by two loving parents. She had that rare combination of grace, determination, and strength, as exemplified by her decision to leave the safety of her hometown in the early 1940s to enlist in the US Navy Nurse Corps. She met my dad, Peter Anthony McGuire, Jr. from Brooklyn, New York, when they were both stationed in New Orleans for training. As the family story goes, Dad spotted this wavy-haired, brown-eyed, brunette beauty one day when they disembarked the same train and asked if she needed a city tour guide.

The war took them in different directions, but they stayed in contact through it all. As a Navy pilot, Dad was assigned to an aircraft carrier, the USS Santee, which engaged in heavy conflicts with the Japanese Navy in the South Pacific. He flew his F6F fighter plane into many battles, including the Battle of Leyte Gulf in the skies above the Philippine islands. Dad never told us that he was nearly shot down by a Japanese Zero pilot; I heard it from his younger brother, Uncle Al, when Al was in his 90s. Dad also never mentioned the Distinguished Flying Cross medal he received from the Navy—awarded for heroism or extraordinary aerial achievement. We found it among his things many years later.

Pete and Marie reunited after the war, committed their love to each other, and married in November 1946. Together they raised five children born in four different states: New York (Mary and Pete), Florida (John), Pennsylvania (me), and Michigan (Ann). We moved a lot based on Dad's career, but Mom always kept the family organized, well fed, and healthy. Her soft, gentle exterior sometimes disguised her inner toughness. Nothing rattled her.

Except the day Dad died: October 4, 1987. For the previous four years, he suffered from a red blood cell disorder that no doctor or clinic could resolve, despite Mom's vigilance. Dad's hard work ethic and endurance were legendary, so when he started to complain that he didn't have the strength to do simple chores around the house, Mom's alarm bells sounded.

She took him to the Mayo Clinic in Minnesota, Scripps in San Diego, California, and any doctor she could find. Routine red blood cell transfusions were the only treatment that worked, which would restore his energy levels for several weeks until they faded again. Over time the positive effects from the transfusions diminished and had to be performed more frequently. His face and body showed the strain of his weakened state.

One Sunday afternoon, as I played in the yard with two-year-old Stephen, Annie called me from inside the house. A nurse from the Tustin Medical Center, where Dad got his blood transfusions, was on the phone. "Your Dad's health is fading fast," she said. "I suggest you make it here to see him as soon as possible."

My brother John and sister Ann, who lived nearby to Mom and Dad, were both in Japan on a trip Dad had arranged with them several weeks earlier. Pete lived in Colorado and Mary lived in New York, so I was the closest. I jumped on a one-hour flight from San Jose to Orange County airport and arrived at the medical center that evening. When I walked in, a nurse with a distressed look on her face escorted me into his room. The nursing staff all had gotten to know Dad over the years and loved his fun sense of humor and engaging personality.

When I saw Dad motionless and flat on the hospital bed, connected to a respirator, my mind and body froze. My throat constricted as tears instantly appeared. I had never seen Dad, our family pillar of strength, so incapacitated. So weak. So vulnerable. Mom leaned over him, trying to provide comfort.

When she saw me, she partially stood up and nodded at me. Sadness and distress covered her face—a look I had never seen before. I took my place next to Dad on the other side of the bed, directly opposite Mom. His eyes were closed, and the respirator covered his mouth and cheeks. I gently held his hand in mine, which felt warm and soft. He squeezed back. I wanted to say something but couldn't talk. "Pete," Mom said, "Bob's here."

I turned my head and saw Mom's black leather Bible, open at the foot of the bed. She asked me to read Psalm 23. I picked up the Bible but couldn't get any words out. I heard Mom's soft voice say, "You're going to be OK, Pete. You're a fighter pilot. You're a fighter."

I had to step out of the room to gather myself. One of the nurses handed me a phone, and I struggled to tell Mary what was happening, then my brother Pete. When I stepped back into the room several minutes later, I saw Mom bent over, softly weeping over Dad's body. A nurse slowly shook her head. He was gone.

As Mom gently wept, I couldn't comprehend or believe what had just happened. Dad, always there for everyone, always the rock—gone? Impossible. It couldn't be.

The rhythmic hiss-stop…hiss-stop…hiss-stop of the respirator and Mom's soft weeping were the only sounds in the room. I stood at the foot of his bed in shock and disbelief. I looked at Mom, still bent over Dad, and my heart broke. I could not imagine Mom without Dad, and vice versa. The two of them were always one together. A team. A duo. How can one possibly be without the other?

I walked over and stood next to Mom. She wasn't a hugger, so I just stood there next to her in the silence. After a few minutes, she slowly stood up and moved to collect her Bible, her purse, and a few things. I moved alongside her in a daze.

The two of us drove home sometime after midnight in complete silence and shock. Once home, I wanted to comfort her but knew she needed space. We said a surreal goodnight to each other and retreated to separate rooms—Mom into her bedroom and me into my old room a short distance down the hall. Silence filled the house. I lay in bed wide awake as my mind spun in circles.

Then I heard a sound I had never heard before. It wasn't the sound of soft weeping I heard at the medical center, nor was it loud wailing. It was the sound of Mom's broken heart that cried out. I knew if I tried to comfort her, she would say something like "I'm OK, Bob," and insist that I go back to my room. So I decided to just be there in spirit with her in her pain, as she wept in the darkness. A while later, silence returned, and I eventually fell asleep.

Starting the next morning, Mom did what she needed to do to mourn, regroup, and move forward with her life at the age of sixty-four. She did it in her own private way; she didn't attend grief support groups or seek out a therapist. She kept her inner thoughts, feelings, and struggles to herself—a family code of conduct. She closed the door of the room she shared with Dad and moved her bedroom to the opposite end of the house. She never remarried and never expressed any interest in companionship. She remained content to live at home alone, babysit her grandchildren, and stay involved with volunteer activities at her church and the public library. She lived happily that way for twenty-one years, until her mind and body began to weaken.

Mom had always been the family's go-to source for any medical advice, but by the time Annie's seizure happened in 2013, Mom had lost most of her ability to communicate, comprehend, and interact. Confined to her bed, she just got through each day, one after another.

In the early evening hours of January 23, 2014, Paz called to alert my brother John that Mom was slipping away. John arrived immediately, and within a few hours, Ann and Pete (who had moved back to southern California from Colorado) joined him at Mom's bedside. They called me and Mary, but this time I couldn't make the immediate trip, and likely would not have made it in time anyway. Mom died peacefully later that night, surrounded by three of her five children.

When I arrived the next day, walked into the house, and saw the empty bed in the living room, it didn't seem possible. How could Mom—the one who was always there for us—be gone? I wanted some sense of her, some way to say good-bye, but felt only emptiness. I stood next to the metal-frame hospital bed and then knelt down on the worn carpeted floor. I remembered the love and devotion that exemplified her life. Her gentle yet strong spirit. The soothing peace that always surrounded her. Silence. Nothing. After a minute I started to feel foolish and imagined Mom saying, "Don't be silly, Bob. Get up. Get moving."

The following month, in February 2014, Annie stood in front of a McGuire family gathering in the Fairhaven Mortuary chapel in Santa Ana, California. She strummed her guitar and sang a song to honor Marie Lawson McGuire, whom she loved dearly. Annie modified the words of a Catholic song about Mary (mother of Jesus) called "Gentle Woman" to fit Mom instead.

As all of us listened to Annie's clear, melodic voice soar through the chapel in loving tribute, I shook my head in astonishment. She had regained nearly everything she had lost ten months earlier. And I could imagine a gentle smile on Mom's face.

Wow. Annie is healing. Healing! This may be manageable after all.

"God grant me the serenity to
accept the things I cannot change,
the courage to change the things I can,
and the wisdom to know the difference.
Living one day at a time;
Enjoying one moment at a time;
Accepting hardship as the
pathway to peace."

—Reinhold Niebuhr

CHAPTER 7

THE UNTHINKABLE

Annie continued to gain strength and support from all sides—friends, colleagues, and family. The outpouring of love and support from the Monterey Diocese, from the bishop to the priests and fellow employees, never stopped, as if she had never left her job there to pursue her therapist dream. She was immersed in every possible church blessing: Anointings of the Sick, Prayers of the Faithful, Masses offered in her name, endless rosaries, and a flood of constant prayers for healing and recovery. People we didn't even know prayed for Annie's healing.

One year after the seizure—almost to the day—she returned to her internship at the local recovery center. On her first day back, she beamed with the excitement of a child on her first day of school. Her eyes sparkled, her full auburn hair had grown back and covered every part of her head, and her face radiated with joy. The moment she had worked, hoped, and prayed for had finally arrived. The moment she feared would never come. But it did.

That morning I stood in the kitchen making coffee—the same spot where the nightmare started—and marveled as she walked in. She looked like nothing had happened to her. Fully alive, smiling, and dressed for work. She wore a blue and white patterned skirt with a black sweater. A royal-blue lanyard wrapped around her neck, attached to her therapist-intern ID badge that had waited for more than a year to be worn again. From a long silver chain around her neck hung a circular silver pendant inscribed with the Serenity Prayer: "God grant me the serenity to accept the things I cannot change, the courage to change the things I can, and the wisdom to know the difference."

Later that day, when I returned home from work, the look of jubilant exhaustion on her face said it all—her first day back had been a complete success. Although she couldn't work at full capacity, the entire staff supported her 100 percent and welcomed her back with open arms.

Over the following weeks and months, life started to feel almost normal again. Aside from regular doctor appointments and monthly MRI scans, things looked bright. The chemo treatments seemed to have worked.

Then the next wave hit.

In mid-August 2014, we sat in an exam room in Monterey with the oncologist as he delivered the results from the latest MRI. The cancer cells had reappeared. A look of concern covered his face: "I'm going to refer you to Stanford Medical Center for follow-up and next steps. Even though this is a very small amount of growth, it cannot be ignored. We have to follow up, and you'll be in good hands at Stanford."

The relaxed and joyful look on Annie's face instantly turned to sorrow. My stomach twisted back into that sickening spot. Our glorious "vacation" away from everything related to cancer suddenly ended. I didn't want to hear it. I didn't want to accept it. *What happened to the "famously slow," low-grade tumor? Did we do something wrong? Did God just abandon us again? Did He not see how great Annie was doing the last three months? What the hell is going on?*

Annie stayed silent. She didn't cry. I tried to listen as the doctor explained the Stanford referral process, what medical information they would need, and the next steps. I saw Annie shift her face from sadness to determination. She looked at me, then the doctor, and said, "OK, let's get this thing going."

Two weeks later we sat in an exam room at the Stanford Medical Center with several doctors, including the lead neuro-oncologist. She had conducted a detailed review of Annie's latest MRI. "The MRI shows a strange enhancement within your brain," she said, "which indicates a more aggressive type of tumor. I'm sorry to tell you this, but the tumor is changing from a low-grade, slow-growing tumor into a higher-grade, aggressive tumor called glioblastoma. A decision needs to be made right away regarding treatment."

We sat in stunned silence as she spoke. Her words, though spoken with kindness and care, exploded like bombs. Then she said, "The prognosis for this type of cancer is three to five years."

That instant, something yanked me underwater. I couldn't hear any sound except a faint, muted noise. The doctor's voice became muffled and unintelligible. I couldn't breathe. Panic rose from my chest and expanded into every limb in my body. My heart raced. A cold sweat broke out and soaked into my shirt. I couldn't think. I couldn't see anything. I could only feel the weight that pulled me down and kept me under. I didn't know if I would vomit or faint.

Slowly, I started to surface into a sickened state of shock. I could barely see the look on Annie's face through the tears that burned my eyes. I couldn't talk through my strangled throat. Annie had just received a death sentence. Three to five years. Three to five years of life left. *How is this possible? How can this even be possible?*

Something unthinkable entered the room and my consciousness for the first time: death. The end of life. Annie's life. Our life. A dark and heavy cloud fell over us. The actual thought that Annie's life—our life—was going to end did not even seem real, did not seem possible. We sat in darkened silence as the doctors spoke other unintelligible words.

As the meeting concluded, the doctor's words started to become audible again. She presented a three-headed approach: surgery, radiation, and chemo. More consultations had to be scheduled. Another MRI was ordered—an advanced MRI with the highest resolution available that would show the most detail.

Numb with grief and shock, we soon found ourselves on board the shuttle bus that would take us from the Stanford Cancer Center back to the main parking lot. I looked around at the other passengers on the bus. Some wore large air respirator masks strapped to their faces, with bright green or blue-colored round filters on each side. Some wore headscarves on their bald heads. Some were elderly, barely able to walk up the bus steps. Some in wheelchairs. Some with caregivers. Some alone. All had the same look on their faces that Annie now had on hers:

the look of a recipient of a death sentence, and their resolve to fight against it.

I sat there humbled amid these courageous souls who fought for their lives every single day, regardless of the odds. Without saying a word, they taught me to look at life with a whole new perspective: to cherish the priceless gift of every single moment.

After we stepped down from the shuttle bus at the parking lot, Annie stopped and said, "I need to walk." We walked into an adjacent garden area full of planter boxes and walkways. She held onto my arm as we walked in silence in the warm afternoon sun. When we reached the end of a pathway, we sat down on a wooden bench. Annie softly wept in despair. Her hopes and dreams shattered. Her new life shattered. Instead of a future, the end of her life appeared.

Despair flooded into me as I held onto her and tried to provide comfort. I despaired for her life and for our life. But unlike me, she had to face the end of her own life. I could not imagine the suffering she endured at that moment. All I could do was to be there for her. I could listen, love, hold, and comfort her—through whatever or wherever the path would take us.

We couldn't sleep that night. I wrestled with thoughts of life and death, and the unknowns of what awaited us. She lay wide awake as she faced her own mortality.

The next day, we both forced ourselves to go to work and try to move forward with a "normal" day. But nothing felt normal anymore.

That evening, Annie told me how she talked to her colleagues at the recovery center and struggled to tell them her prognosis. Her devastated co-workers surrounded her with tears of sadness and hugs of encouragement. Her supervisor, Karen, told Annie that she was the best therapist and counselor there, and no matter what happened, they would always hold a place for her.

And yet again, Annie set her mind straight ahead to what needed to be done. This time, a second surgery followed by a combination of radiation and chemo would be required. The doctors explained how the craniotomy would work. She would be awake during the surgery, and the medical technology allowed them to remove the tumor cells without impacting her speech center. She would be comfortable and pain-free during the entire process, and even able to talk to the doctors to confirm her speech function. The doctors assured her that the recovery time would be much faster than the first surgery—a matter of days.

The only good news was that Stephen's life had turned in a positive direction. He had been hired by an out-of-state construction-survey crew through a friend and enjoyed the work. Once we contacted him, he assured us he would return to be with us for the surgery.

Sure enough, he did. When he walked into our hotel room located near Stanford Hospital in late October 2014, his energy filled the room. He wore a black and white baseball cap over his short-cropped brown hair, a black T-shirt with the San Francisco Giants logo across the front, blue jeans, and red athletic shoes. His brown-stubble beard made his face look rugged and strong. He hugged us both and paid special attention to his mom.

"Hey, Mom," he said as he sat on the hotel bed facing her. "Sorry I haven't been so easy to contact, but it's all good. The survey job is good. I'm learning a lot and like the outdoors. The guys are cool." Then he said, "You're going to kick this thing's ass, Mom. You got this. Hey, what's up with the new hairstyle? That's a cool look you got."

He referred to Annie's shaved left temple, dotted with one-inch square adhesive pads, which would be connected to the brain-mapping sensors early the next morning. She just nodded and smiled at him. I sat back and watched the two of them interact. He loved to gently tease her, and she just smiled and rolled with it.

The next day, the surgery proceeded flawlessly, and we returned home two days later. As promised, her recovery time was almost instantaneous compared to the first one. Then came the follow-up phone call from the surgeon. The three of us squeezed together in a semicircle on the living room couch and looked at the phone in front of us. "The pathology test results have been confirmed," the surgeon said softly. "I'm very sorry to say that the cancer has progressed to a Grade 4 glioblastoma multiforme, the most aggressive type. I am so very sorry."

Silence. The three of us just stared at the phone. Tears burned my eyes, and my throat tightened. Annie sat quietly. Stephen hung his head. I looked at Annie and saw the sadness in her eyes get shoved out by sheer determination and her will to live. She still didn't say anything but didn't have to. Just like her approach to every obstacle, she made up her mind to bring everything inside her to fight this. She would not back down or surrender. I felt a surge of strength inside me as I made my own choice to join that fight. God was still with us. We would push forward, one step at a time, no matter what.

This time, Stephen didn't run. He stayed at home with us.

Several days later, around 4:30 a.m., I heard a commotion coming from the living room. As I emerged from sleep, I realized Annie wasn't in bed, so I got up to check. She stood next to Stephen, laid out on the couch. She shouted words at his listless body. Coaster-size squares of crinkled, blackened aluminum foil and a Bic lighter sat in front of Stephen on the ottoman—telltale signs of smoking heroin. Nausea hit my stomach and throat. Stephen stayed in an incoherent stupor on the couch. Annie's face and body clenched with anger.

"I can't believe this," she fumed. "How many times have we told him? He knows the rules. He knows he can't use in the house! He knows! That's it. He has to leave."

"OK," I said, "let's go back to bed and talk to him about it in a few hours. You need to rest. How did you even know?"

"I just felt something was wrong," she said.

I couldn't believe how aware and coherent Annie was only days after her second brain surgery. We returned to bed and tried to sleep, but an elephant now occupied the house. She was right. We had talked to him multiple times over the years about the rules of the house. He could stay here as long as he was clean. We supported his recovery but couldn't support his drug use. But we had never acted. We just looked the other way, bought drug-testing kits, warned him, gave ultimatums, and tolerated it. But this time was different.

When we got up a few hours later, we discovered Stephen had moved into his bedroom where he remained in a stupor. Every hour of the day dragged on until the early evening hours when he finally woke up. Around 6:00 p.m., as Annie and I sat in the living room, she looked at me and said, "So are you going to tell him, or me?" I froze. This was the moment I had always dreaded. But Annie was 100 percent deter- mined, as if her therapist training had crystalized her approach. It had to happen. I didn't want to do it, but I didn't want her to do it. I couldn't, but I had to. "I'll do it," I said.

Every fiber in my body kicked back, punched back, and screamed "*No!*" Every single aspect of me as a father, as a dad, shouted "*No! Don't do this!*" But another part of me said, "*You have to. You have to deal with the addict inside Stephen. You have to.*"

I grabbed two or three large black plastic garbage bags and knocked on his door. "Hey, Steve," I said. My body tightened with fear. My heart pounded in my chest and throat.

"Yeah, come in," he said.

I opened the door and took one step inside. He lay on top of his bed covers, still groggy and ruffled. "Steve, you know you can't stay here if you're using," I said. "This morning, Mom found—"

"I know, I know," Stephen said. "I'll leave in the next day or two."

"No, you have to leave now." I couldn't believe the words came out of my mouth. I wanted to take them back. But I just stood there, shaking inside.

"What?" he said as he looked at me with a sudden alertness.

"You have to leave now," I said. "We've decided this has to happen now. Here are some bags to put your stuff in."

Stephen sat up straight with a look of shock and anger on his face. "What the fuck!?"

"I'm sorry, Steve, but this has to happen now."

"Where the hell am I going to go?" he said as his eyes burned into me.

"I don't know," I said as my stomach roiled with fear.

He threw a metal wristwatch across the room, which ricocheted off the wall and hit me. "This is fucking bullshit!" he shouted.

"I'm sorry, Steve, but this has to happen." I closed the door and walked back into the living room. My entire body shook. *What am I doing? What are we doing? What the hell am I doing?*

I looked at Annie, who had a calm but determined look on her face. I sat down and tried to breathe. "I know this is hard, but we have to do this," she said.

I heard banging noises from Stephen's bedroom. Several more minutes of sickening fear elapsed. *Can I undo this? Can I pull it back?*

Stephen opened his door with angry force and stomped into the living room carrying bags of clothes and things. "This is fucking bullshit," he said as he steamed toward the front door. By sheer force I stood up and moved my body to the front door and out to his rental car, a white sedan. Stephen threw the bags in the trunk and slammed it shut. He kicked a dent into the side of the car, then opened the front door, climbed inside, slammed it shut, and drove off.

The ground under my feet turned into a pit of quicksand, which swallowed me alive in guilt and shame.

What have I done? What kind of a father kicks his son out of the house? How could I do this to him? How could I kick him out?

But I had to. We had to. It was the addict, not Stephen.

I would NEVER kick Stephen out of the house. Ever. This wasn't him. The addict had taken over his life and had to go—not Stephen.

But they're the same person!

No, they're not. The addict is NOT Stephen. But it has taken over. Stephen would never do this to his mom or me. The addict would, but not Stephen.

I walked back into the house, numb and nauseated. Annie remained on the couch, her head lowered in sadness. "We did the right thing," she said. "As hard as it is, we did the right thing." I didn't know what to think, do, or say. The numbness and nausea lingered for days.

I wanted to reach out and pull Stephen back home. I wanted *Stephen* back. I wanted to but couldn't deal with his addiction, life, and decisions. I wanted to but couldn't fix it. I had enough to deal with. I had to let him figure it out. I had to learn how to detach with love, the ultimate oxymoron of family recovery.

Weeks went by without hearing from Stephen. A friend told us they had seen him in a food line while they served the homeless free food at Dorothy's Place, a shelter in downtown Salinas.

Every day the heaviness of what we had done shoved me to the ground. But I kept hearing from fellow parents of addicts that we did the right thing. "You have to let him hit bottom," they would say. All I could do was keep releasing him, keep praying for him to choose recovery in some way. I couldn't do it for him. But my heart couldn't stop aching.

When he finally contacted us, we met him at a Mexican restaurant in Salinas one late Saturday afternoon. Our hearts broke when we saw him. Homeless, worn clothing, dirty, disheveled, with a defeated look in his eyes. We hugged him, fed him, and sat together for hours.

I racked my brain to figure out what to do. He could come home, but would that end up any different than last time? He needed a recovery program. When Annie suggested a local residential program in Salinas, he jumped and agreed to go.

A few days later, after he was admitted to the program and checked in, I felt a welcome surge of hope. Maybe he had finally hit bottom and was ready for recovery. Maybe we could begin to put this nightmare behind us.

"All is miracle. The stupendous order of nature, the revolution of a hundred million of worlds around a million of suns, the activity of light, the life of animals, all are grand and perpetual miracles."

—VOLATIRE

CHAPTER 8

LOURDES

A few weeks later, in late December 2014, Annie came home from one of her local radiation treatments bursting with excitement and energy. "Bob," she said, "you won't believe this. I mentioned something about my Catholic faith to the doctor, and at the end of my treatment, he asked me if I had ever thought about going to Lourdes in France. The healing place! Saint Bernadette." She continued, "I was shocked, but said I would love to go, but didn't know how to go about it, or what to do."

The doctor went on to tell her about an annual pilgrimage to Lourdes, organized through the Knights of Malta. Every year in the spring, fifty people in the western United States are selected for an all-expenses-paid trip to Lourdes. The people selected have serious or terminal illnesses and are active in their Catholic faith. Then he explained the application process and who to contact.

We both knew about Lourdes from our Catholic upbringing and had both seen the 1940s era movie *The Song of Bernadette*. We knew the basics of Saint Bernadette and the healing water from a spring in a rock grotto. Lourdes stood among the most holy pilgrimage sites in the world, and many people received healing from cancer or other maladies.

A few days later we sat at a local Chinese restaurant with Paul, a member of Carmel Mission's Knights of Malta chapter, to discuss the application process for the Lourdes pilgrimage. He told us that hundreds of applications were submitted each year, and that the selection process took months to complete. In the end, a total of fifty people would be accepted, and each could bring a companion, who would pay their own way. He went on to tell us about his experience of Lourdes as a volunteer helper, and how deeply spiritual and inspiring it was for him. "Not everyone is healed," he said, "but everyone is changed in some way."

As I listened, I thought about the miraculous healing stories in the Bible, some in which Jesus merely touched the person. I looked at Annie and said, "Wow, how awesome would that be?"

She paused and said, "If I get selected for a trip to Lourdes, all I want is peace. Healing would be wonderful, but what I want is a sense of peace." The three of us sat in silence—and stayed quiet for a long moment as her words sank in.

At the end of our meeting, we thanked Paul and said our farewells. He told us we would be in his prayers and wished us well in the application process.

Radiation and chemo treatments progressed as we waited to hear the decision on Annie's application. Every few weeks, the black and white MRI images continued to show the good news of no tumor growth. *Stable* became our favorite word.

Then the decision arrived: Annie had been selected to go to Lourdes!

On our next exam day at Stanford, Annie looked at her doctor and said, "I have the opportunity to go to Lourdes. It's a special and holy place, and I really want to go." The doctor nodded her head as she listened. She completely endorsed the trip and said she knew about Lourdes from her Catholic upbringing.

So, in late April 2015, we boarded a plane headed to the Tarbes-Lourdes-Pyrénées Airport in southern France. Fifty *malades* (person with an illness or malady), who ranged from six to seventy-five years old, and their family companions, along with about two hundred others—clergy members and Knights of Malta volunteers—filled the chartered jumbo jet.

When we arrived in the town and sanctuary of Lourdes, I realized how our little western United States group was just one part of a worldwide pilgrimage. Thousands of people from all over the world—from many faiths—malades and those who were there to love and support them, sought healing. Through the dizzying crowds of people, I turned my focus to one thing: Annie's healing, in whatever form it would take.

At the heart of the Lourdes 126-acre sanctuary sat the grotto, a rocky, semicave area on the side of a hill where in 1858 a fourteen-year-old Bernadette Soubirous experienced supernatural encounters with Mary, mother of Jesus. During one encounter, Bernadette uncovered a continuous spring of water which seemed to possess healing powers. Once word got out of the healing miracles received there, people from all over the world started to arrive. Eventually, a series of baths were constructed adjacent to the grotto where one could be immersed in the water, almost like a baptism.

More than anything, Annie wanted that immersion, and on the second day there, she got it. And so did I.

Hundreds of people queued up on either side of two curtained-off bath areas—a women's side and a men's side. They sat in wheelchairs or rickshaw-type carts, accompanied by their nurse or caregiver. A short railing separated those awaiting the baths from family members or observers.

I marveled at the sight: malades from around the globe, so many with sadness in their eyes, along with a glimmer of hope. They were young and old, black, white, and brown. The faces of the volunteers and family members had a similar look of sadness and hope. An overriding sense of peace and loving service prevailed over the entire mass of people. The focus was on the loved one—the spouse, the family member, the friend or companion. And everyone prayed for healing, for a miracle.

When our escorts pulled Annie's carriage up to the women's waiting area, they told me I needed to go to the men's side where I would experience the bath for myself. I leaned down and looked at Annie inside her cart to wish her well. She smiled with her "I'm ready for this" look.

The men's side wasn't as crowded as the women's, and when I got to the front of the queue, I approached an older man with gray hair who stood at the entrance. A blue and white curtain covered the six-foot-wide and eight-foot-high doorway, which he opened and closed as men came in and out of the baths.

"Hi," I said. "Are you a volunteer?"

"Yes," the man said with an Italian accent. "I've been a volunteer in the baths for over twenty years now. I love it. I see people from all over the world—from every religion and background. The Virgin Mary appeals to so many people. You don't have to be a Catholic. You don't have to be anything. There are no barriers. People just come."

He then motioned to me and a group of four other men to enter. Once I walked through the curtained doorway, a man directed me to an area to undress, and gave me a towel to wrap around my waist. When I stepped out of the undressing area, I was escorted to a rectangular, recessed pool about three feet wide and seven feet long. Concrete steps led into the water, and short concrete walls lined the left and right sides.

Three men gathered around me, and one of them spoke with a German accent. "We are here to assist you and pray with you," he said. "Take your time. There's no rush. After we pray together, you can pray silently until you are ready to step into the bath. Just give us a sign, and we will help you into the bath." I nodded to them that I understood, and we all prayed the Our Father out loud: "Our Father, who art in Heaven, hallowed be Thy name..."

When the prayer finished, the three men stepped away from me, giving me space to pray silently. I prayed for Annie's healing, for Stephen's healing, and for my healing. I prayed for God's guidance and direction. I prayed for God's mercy, healing, and forgiveness.

Then I nodded, and they stepped forward to guide me into the bath. When I stepped onto the first step, the cold water bit into my skin. But as I stepped down onto the second and third steps, and then onto the floor of the tiled bath, waist deep in the water, I didn't shiver or feel cold. It felt so clean, so pure, so perfect. I could hear other men praying in adjoining baths and the sound of water as a body submerged and surfaced.

I looked straight ahead and saw a small statue of Mary on a ledge. I took a deep breath and continued my prayer. The German man said, "OK, we are going to support you as we lean you backward into the water, up to your neck. Just relax. Here we go." The men reached over the short bath walls with their hands on my chest and back, and leaned me backward. I inhaled another deep breath as my body entered the cold water, which still didn't feel cold. The clean and pure water penetrated my body and soul in an invigorating way, a healing way. The men lifted me back up to a standing position. I stood dripping wet but realized my head was still dry. I reached down and splashed water up onto my head, in solidarity with Annie, as I prayed again for her healing.

The men helped me up the stairs of the bath to the wet tiled floor. I felt strong, invigorated, and alive. I felt clean and lifted up. Happy. Exhilarated.

They directed me to the dressing area, where my clothes and shoes waited. I looked for a dry towel, but the only towel was the one around my waist, soaking wet. It didn't matter. I took it off and started getting dressed into my clothes. The water seemed to dry off instantly. Maybe it soaked into me. I didn't care. I was in this holy place, surrounded by God's holy presence, and had just been immersed in the healing water from the miraculous spring inside the grotto. After getting dressed, I thanked the men who assisted me, and half-walked, half-floated, out of the bath area to find Annie.

I spotted her near the front of the women's section and, before long, watched her enter the curtained doorway into the baths. I positioned myself in front of the area where she would exit. When she emerged from the curtained area, I waved my arms until she caught sight of me. She had a mix of happiness and sadness on her face. She walked up and fell into my arms.

She dropped her head into my chest and wept. "I couldn't stop crying, Bob," she sobbed. "I couldn't stop crying. They asked if I wanted to pray...I wanted to...I wanted to do things a certain way...but all I could do was cry." She took a breath and said, "After the bath part, I asked them to pour water on my head, and they did. I felt so close to God, to Mary, to the Lord. I just couldn't help from crying."

For the next seven days, our wonderful hosts guided us through a spiritual pilgrimage of Lourdes: a visit to Bernadette's childhood home and village church, special Masses at various church venues, tours of the area, and special prayer and anointing events. Every moment was special, but nothing impacted Annie more than her experience that day in the baths.

As we boarded the plane to return home, I wondered if healing—physical healing—had taken place. Did God remove the cancer? All I knew for sure was that God touched both of us in similar yet different ways. He made His love crystal clear. I felt it. I know Annie felt it.

Whatever awaited us on the road ahead, this pilgrimage had given us strength to face it. But I also wondered if it would be enough.

"Loss and possession, death and life are one.
There falls no shadow where there shines no sun."

—Hilaire Belloc

CHAPTER 9

THIS CAN'T BE

On a Friday afternoon in early May, we sat in the Stanford exam room with the doctor and looked at the black-and-white images of Annie's brain. The MRI showed the cancer still intact. A miracle healing hadn't happened in Lourdes, despite all the prayers, petitions, devotions, anointings, blessings, and immersions. But as I looked at the images, I realized I had to change my perspective. Although the cancer had not been erased, it was stable and dormant. The fact that this type of cancer—the most aggressive form of brain cancer—had been stabilized was great news. The cancer may not be gone, but it wasn't going to stop Annie from living or from pursuing her dream. Could this be another form of healing?

Annie smiled at the news. Even more than a smile, I saw something else: Belief. Faith. Peace. Her prayer for peace was certainly answered. She glowed with God's peace, more than I had ever seen before. More than anything, she wanted to press on toward the fulfillment of her dream to become a therapist.

We returned from Stanford and settled into a weekend at home. We still felt the glow from Lourdes and couldn't wait to tell our friends everything about our experiences there. Annie loved to tell the story of the baths, and how God touched her. She talked about healing in a calm, reverent way: "I feel like I have been healed. I don't know if the healing is physical or spiritual, but I feel like I have been healed." My faith wasn't as strong as hers, but I started to wonder if perhaps healing somehow happened or was happening in slow motion. Our friends and family cheered her on and surrounded us with love and support.

In late May 2015, life started to return to normal—glorious normal—once again. I returned to work. Annie went back to work part time at the recovery center, where her fellow therapists embraced her and welcomed her back. They wanted to know all the details about her trip. The best part was that Annie got to return to her element and could continue the work she loved. Some workdays took their toll on Annie's chemo-weakened state, but she would say, "I love this work. I want so badly to become a therapist."

July, August, and September rolled on in glorious normal mode. The MRIs and checkups at Stanford continued to deliver good news. The cancer showed no signs of growth and remained stable. Annie continued to make excellent progress toward her marriage and family therapist goal. Out of the required total of 3,000 supervised internship hours, she had made it past the 2,500 mark. She started to make study plans for the final state exam, the last requirement to get officially licensed.

In late September I wrote in my journal: "The time we've had over the past several months has been like a pleasant stay in a peaceful inn off the beaten path. Off the road of chemo, surgery, radiation, constant doctor visits, and never knowing what was next. God has blessed us with an off-ramp and a quiet place to stay. We have been able to rest, regroup, reconnect, breathe, be with each other, and relish a restful, peaceful existence. Just be. Not do. Just be. It has been such a blessing. So simple. So wonderful. Will we be asked to get back on the crazy road of battling cancer? God only knows. But we will go where God leads us."

Then, on Monday, October 19, we met with our local oncologist to review the results of her latest MRI. We walked into the exam room full of faith that the results would show the same stable state as the previous MRI. Full of faith that healing continued to happen.

But no. The MRI showed an "increased level of enhancement" in the tumor.

In an instant, our glorious normal crashed to a halt. The peaceful inn completely vanished and we were catapulted back onto the chaotic road as if we had never left it. The horrible, familiar feeling of dread grabbed me by the throat and punched me in the stomach. Dizziness filled my head.

CRACK.

We sat silently in the exam room, stunned and in disbelief. After a few minutes, Annie spoke. "How can this be?" she moaned. "In Lourdes...I was healed. I was healed."

Where did You go, God? How can You suddenly leave us? Where the hell are You? What's the point of doing anything? Of any of this?

As we waited over the next week for the next Stanford appointment, ugly symptoms of the brain tumor smashed into our lives once again. Annie's speech completely locked up one night. Only fragments came out:

"The thing..."

"I..."

"It looks..."

She stopped in frustration, confusion, sadness, anger. My heart dropped into my churning stomach. My head pounded.

Suddenly she struggled to read or understand work-related paperwork, something so easy and natural before. She looked blankly at the words. Sad vulnerability filled her eyes.

We attended Mass on Saturday evening at San Carlos Church. When the cantor announced, "Our Offertory song is number 265," Annie leafed through the hymnal, unable to find it. Heartsick, I gently pointed to the song in my hymnal. Still struggling, she eventually found it. But rather than sing in her lovely voice, I heard the sound of soft weeping. Annie's heart and spirit were breaking. I was breaking.

Chained to the shore, I watched in agony as the river current pulled Annie away from me.

In early November 2015 we returned to Stanford for the next level of diagnosis and treatment options. The doctor tried to put some optimism in her voice as she explained a new set of options, including clinical trials, more aggressive chemo, and even an electrical treatment device. But every option brought only more confusion over which way to go. We had a mountain of information to consider, but we didn't have the luxury of time. We needed to decide soon. Each day that passed represented more tumor growth.

On our drive home from Stanford, she blurted out, "I don't even want to hear the word Lourdes. I was healed! Damn it! So, what is this?" Then she said, "Help me to understand...why this...is happening to me. Help me understand."

Based on recommendations from the doctors, we decided to enroll in a clinical trial with Stanford that involved a third brain surgery followed by treatment with an experimental drug. Due to the uncertain nature of the trial, we had to sign multiple legal disclosure and consent forms and return weekly to Stanford for follow-up testing and treatment.

After the third brain surgery and return home on Thanksgiving weekend 2015, we tried to have a normal December when nothing was normal. Each week that passed as we waited for the drug trial to start brought me an increasing sense of dread as I tried to cling to shreds of hope. Somehow Annie was able to rebound in her faith and landed in a place of peace and calm. She was able to smile when I felt like a nervous wreck. *How can she be so calm? How can she manage to smile? What does she see or know that I don't?*

In mid-December, Stephen arrived at the house with a young woman he met in southern California. In the year since he entered the Salinas drug rehab program, where he lasted six weeks before a relapse and subsequent discharge, he had moved back to Anaheim in southern California, then reconnected with his friend who rehired him to work on a construction-survey crew in Pennsylvania. That lasted until winter arrived, when he returned back to Anaheim.

Although this was his first time back at the house since his eviction, the girlfriend dynamic provided a welcome distraction that prevented it from becoming a topic. After dinner, the four of us spent the evening looking at Stephen's baby photographs, which his girlfriend begged to see. As much as I wanted the visit to be normal, it wasn't. Her erratic behavior and on-and-off incoherence telegraphed that she struggled with addiction as much as he did—maybe worse. I tried to relate and enjoy our time but couldn't, whereas Annie seemed so calm and present to them. By the time they left the next morning, I sighed in relief.

I heaved another sigh of relief once the clinical trial drug treatments started in late December. Now at least something fought the brain tumor. Each week, we made the four-hour round trip to Stanford.

One day in late January, after one of the weekly visits, as we got into our car for the drive back home, my phone rang. I didn't recognize the number, so I ignored it. It rang a few minutes later, and I ignored it again. When it rang a third time, I answered. "Hello, this is a collect call from the Inmate Calling Service from the Orange County Jail. The person <Stephen>"—pronounced with his own voice—"is calling. Press 1 to answer or press 0 to decline the call." *What the hell?*

My blood boiled as anger erupted inside me. I wanted to scream. I wanted to push Stephen out of my life. With anger and disgust, I pressed 1.

"Dad?" Stephen said.

"Yeah… What the…" I could barely talk.

"Uhh…yeah…it's fucked up, I know, but I got arrested and put in jail. But I need some money for the commissary so I can buy some hygiene stuff. Can you help me out? I'll explain it all later." I bit my tongue and looked over at Annie in the passenger seat. She looked exhausted. Confused. But an unshakeable sense of peace and acceptance still surrounded her. *How can you do this to us, Stephen? How can you do this to your mom of all people, who's fighting for her life?*

Days, weeks, and months dragged on as the current pulled Annie further and further away.

In early March 2016, Annie's doctor entered the exam room and greeted us. As she conducted the usual neurological exam, a concerned look appeared on her face as Annie struggled through every step. She couldn't come up with any of the answers to any of the questions and looked blankly at the papers. Sadness filled her eyes.

I watched in powerless agony as parts of Annie fell away like giant pieces of glacier ice that crash into the sea. Permanent parts: the ability to think, talk, and function.

After the exam, the doctor hugged Annie and exited the room. Within minutes another knock sounded on the exam room door, and our coordinator from the Clinical Trial Unit entered. She, too, had a troubled look on her face. "I'm sorry, but I have some bad news," she said. "The blood test shows a high enzyme count in your liver. It's one of the indicators we watch each week. It's a measure of how the body is reacting to the study drug. We have to suspend the clinical trial until that indicator gets back to normal."

This removed the only thing that stood between her and the relentless invasion of the cancer. The medication could no longer protect her. The best doctors and surgeons could no longer protect her. I could not protect her. At that moment the last vestige of hope within me died, leaving an empty void.

CRACK! Deafening and final.

She looked at Annie with a deep kindness and said, "You have an aura about you. It's remarkable. You have a presence, an energy, that makes people love you without even knowing you. You're very special." She continued, "I'm very sorry about this news. We just cannot continue the drug until the liver enzyme level goes down. We will set our sights on next week's blood test and go from there. This is difficult. Your speech will get worse as the cancer progresses. While you can still talk, make sure you say things that need to be said to the people in your life who need to hear them."

She knew about Stephen's addiction and our family struggles. I nodded a thank-you, and we finished our appointment and drove home in silence. A few miles down the road, I looked over at Annie and noticed a peaceful look on her face. Somehow, through it all, she was being protected. Insulated. Comforted. *How is that even possible?* A mixture of relief, confusion, and trepidation filled me.

I looked again a few minutes later and noticed she had fallen gently asleep.

"Even though I walk through the valley of the shadow of death, I will fear no evil, for You are with me; your rod and your staff comfort me."

—Psalm 23:4

CHAPTER 10

FREE FALL

Monday, 10 P.M., April 25, 2016.

Darkness engulfed the lifeless house. Silence permeated every room, except for the low hum of the kitchen refrigerator. Ten hours earlier I held onto Annie's hand as she crossed the threshold into eternity at the age of sixty. Trembling and alone, I looked on as death took Annie away. From the instant I witnessed her last breath and her life force vanish from my sight, my world shattered.

Life without her was unthinkable. A reality I couldn't imagine.

Now, on my first night alone, I held on for dear life, as if I clung to a raft in a storm at sea. Grief gagged me like gulps of seawater. My empty stomach churned in knots. My head pounded as it tried in vain to grasp what had happened. My body begged for any kind of relief or sleep, but the torment inside raged on.

Dark images from only hours ago flooded my mind: The hospice nurse whom I had desperately called for but who arrived thirty minutes too late stood over Annie's lifeless body in the medical bed in our bedroom, declaring the time of her death. The two men from the mortuary as they lifted her dead body from the bed, placed it inside a black body bag, zipped it up, strapped it to the gurney, and wheeled it out of the house. The sight of the mortuary vehicle driving away and disappearing around the corner. The images cycled nonstop over and over in my brain. *Stop! Stop! My God. Oh God. Did this really happen?*

In the final days leading up to Annie's death, as she lay dying, I found myself in a small rowboat inside the grip of a roaring river as it hurtled me toward a powerful waterfall. Death approached. The sound of the waterfall ahead grew louder and louder with each passing day as it pulled me into its grip. The tiny boat was no match for the violent white water that soaked me and tossed the boat. Powerless to fight the waves or row against the rushing current, all I could do was hang on, watch, and wait in dread. Nothing could stop it or slow it down.

Now, the waterfall swallowed me. It pulled me over its edge into a free fall. I squirmed and twisted in the empty bed—our bed, the bed we shared for thirty-five years—as I plunged into the darkness. My shattered heart pounded inside my chest. My mind raced in panic as it tried to face the new nightmare reality of life without Annie. There was no escape. No rescue. No relief. She was gone. Forever.

In the darkness I reached my hand across the bed in a vain attempt to feel her next to me. I grabbed the pillow and tried to get a smell. A sense. A feeling. Anything. But nothing was there other than a dark, empty void. After life together for so many years, part of me had been amputated—pulled, stretched, and yanked until it tore off completely. I now faced life alone.

As I fell in agony, the only thing I could hang onto—the only thing I could see—were four small words from Psalm 23 that flickered like a faint light inside the abyss: "...you are with me." *You are with me. Oh God, please be with me. Please be with me in this darkness. You are with me. Please be with me. You are all I have.*

In the middle of the night I jerked awake to the suffocating heat of my sweat-soaked sheets and pillow. I threw the sheets off my wet skin and stumbled to the bathroom to dry off. I grabbed a towel and looked in the mirror in the dim light. I looked blurred, ghostlike, almost invisible. *What the hell is happening to me?*

I wiped the sweat off my chest and splashed cold water on my face and hands. I took a deep breath through my dry mouth as I looked again at my reflection. My stomach twisted. I wanted to scream, or cry, or both. But I didn't have the energy. After I used and flushed the toilet, I heard the familiar sound of water refilling it, like I had heard hundreds of times before. That same sound happened during good times, normal times. I felt a momentary sense of familiar comfort, a tiny sense of normal. Then the water stopped. The dreaded, empty silence returned.

Loneliness mocked me: "*You are alone now. That's right. Alone. There is no one here but you. And me. Get used to it. This is not a dream. It's real. And I'm not going away.*"

Now wide awake with my heart pounding, I worked my way out of the dark bedroom toward the kitchen. The empty house felt cold and foreign, like I no longer belonged. The soft light from the neighborhood streetlamps was enough for me to find my way to the kitchen, to the hum of the refrigerator.

I thought of my next-door neighbors, oblivious to my pain and sound asleep in their homes, like any other night. It wasn't their fault. They had their own lives. They couldn't help me.

My eyes burned from the white light of the refrigerator when I opened the door and pulled out the plastic milk carton. I unscrewed the blue plastic cap, lifted the opening to my numb lips, and poured it in. The cold, white liquid soothed my dry mouth and throat as it went down. The muscles in my body relaxed a bit, then I felt a strange sensation in my stomach—a tinge of hunger I hadn't felt all day. I opened a kitchen cabinet and pulled out a package of cookies and dug in. I sighed in relief with each bite chased by cold milk. After a few minutes, my stomach hit the brakes. I stood in the dark kitchen and inhaled a deep breath.

I had to face the empty bed again.

When I crawled in, my skin recoiled at the cold, sweat-soaked sheets and pillow. I moved to a dry spot in the middle, flipped over my pillow, and lay on my back. I stared at the ceiling. I looked at the blue glow of my bedside digital clock: 2:23 a.m. Then 2:31 a.m. Then 2:37 a.m. Time needled me with each glance, over and over, again and again. 3:02. 3:11. 4:03. Finally, morning light started to appear through the bedroom window and ushered in nothing but emptiness.

Numbness permeated my body as I climbed out of bed on my first morning alone. I don't remember taking a shower, getting dressed, or forcing myself to eat, but I must have. The only activity my brain could conjure up was physical exercise. I had to get out of the torture chamber that my house had suddenly become. Using pure muscle memory, I put on my workout clothes and drove my car to the gym.

Cardio exercise always kept me anchored, especially over the prior three years. It gave me a sense of control in the chaos. I could put on the headphones, listen to music, and lose myself on the elliptical, or the bike, or the stair climber. Afterward I had some strength to face whatever came next. But this time was different. I was alone now. A widower. The ground under my feet had turned upside down. The clean, crisp morning air may as well have been smoke-filled; I wouldn't have known the difference. *Where am I? What planet?*

I entered the gym's glass entrance doors in a fog. I checked in at the front desk. The girl checked my ID card and handed me a white workout towel. I walked through the next set of glass doors into the facility, which opened to a large hallway with a sunlit, thirty-foot ceiling. Muffled sounds of people talking, the echo of a basketball being dribbled against the gym floor, and the whirling of cardio machines filled the space. I had to consciously tell myself where to go. *Turn right for the swimming pool, go straight for the basketball courts, and turn left for the cardio and weight room.*

I turned left for the cardio room, which was just past the snack bar area dotted with tables and chairs. I noticed a family of four seated at a table nearby. Out of the blue, a little red-haired girl I had never seen before turned completely around in her chair and looked straight at me. She smiled and waved at me with all the innocence of a child. My knees buckled. My heart stopped. Somehow, I managed to smile and wave back. She then turned back to join her family, and I just stood there as people buzzed past me. *It's OK, Bob. I made it safe and sound. I'm OK.*

After the momentary shock wore off, I realized it wasn't OK. *I'm not OK. Nothing is OK. How can I possibly endure this?*

"Here at the bottom of the world,
everything was upside down."

—LESLEY HOWARTH

—◆—

CHAPTER 11

MY UPSIDE-DOWN WORLD

The world around me looked strange and unfamiliar. Nothing had physically changed, but everything had changed. My life plans, hopes, and dreams—my identity—all lay shattered on the floor like glass fragments from a broken vase. For the first time in forty years, I faced an unknown future alone with zero sense of direction or what to do. Overnight, I found myself aimless. No focus. No role. No one to love and protect. Unlike the last three years, in which every moment revolved around my role as Annie's primary caregiver, everything had instantly stopped.

The sudden void left me paralyzed. I could no longer pray with her, hug or comfort her. I could no longer care for her—brush her hair, tuck her into bed, or help her get cleaned and dressed. I could no longer sing to her or feed her. I could no longer whisper to her that everything would be OK. I no longer needed to handle all the details, the appointments, the trips to doctors and medical centers, the medications, the insurance billing, and whatever else needed to be done. None of that remained.

Day after day, hour after hour, life compressed itself into one pain-filled moment after another. My sense of smell and taste disappeared, along with any appetite. Invisible chains pinned me down, immobilizing me. Dense fog surrounded me. I continued to cling to any sense of God's presence, but felt only a throbbing, dull ache that wouldn't go away.

Gravity doubled its force on me. My six-foot, 200-pound frame now felt like 400 pounds. I moved in slow motion through a maze of thorns

I didn't want to navigate but had to: decisions on funeral arrangements, mortuary and cemetery services and payments, notifications and phone calls to family and friends, obituary details, bank account and insurance policy notifications, proper disposal of all medications no longer needed, and on and on.

Grief forced a new set of glasses on me that turned everything upside down, like the man I saw in a school science class film. The man put on lenses that flipped everything upside down on the retina. He bumped into things, lost his balance continually, and could barely function. I had become that man. Eventually, his optic nerves and brain compensated for the distorted orientation and turned everything right side up again. He regained his equilibrium and returned to normal life. I wondered if that would ever happen for me.

Exhaustion pervaded my body, but sleep continued to elude me. At night, when my squirming in bed became unbearable, I grabbed one of Annie's sleeping pills from the brown prescription jar in the medicine cabinet.

The knot in my stomach didn't let up, along with my lack of appetite. But I knew I had to eat, so I forced myself, which made me feel sick. The only food items I could manage were protein drinks, milk, yogurt, and peanut butter and jelly on toasted bread.

One day I tried to rest on the living room couch. I sat on the plush surface, where I had found so much comfort before. I slumped sideways and laid my head on a pillow but felt seasick. My body had forgotten how to relax. I closed my eyes in exhaustion, but images of what had happened slapped me back into my new reality. I turned on the TV for a distraction, but it sounded like meaningless noise. Unable to relax, I rolled off the couch and went outside for a walk. Maybe it would help me breathe.

Despite my excellent physical condition, exhaustion stopped me halfway up the neighborhood walking trail. The easy trail felt daunting.

On the morning of the funeral, my body moved robotically on its own. I got out of my bed, showered, forced down something to eat, got dressed, and drove myself to the old mission church in Monterey. As I opened the car door, the cold, damp air hit my face. A mixture of fog and clouds cast their gloom on the day. Everything looked and felt gray. I struggled to breathe as I turned to make my way to the church.

I saw Stephen on the sidewalk. He had arrived the day before, driven into town from southern California by Annie's brother, Bill. He had finished his jail term a few weeks earlier and had been living on the streets since. When he arrived at the house, I was at a complete loss on how to respond to him. When I reached out to hug him, his body slumped into mine. His ragged clothes smelled foul, his dirty brown hair hung in strands around his face, and his eyes looked hollow and sad. His muscular arms had tattoos and blood marks where I assumed needles had penetrated. His spirit sagged into the depths of despair and shame.

"Stephen," I said, "I am barely hanging on here. I cannot deal with anything from you. I can't. I'll set you up in a hotel room, but that's all I can manage." He just nodded as he looked at the ground. My heart sobbed in agony as I looked at what our son had become.

I thought back to the last time Stephen saw his mom. Shortly after another release from jail, I told him to come up and see Annie as soon as possible, before she had completely lost her ability to talk. The brain tumor had invaded her speech center, which faded away, day by day, as she entered her final weeks.

"OK, Dad," Stephen said. "I'll be there next weekend."

He never showed. After two agonizing weeks, he finally called and I made arrangements for him to take an Amtrak train from southern California to Salinas. My friend Tim picked him up when he arrived and drove him to the house. When Stephen walked into the house, I gagged. He looked and smelled like a lost soul, a pariah. Barefoot, dirty, torn jeans and shabby T-shirt, stringy hair, and the look of despair and deadness on his face.

Dizzy and wobbly from the shock of seeing him, I led him into our bedroom where Annie lay in the medical bed next to our bed. She turned her head to look at him but couldn't speak a word. She strained to speak with her eyes, using the last bits of energy she had. Stephen stood alongside her bed next to her, and then sobbed as he collapsed to his knees on the floor.

Now, as I saw him outside the church, his shoulders slumped, his head bent down, his hands stuffed in his pockets. He wore a pair of shoes, pants, and collared shirt he found in his old bedroom closet. His straggly hair hung over his forlorn face. He looked so lost. But I couldn't help him. It took all I had to walk in alone.

A flow of people moved toward the church from different directions. As I approached the entrance, voices greeted me and hugged me or shook my hand. I greeted them back and thanked them for coming. Faces and bodies blurred. I took my seat in the second row from the front in the small church, near the altar. I couldn't bring myself to sit in the front row, directly in front of the casket. Stephen took a seat a few feet to my right. Annie's mother, Germaine, her brother Bill, his wife Susan, and their two adult daughters, Kelly and Jessie, sat in the front row.

Music started to play, and the Catholic funeral Mass began. The polished wooden casket sat less than ten feet in front of me, three feet off the ground on a draped four-wheel cart. Two statues mounted on the far side church walls appeared to bracket the casket at the head and foot: on the right side, a statue of Jesus with arms stretched out in front, and on the left, a statue of Mary. Maybe the juxtaposition was meant to comfort me, but it didn't. Nothing could. I tried to focus on something else. Anything but the casket.

When the moment came for me to say a few words, I stood and walked up to the podium. Father Patrick, the priest and friend who walked the entire brain cancer journey with us, whispered to me, "It's OK, Bob. Just speak from your heart. We are all here for you. Whatever you say is fine."

I looked out at the sea of faces, but none registered except Germaine and Bill. At eighty-nine years old, Germaine's five-foot, eight-inch solid German frame sat stoically in the pew, but her wrinkled face showed the deep pain of sorrow and disbelief underneath her short, white-gray hair. "This shouldn't have happened to her," Germaine had bemoaned over and over. "I've lived my life. God should have taken me, not my baby. Not my Annie."

Bill also sat upright next to Germaine. His strong face, neat gray hair, and stocky frame faced the casket. His disciplined background in U.S. Navy submarines and nuclear engineering enabled him to stay strong, but I knew his heart was broken inside. He loved his little sister with his entire being and had always looked out for her.

Bill took after their father, Harvey, a rough, tough, ex-WWII Marine gunnery sergeant of Spanish-Mexican descent. He took care of his family with a fiercely strong love. He died of a sudden heart attack while albacore fishing with Bill on a boat off the Sea of Cortez sixteen years earlier. He managed to land a big fish, then sat down on the boat deck and died.

But if one person could melt Harvey's tough exterior, it was Annie. She was his little girl, and no one was good enough for her. He grudgingly gave his permission for us to marry only after I survived years of his resistance, and then he became my biggest ally.

I spoke for a few minutes as I held onto the wooden sides of the podium. I didn't cry or break down, but I don't remember what I said.

Soon afterward, the service ended. The moment had come for the final good-bye. My body got up from its seat and moved alongside the casket along with Stephen and two other pallbearers. The musicians sang "Lead Me, Lord" as we escorted the casket down the center aisle past the rows of faceless attendees.

I struggled to breathe through my dry mouth as we exited the church into the sprinkling rain. My rigid body vibrated from head to toe, my head throbbed, my eyes burned, and my empty stomach churned. The mortuary attendant stood calmly outside the church and directed us to the rear of a large black hearse that idled curbside. Once we arrived at the vehicle, he said, "On the count of three, lift up and place the front onto this railing. Then we'll push it inside. Ready? 1-2-3, *lift*."

The four of us lifted the heavy casket off the cart and onto the hearse. Once the front edge landed, the two men at the rear slowly pushed it into the vehicle. As the casket slid past me, raindrops on the smooth, wooden surface soaked my left hand. *This is it.*

Once the casket was fully inside, the attendant stepped forward. I stepped back as he slammed the two rear doors shut. *Bang! Bang!* My body recoiled. None of it seemed real. I stood and watched as it drove away and disappeared around the corner. I turned to face my family and friends gathered to support me. I wanted to scream. Or yell. Or cry. Or all three. But no life pulsed in me. Just a dull throbbing pain. *Suck it up. Be strong.*

I moved in a daze across the wet street, accompanied by friends, family, and co-workers, to the church's community hall. The large, carpeted room was set up with tables of food and beverages, and a large area in the middle where we all gathered. I didn't see Stephen. People expressed their support and condolences the best way they could.

"I am so sorry, Bob."

"Please let me know if you need anything."

"She was an amazing woman and is now at peace."

My boss told me to take as much time as I needed away from work. Each loving encounter was meant to comfort me, but I felt nothing but numbness. After a while, after all the hugs and words of encouragement, the spinning room emptied as everyone dispersed and went their own separate ways, back to their own lives.

Annie's brother, Bill, hugged me farewell and assured me that he would take Stephen back to southern California. I hugged Stephen good-bye but didn't know what to say other than "Take care of yourself."

The time had come for me to go back home. *Home? What home? What was I going back to?* As I walked to my wet car in the empty parking lot, dizziness spun me around in nauseous circles. *What now? What do I do now?*

I had absolutely nothing left to do. No tasks. All the arrangements, interactions with people, and to-do activities leading up to the funeral were now over. Done. The cremation and interment of the ashes were weeks away. There was nothing left to protect and distract me from the empty loneliness. I had nowhere to run or hide. I had to face it, and the thought terrified me. *How can I do this? How can I face this alone?*

"For in grief nothing 'stays put.' One keeps on emerging from a phase, but it always recurs. Round and round. Everything repeats. Am I going in circles, or dare I hope I am on a spiral? But if a spiral, am I going up or down it?"

—C. S. Lewis

CHAPTER 12

THE GRIEF CAVE

I quickly discovered that my experience of grief isolated me in a way I had never experienced. My friends and family wanted to help and did everything they could to support me. I received countless expressions of love and encouragement: letters, cards, phone calls, flowers, emails, invitations to dinner or a walk, or "whatever you need." My two older brothers, Pete and John, drove up from southern California for a moral support weekend. My two sisters who lived in New York and North Carolina, Mary and Ann, supported me with phone calls.

But despite the support, I found myself in a totally different orbit from everyone. As much as they wanted to help me, they could only do so much. Even those who had suffered the death of a loved one were limited. They listened to me. They sympathized. But they had already walked their own grief journey. Now I had to walk mine.

I had been plunged into a dark cave with no map, no guide, and no flashlight. I had to acclimate to the darkness and somehow find my way through.

My subterranean world also made me invisible to most people. I existed in a grief dimension that most people couldn't see unless they were in it themselves. With few exceptions, most people started to leave me alone, as if I didn't exist. Maybe they were giving me space. Maybe the cloud of mortality hovered over me, which subconsciously repelled them. Whatever it was, I no longer fit in with the world around me. Already disoriented, I felt the confusion and despair of being an isolated outcast.

My worst torment came from permeating aloneness. I lived in constant mental, spiritual, emotional and physical pain. It hurt so much that my moment-to-moment existence boiled down to how and where to find any kind of relief. I couldn't relax.

The comforting home we had lived in for the last twelve years became a torture chamber. I stood in the living room, in the middle of a pressure-cooker of dead emptiness. No voices. No movement. No noises. No life. Just me and complete stillness. Reminders and memories of the life we had built together surrounded me—every piece of furniture, every photo on the wall, every single item in the house connected me to a life that no longer existed.

Exhausted, I flopped down on a living room chair and tried to gather myself. My eyes settled across the room on an 8 by 10 photo propped on the coffee table, a framed picture of the two of us together smiling. *Bang!* The walls started to close in. Fear and panic gripped me. I bolted across the room and slammed the photo face down. I couldn't look at it.

To find relief, I would sit in bumper-to-bumper traffic, where at least I could feel cars and people around me. I attended crowded Masses at church, I walked through stores at the mall, sat at the countertop in restaurants and bars where at least the bartender would interact with me.

I couldn't bring myself to call friends or co-workers and say, "I'm lonely. Can I come over?" I had to do this on my own. They had their own lives, and I didn't want to be a charity case.

I wanted to feel God's presence and comfort so desperately, but I didn't. Or couldn't. I had to find something to hang onto, to give my soul just an ounce of peace. Each night I clung to some scripture verses that I could relate to and find a morsel of comfort:

"Be merciful to me, O Lord, for I am in distress; my eyes grow weak with sorrow, my soul and my body with grief." —Psalm 31:9

"The Lord is close to the brokenhearted, and saves those who are crushed in spirit." —Psalm 34:18

"You will grieve, but your grief will become joy." —John 16:20

But these weren't enough. The relentless demon of loneliness plagued me day and night. I needed human interaction and human companionship.

I immediately returned to my job at the Monterey County IT (Information Technology) Department, just so I could get some distraction from the pain, even if only for eight hours a day. The IT Department was filled with more than a hundred smart, friendly, and supportive employees, and I knew they would give me a warm welcome back. As a centralized group, we provided computer and software support services for the other county departments and were housed in a large single-story building. We banded together like IT geeks tend to do.

Although I didn't identify myself as a computer nerd, I enjoyed the technical world of computers and software and spent more than ten years as a computer training instructor—back in the growth days of the personal computer, computer networks, and the Internet itself—from 1990 to 2002. My work in the IT field made for a solid career and paid well, but it didn't represent my passion or fulfill any deep purpose in life.

I always looked at my work life as a choice on a menu—pick something that looks good and work hard at it to provide for my family—not a passion to pursue. After graduating from college with a bachelor's degree in construction management, I spent the first ten years of my career in the construction-engineering field where I worked in power plant construction (geothermal, hydroelectric, and natural gas) in northern California. When my employer decided to vacate the power plant building business, however, I had to find a new path.

Through Annie I met Tim and Alice, a husband-wife team who had hired her to teach classes for their new computer training company. Eventually, in May of 1990, I resigned from my initial career path and started over in my computer-hardware-software career.

My return to the IT Department gave me a reason to wake up in the morning. The once burdensome routine now gave me incredible comfort: wake up to the alarm at 5:45 a.m., take a shower, get dressed, pray/meditate/breathe, eat something for breakfast, make coffee, and drive to work.

As soon as I walked into the building on my first day back, my co-workers responded with warm greetings, often accompanied by big hugs:

"Hi, Bob! It's so great to see you!"

"Hey, dude! Welcome back!"

"We've missed you around here!"

"I'm so sorry for your loss. Please let me know if you need anything."

What helped me most, however, was the mental focus on work stuff. As an IT manager, I supervised a group of IT support analysts and got involved with a wide variety of issues. Everything from technical hardware-software issues to human resources and job performance. I got to see and talk with people on solving work problems. I got to sit, stand, walk, talk, meet, discuss, strategize, solve, and fix. From day one I felt some equilibrium come back into my life. I even ate lunch with a slowly emerging appetite.

But as the clock neared 5:00 p.m. and the end of the workday approached, my stomach twisted and churned. For the first time in my life I didn't want the workday to end. I would have slept there if I could.

Instead, I heard the office building doors close as people exited one by one. I heard the happy farewell greetings: "See you tomorrow!" or "I'm off to my son's game. Have a great night!" I fidgeted in my office chair and tried to focus on the email on my computer screen as the sound of the night janitor's vacuum filled the void. I had no reason to stay late. I delayed as long as possible but eventually faced the fact that I had to go home. I logged out of my desk computer, gathered my empty lunch box, turned off the office light, and closed the door. As I walked to my car in the empty parking lot, an anchor pulled me downward.

When I returned to the empty house, I crawled back into the cage to fight another round. I looked at the two pillows on the bed. Why two? That's no longer true. I took one pillow off and put it in a closet. I moved my pillow to the middle of the bed, by itself. A single pillow on our large bed looked so sickening.

I looked at the wedding ring on my finger. The ring I wore for thirty-five years. Why is it there? It's no longer true. It no longer applies. I took a final glance at it on my finger, and then pulled it off. I sat and stared at my bare finger. It wasn't just a ring. It was an identity. A role. An honor. A joy. And now gone.

Who am I alone? Everyone and everything in my life was so connected to Annie. We were so connected, so much a part of each other, going all the way back to our wedding vows that stated, "the two shall become one flesh" (Genesis 2:24). How can flour and salt be separated once they're baked together into bread? How can I be separate again? I can't. But she's gone. I had no choice. I didn't understand. Nothing made sense anymore.

When I saw happy families around the neighborhood or at the store, I had to look the other way. They reminded me of what I had lost. I burned inside. Everyone had a family of some kind. Everyone belonged to someone. Friends asked me if I was getting support from Stephen, and I groaned. I hadn't heard from him since the funeral, and even if I wanted to, I had no way to contact him. I just tried to survive and assumed he did the same. We were both on our own. *Is anybody out there who would understand this? Anyone who gets it? Anyone who knows what this is like? Anyone who can help?*

I had to find others who slogged through their own grief caves. Did such a thing exist? I heard about a local grief support group and decided to attend. I didn't expect anything miraculous, but I did expect to come away with something—anything—positive and helpful. But I also felt like a leper in search of a colony.

One day after work, I drove with nervous anticipation to the meeting. I found the building in downtown Monterey and parked in the black asphalt parking lot. I took a deep breath and stepped out of the car. *Here we go.*

My nervousness grew as I walked around the building trying to find the entrance. Once I found the entry door, I stepped inside and climbed a narrow flight of carpeted stairs to the second floor, which led me to a closed door with the correct suite number. I opened the door and stepped into a meeting room.

Several people mingled in the room and talked in hushed tones. I noticed about fifteen folding chairs arranged in a circle. A woman walked over and welcomed me to the meeting. After a brief introduction, she pointed out an adjoining room where I could find water, coffee, tea, and various food items. I thanked her and walked over.

Seven or eight people gathered around the long, rectangular snack table. More hushed tones. Sad smiles and a sense of heaviness permeated the room. I introduced myself to a few people, but the greetings were brief with few words and little if any eye contact. After a few awkward minutes, the facilitator called everyone into the main room to begin the meeting. I took a seat in the circle of chairs and noticed the coffee table in the middle, which had tissue boxes, some plastic drinking water bottles, and a bowl of candy. Soon the circle of chairs filled in as people took their seats.

The facilitator opened the meeting: "Thank you all for coming. It's not easy for any of us to be here, but it's a place where healing can begin. Let's start by going around the circle. Please introduce yourself and tell us what brought you here this evening." By the time it got to me, I blurted out these words for the first time: "My name is Bob and my wife passed away from brain cancer about a week ago." The reality and impact of the words shocked me, as if someone else spoke them. I heard a few gasps from the group.

The introductions continued around the circle until everyone finished. The facilitator thanked everyone and opened the floor to anyone who wanted to share what they were going through. For the next hour or so, I sat and listened to people sob, weep, and agonize over their loss and the intense pain they felt. With each person's share I felt a deeper sense of despair. I kept waiting for some helpful words from the facilitator—something to ease the pain, some helpful insight or revelation—but nothing was offered except a listening ear and an acknowledgment of each person's pain.

I squirmed in my seat as I witnessed the pain around me, like witnessing seasick people vomit on a heaving boat. I started to feel sick myself. Anguish flooded the room. When my turn came, I passed. I wanted to get up and walk out. But I just held on and waited for the meeting to end. When it finally did, I couldn't get away fast enough. Panic gripped me. Instead of some light, I found only more darkness. No light. No hope. No tools. No sign of life. *How deep is this pit? Am I trapped here? Will I ever get out?*

All I knew is that I couldn't go back to that meeting. I had to find another way. Anything that would help. That night I tried to force myself to a better frame of mind and wrote in my journal: "*I can get through this. I can do it, with God's help. God is with me 24 x 7, 365. He is with me. Breathe deep. Fill your mind with good thoughts. I am not alone—God is with me. I have true friends who want to help me. God has a plan for my life.*"

Desperate to find support, I searched online for local grief support groups and found one offered through the local hospital, where we had found so many support resources over the last three years. Lectures, events, books, videos, support groups, nutrition guides, and counseling—all offered at no charge. Surely the grief support group they offered would help me now. The meeting was held at the Westland House, a short drive from the hospital.

A week later I drove along a curved road through a quiet, forested area. It felt like I had entered a retreat center. After I parked, I sat in the car for a few minutes with the windows open and breathed in the clean and peaceful air. I walked toward the entrance and held my breath that it wouldn't be like my first meeting. The late afternoon summer sunlight filled the entry lobby of the modern building. I saw a handwritten sign with an arrow that pointed toward the room for the Grief Support group.

I entered a large room that felt like a comfortable library. A stone fireplace accented the space that had about ten chairs and six people arranged in a circle. A middle-aged woman with short brown hair smiled, greeted me warmly, and asked me to take a seat. As I sat down, I glanced at the others in the circle and nodded a silent greeting. Some nodded back. Others just looked straight ahead with blank expressions on their faces.

The facilitator handed out a worksheet with some guidelines and discussion questions for the meeting. She sat in the circle and welcomed us. "Thank you for coming today, everyone. My name is Barbara, and I'm here to facilitate our discussion. Before we begin, let's go around the circle and introduce ourselves. Please tell us your name and the loss that brought you here."

I immediately felt more comfortable than I had at my first meeting. Maybe it was the format, or the smaller group size, but many of us shared our answers to the questions printed on the handout. Questions such as: "What emotions are you experiencing in your grief?" "What challenges are you encountering in your grief?" The facilitator provided feedback and insights at appropriate times, and the participants shared openly. Some people cried and sobbed as they tried to speak. Others passed on verbal sharing, but their body told their story: head down, shoulders slumped, and their eyes focused down at the floor.

When my turn came, I spoke up and answered the questions, but felt hollow and numb inside. The articulation of words describing how I felt did not provide any instant healing power. It wasn't going to be that easy. If anything, I became more aware of the inner turmoil throughout my body. How deep was this hole? *What's the point? What am I doing here? I'm barely treading water.* But still, I wanted to participate in the process. I knew I had to attack this thing, even though I had no idea how. What other choice did I have?

For the next six weeks, I dug into the questions on the handouts, hoping to find some relief and guidance. Anything to help me face my pain. But each week I left with the same pain, and nothing but emptiness inside. I felt like a rookie bullfighter pitted against an attacking bull. A few friends and family watched from the stands, cheered me on, and tried to help, but this was my fight. No one could step into the arena and take my place. I had to find a way out or through this. I had to find an escape or learn how to fight the bull. I had to keep trying.

In the last meeting I attended, a woman in her mid-thirties shared how she lost her husband to a sudden illness. Sadness and misery enveloped her like a shroud. When the meeting ended, I walked out with her, and we stopped after we exited the front door. She just looked down at the ground and said, "I cannot believe how painful this loneliness is. It's overwhelming…it's unbearable…I miss my husband so much."

I nodded and said, "I know."

We each walked away, back to our own cars, in the same agony. I was going in circles. *Am I just going to discuss my misery each week with fellow sufferers and then go on my way? How does this help?* I had to find a better grief recovery meeting if it existed. This one was more helpful than the first, but I needed something more.

At the three-month mark, the daily grind of grief pain continued unabated. One moment overwhelming sorrow and sadness invaded, followed by a crippling wave of fear. The dull, gut ache of confusion and emptiness were constant. Grief infected my entire mind, body, and soul.

Pain relief eluded me as I searched for anything to take my mind in another direction. For some fortunate reason, I wasn't drawn to alcohol or drugs. In normal times I enjoy a few beers or glasses of wine, but they held no appeal in grief. Simple pleasures or enjoyment of any kind had become foreign concepts to me.

I continued to take walks and go to the health club for exercise, which helped to clear my head momentarily. Occasionally I would take a walk with a friend, but most of the time I went solo. I didn't want to be alone, but I had to be alone to think. To process. To wrestle.

My daily work life pattern of Monday through Friday helped distract me from my pain, but that's all it was—a distraction. I dreaded weekends, holidays, and days off from work. I finally understood the appeal of a workaholic lifestyle. *It may not be the worst thing to become a workaholic. Instead of a mere forty hours a week, I could work myself to exhaustion, fall asleep, get up, and repeat the process every single day of the week. I could bury myself in work and escape the pain.*

But something inside told me that would just make my misery worse. It would be the equivalent of running away from the bull, and then it would chase me. I knew I had to continue to face it, even though it continued to kick my ass.

One day in the mail, I noticed an envelope from VNA (Visiting Nurse Association), which immediately grabbed my attention. VNA not only provided in-home hospice care to Annie in her final days, but they supported me through all the associated fog and despair. I had leaned heavily on their 24-hour support number to get help on how to respond to specific symptoms Annie exhibited as she approached death. I would frantically dial the number in the middle of the night as my heart pounded in fear. A kind, patient, and supportive nurse calmly listened as I choked out the issue. Then the nurse guided me through the steps I needed to take, waited patiently for me, and helped me calm down. I couldn't have gotten through it without their help.

The VNA envelope contained a single piece of paper that listed the grief support services they offered, including dates, times, and locations. A glimmer of hope lit up inside me. Maybe they can help me now like they helped me before! At the very least, I had to find out. I immediately made plans to attend the next meeting, scheduled for the very next day at 7:00 p.m.

After work, I drove into an empty parking lot of a Presbyterian church in Monterey and recognized it as the place where I once attended a funeral for a friend's husband. I walked down a corridor adjacent to the church where I found several classroom doors. Halfway down I noticed one slightly open door. I peeked in and saw a few people gathered around a table in the middle of a small room.

"Hello, is this the grief support group?" I asked.

"Yes, it is," responded a middle-aged man with short, gray hair. "Please come in and have a seat."

I took a seat in a simple chair and looked around at the four or five people gathered at the table. Other than the man who greeted me, the group was all middle-aged or older women. They smiled and welcomed me, and I immediately felt comfortable. The man then brought the meeting to order. "Welcome to our grief support meeting, everyone. My name is Mike, and I'm a hospice chaplain. We're here to support each other in our time of grief. Let's go around the table and introduce yourself and tell us why you're here."

The support group meeting dynamic started to feel familiar to me. Each person introduced themselves, and when my turn came, I explained my circumstance without emotion:

"My name is Bob, and on April 25 I lost my wife of thirty-five years to brain cancer." No drama. No emotional outbursts from anyone. Nothing but nodding heads and sympathetic faces. The evening continued smoothly as Mike led a discussion on grief. He talked about the various responses people have to grief: anger, sadness, remorse, despair, and so on. Then he asked, "But do you know what the most common response to grief is?"

No one answered.

"Denial," he said. "Most people deny their grief and don't deal with it directly. They numb it, distract themselves from it, or stuff it inside. Why? Because it's painful. It hurts. It's difficult. But the more directly you deal with it, the faster you can work through it. If you don't, it will linger for years and show up in strange and disturbing ways. It takes courage to deal with grief, but it's worth the pain and effort."

He continued: "How you approach grief is a very individual decision. But it's a decision everyone in grief makes, whether they realize it or not. I encourage you to decide to take grief head on. Step into it and go *through* it. It won't last forever. You'll come out a stronger person into a new life."

Finally, I heard some words of guidance and encouragement. For the first time on my grief journey, I felt an injection of strength. Then it got even better. At the end of the meeting, Mike said, "Let's close our meeting tonight with a brief prayer: Dear God, we ask that you strengthen everyone here tonight as they endure their grief. Give them hope, courage, and peace, and keep them safe until we gather together again. Amen."

The moment the prayer concluded, my heart jumped inside my chest. A brief but unmistakable light sparked in the darkness of my grief cave, then disappeared—like the strike of steel on a piece of flint. But I saw it! I felt it! The tiny flash only lasted for an instant, but it gave me something priceless—a jolt of hope and comfort. Hope that I might make it through this. Comfort at the thought that God, my Higher Power, may help me carry the load that felt like I had been carrying alone. And hope that this grief support group might give me the help I needed.

I drove back to my empty house that night a little stronger, a little braver. My demon awaited me, but this time I carried something with me. Could it be the first layer of my bullfighter's cape?

"You will grieve,
but your grief will become joy."

—John 16:20

———————

CHAPTER 13

A SEASON?

As I entered the fourth month, despite the fact I had found a good support group, the dull pain and disorientation didn't disappear; they had become my new normal. An ever-present sense of being lost and alone kept fear and low-level panic brewing in my mind and stomach. I had no vision of the future, and nothing to look forward to. *How long will this last? Will I ever get out of here? Which way do I go?*

As I attended the VNA support meetings week after week, I started to gain a better understanding of the challenge I was up against, as well as some perspective. One widow in her late sixties shared how difficult it was for her to sleep in the same bed she had shared with her husband for the past forty-plus years. "For the first few weeks," she said, "I had to sleep on the couch in the living room. I couldn't bring myself to get inside our bed under our covers. But one day I rested on top of the covers and got through it. Then another day I laid my head on my pillow and got through that. Finally, one day I pulled down the covers and crawled inside. I cried my eyes out but got through it. I'm sleeping in our bed every night now." As I listened to her share her story, it dawned on me how huge it was for me to climb back into bed on that first night.

As I slowly regained consciousness from grief's initial knockout punch, I started to recover my ability to think. I knew I was inside a cave, a pit, a tunnel—and had to work through it—but I started to hope and believe that it ended somewhere. There had to be an exit.

I also imagined a place that would bring me great relief, if it only existed: a getaway place, like a resort hotel, that only allowed widows and widowers. A grief getaway resort. Somewhere safe to be with others who suffered similar loss. Somewhere for the bereaved to find simple companionship, to gain strength and comfort from each other. I needed more than brief weekly meetings. This place would allow for 24/7 interaction, intimacy, solitude, or some combination of all three. I imagined talking with a few people around a fire pit in the middle of the night, and then going for a walk alone or with someone. Maybe it wouldn't work. Maybe it would be disastrous and become the subject of a true crime novel. But I would have signed up for it in a split second.

I started to realize I needed to find my identity as just me. Not married or with someone, but alone. That realization overwhelmed me. How do I find out who I am now, after being married for thirty-five years? My identity had been so intertwined with my wife. Nearly everyone in my life knew me as "the other half." But now it's just me. Who am I as just me?

In my search for guidance and direction, I purchased books on grief recovery. One of them, titled *Grieving Mindfully* by Sameet Kumar, helped me to breathe, relax, and try to look beyond the suffering to the ways grief could transform my life. The thought that grief could transform me into a stronger and better person seemed like pure fantasy. But I sat up and reread that section again and again. Grief had thrown me into an upside-down world that, if I worked through it, would change me in ways I couldn't imagine. The final sentence exhorted me to "seize the vastness of this moment." What a concept. *OK, I'll try, but I have no clue what you're talking about.*

One book inspired me just by the title: *The Courage to Grieve* by Judy Tatelbaum. I constantly prayed for courage. Another book's title: *Through a Season of Grief: 365 Devotions for Your Journey from Mourning to Joy* by Bill Dunn and Kathy Leonard. I read the title over and over. "Through a season of grief." Like fall, winter, spring, and summer? Seasons don't last. They transition. I'm going through a season. It won't last. It will transition. It will? "Your journey from mourning to joy." I'm in mourning, but is there actually joy at the end? Am I moving toward joy?

I met with Margaret, a therapist at the local hospital. She told me that grief can transform over time, but she also reiterated something Mike said in the grief support group: "Be willing to go through the darkness. Enter into it. Give it its due. Set aside time to grieve each day."

I wish I could tell my grief to show up for only an hour or two each day. It's just the opposite. It's with me 24/7.

Gregor, a therapist I saw on a regular basis, talked to me about the "discipline of loneliness." Work through it. Read. Focus. I doubted I had the discipline needed to tame loneliness, which overpowered me every moment of every day.

All the books and therapists helped, but only for brief moments. Most of the time, loneliness, weakness, and fear continued to plague me. I couldn't escape the bull. People would ask, "Hi, Bob. How's it going? What are you up to?" I would reply, "I'm just taking it one day at a time. I'm working on my grief the best I can. It's a full-time job." That usually ended the conversation, except for a few people who really wanted to know.

I kept trying to have a "normal" experience, like going to a restaurant for a simple dinner, which we used to enjoy so much together. One evening I drove to one of my favorite places, sat at the front counter, and ordered comfort food: meatloaf with mashed potatoes and vegetables. But when the food arrived, my appetite vanished. I tried to eat and act normally, but my stomach twisted and tightened. I couldn't do it. I didn't fit here anymore.

My own neighborhood, where we lived for the past twelve years, suddenly changed now that I was alone. In the old days, everyone would wave and smile as we pulled in or out of our driveway. We enjoyed neighborhood gatherings like Fourth of July fireworks in the street as fun music blasted and kids jumped for joy. But now, I was the odd one out. The one off. The misfit. The man who lived alone in a family home. Neighbors didn't know how to approach me, or what to say, or what to do. For the most part, they just left me alone. It wasn't their fault. They had their own lives to live. But when I saw them, it only reminded me of the life I had lost. I didn't want to resent them, or be angry, or even think about it. I just knew I didn't belong there anymore. I had become an invisible stranger in my own neighborhood.

I tried going to the movie theater, another thing we loved to do, but I felt so conspicuous being alone. It felt like everyone looked at me with suspicion and thought, "Why is that guy alone?" My second attempt was no better than the first, so I didn't go anymore.

It felt like the world I once knew was forever beyond my grasp.

I had to carve my own path through the cave, but I didn't know which way to go. I needed guidance. I needed a compass, something that would give me a sense of direction. I needed tools to help me find my way out of the cave. I heard the words "Time heals all wounds," but that rang hollow. I needed tools more than time, but didn't have much of either.

I did, however, start to develop my own "Comfort Compass," which helped me navigate at a basic level. The needle of the compass guided me in every situation I encountered if I paid attention to it. The compass had three zones: Comfortable, Uncomfortable, and Neutral.

Examples:
- Taking a walk outside: Comfortable.
- Seeing happy couples and happy families: Uncomfortable.
- Going out alone in public: On the edge between Neutral and Uncomfortable.
- Being alone in the house: Uncomfortable.
- Eating alone in a restaurant or going to the movies alone: Uncomfortable.
- Talking to close friends: Comfortable.
- Going to work and interacting with people: Comfortable.

I referred to my compass each day, each encounter, and each experience. I steered away from the uncomfortable and toward the comfortable. It seemed so obvious, but it felt like progress.

One day I got a call from some close friends, Mike and Lori. They were kind enough to check in on me and invite me to dinner at a local brew pub. My compass pointed enough in the comfort zone for me to go, but as we talked over beer and food, the compass fluctuated between comfortable and uncomfortable.

What am I doing here alone?
You're not alone; you're with friends.
I know, but I'm here alone with friends. It feels good, but off.
Who am I now?
The beer tastes great. It's been a long time.
Is this my future? Being a third wheel?
I don't know, but it feels good to be out.

At the end of the evening an attractive woman in her forties with shoulder-length brown hair sat down at the bar next to us. Soon a conversation started, and we all introduced ourselves. Her name was Lara. The discussion eventually got to Annie. I showed Lara a picture, and she expressed her sincere condolences. Minutes later a man walked up to Lara, and it became obvious they knew each other. I guessed boyfriend-girlfriend. Eventually she stood up to leave as the man waited for her near the exit door.

Lara started to walk away, but then turned and looked at me and said, "Do you mind if I give you a hug?"

A shocked smile came over my face, and I jumped at the chance. "Of course not," I blurted out. "I would love a hug."

I stood up from my bar stool as she approached me. She stood roughly six inches shorter than me, and her head and chin fit perfectly on my right shoulder and against the side of my neck. I wrapped my arms around her waist and gently tightened her body against mine. I felt her soft, brown hair against my right cheek and temple. A gentle, feminine fragrance of perfume or shampoo or hair spray filled my nostrils and lungs. I felt the warmth of her body beneath her thick outer coat and melted into her. I felt an intoxicating female energy that I hadn't felt for so long and missed so much.

I held on for a few seconds and whispered, "Thank you for the hug," then forced myself to let go. I didn't want to be that weird, needy guy who creeps everyone out. I stood back from her, took a deep breath, and smiled. She smiled back and said, "We should go dancing sometime."

I never saw her again, but for the rest of the night I couldn't stop thinking about the hug. I couldn't believe how much comfort a hug from a total stranger gave me. Even healing. It made me painfully aware of my need for human touch and female companionship.

Another thought haunted me that night: What was happening with Stephen? It had been five months with zero communication from him. Is he OK? Or is he trapped somewhere inside his own cave?

*"The betrayal of a belief is not
the same thing as ceasing to believe."*

—JAMES BALDWIN,
NOTES OF A NATIVE SON

CHAPTER 14

A GLIMPSE OUTSIDE

At six o'clock on a Friday evening, I looked at myself in the mirror as I prepared to go out for an evening alone. *Is this the right shirt? The right jacket? Do I look OK? Are you sure you want to do this?*

My fingers nervously tapped the steering wheel as I drove toward Fisherman's Wharf in Monterey in early September 2016. I was heading to the annual Italiano Festival, a three-day event full of great food, wine, music, and happy people—all things that didn't apply to me. But my comfort compass and something inside pulled me to the event. I needed to get out of the house, and this seemed like a good distraction.

When I arrived and walked into the buzzing crowd in the plaza, amid the smells of Italian food and live band music, I felt completely out of place. *What am I doing here? Was this a mistake?* I walked around and faked it the best I could. I smiled at people and tried to act naturally. My eye caught sight of the people standing in line for a glass of wine, and my feet guided me to the rear. *Maybe I need a glass of wine or two to help me relax.*

The line moved forward to a table where festival volunteers collected money for drink tickets. As I approached, I recognized one of the volunteers behind the table as I asked for two tickets. "Hi. You look familiar," I said. "Have we met?"

"You too. I'm Julie. I think we met at a grief support meeting a few months ago."

"Oh yeah, that's right. Are you still attending? That was my first one, and it didn't work for me," I said.

"No, me either, but I found a group that I really like. It's called GriefShare, held at Shoreline Church in Monterey. I like it much better than the other one," Julie said.

People bumped into me from the side and behind as the two of us tried to talk. My mind grabbed onto the word *GriefShare* and connected it to the *Through a Season of Grief* book I had been reading.

"I didn't realize that GriefShare had meetings in the area," I said. "When does it meet?"

"Tuesday nights at seven," Julie said. "We just got started a few weeks ago, so I'm sure it wouldn't be too late to join."

"Great!" I said. "I'll be there! You made my night."

Tuesday night couldn't arrive soon enough. The GriefShare book helped me, so how much more helpful would an actual meeting be?

My breathing quickened as I walked into the large room at 6:45 p.m. on Tuesday at the church complex. A friendly facilitator greeted me and showed me to a table with blank name tags, permanent markers, and GriefShare workbooks. *Wow. This is a completely different ballgame.*

I looked around the room and noticed six round tables, each with about six chairs. Most of the tables were full, with a mixture of men and women, and a positive but nervous energy filled the room. I filled out a nametag, took a workbook, and spotted Julie at a table with a few empty chairs. She waved me over, and I took a seat, relieved to see a familiar face.

The five of us at the table introduced ourselves, and one of them introduced himself as David, the table facilitator. The others were Brad, a man about my age who had lost his wife; Julie, who had lost her husband; and Pam, a woman about my age who lost her husband. I was in the right place. The meeting opened with a short prayer, and the facilitator then led us through an interactive discussion on Session 3 from the workbook. The topics included:

- "Does a new normal mean forgetting?"
- "How and why our experience is unique."
- "Don't rush—and how to deal with people who may try to rush you."
- "You may feel relief."
- "Your pain may get worse."
- "Ambushes of grief."

I felt like a student in a grief school, which made total sense to me—a place where I could get some tools to navigate through the cave. The entire meeting had the right elements: structure, an agenda, a workbook full of content and daily reading-writing exercises, a well-produced video segment in which people shared their personal stories of grief and pain, along with professional therapists and psychologists who shared their insights. The discussions and fellowship at our table, and with others in the room at break time, reinforced the fact that I was not in this alone.

As I drove home, I heaved a sigh of relief to know that I had found the right grief support group. I finally had a solid foothold in the cave.

Each week I learned insights and tools from multiple sources. Some that helped me most included:

Connect with the current moment: When thoughts of Annie's death invaded my head, I answered some basic questions out loud. What's the date today? What time is it? Where am I? What do I see around me? What sounds do I hear? It was so simple, but it grounded me in the here and now instead of the past.

Gratitude: Instead of looking at what I had lost, I could look at the time that we had together and express gratitude.

Don't short-circuit the grief process: Realize there are no shortcuts, so don't try to escape it with a quick, new relationship or substance abuse. The process will take the amount of time it takes, and it can vary for each person. Just stay on the road. Keep working through it. The pain will eventually ease and give way to joy.

Grief is an experience, not an identity: I may be going through pain, depression, anxiety, etc., but they don't define me.

Grief and love are connected: The deeper the love, the deeper the grief. It's OK to feel the pain. It's the very proof of love.

Have faith in God. There is hope. God has a plan for your life.

Bang! *Wait a minute. Stop everything. God?*

As I dug through layers of pain and sorrow in my grief work, I hit something hard and broke through it, like a pressurized steam pipe—and burning anger toward God blasted out of me.

How the hell could You let this happen? Why wasn't Annie healed? Why weren't the hundreds and thousands of prayers for her healing answered?

Why, of all people, could You let this happen to her? She was so faithful to You. She devoted her life to You. And You let her die.

Why did You abandon her? How could You abandon her?

Annie trusted You—fully trusted You—and You broke her heart.

How can I ever trust You again? Where were You when she needed You most? When I needed You most? You bailed. You escaped out the back door. You left us! How does this make any sense at all? What kind of parent abandons their child when they beg and plead for help?

What about all the Bible verses that we believed—we fully trusted—to be true?

"If a son shall ask for bread from any of you that is a father, will he give him a stone?" —Luke 11:11

"If you remain in me and my words remain in you, ask whatever you wish, and it will be done for you." —John 15:7

"Truly I tell you, if you have faith as small as a mustard seed, you can say to this mountain, 'Move from here to there,' and it will move. Nothing will be impossible for you." —Matthew 17:20

"Therefore I tell you, whatever you ask for in prayer, believe that you have received it, and it will be yours." —Mark 11:24

"Ask and it will be given to you; seek and you will find; knock and the door will be opened to you." —Matthew 7:7

These are all lies! These words are nothing but a cruel deception to create false hope. What kind of a god would say these things? What kind of a god are You?

I turned my back on God. I seethed inside, and I didn't care if I violated some sacred rules in the process. It wasn't right. It made zero sense. I cursed and screamed at God. And heard no reply.

But then, on a walk one evening in the Fort Ord Wilderness area, as I continued my rant, I sensed a presence alongside me. Orange sunlight from the early evening softened the hills and trees around me. I heard an inner voice say: *"I know you're angry. I know none of this makes any sense. I know you're in pain. I know. But answer this one question: Will you allow me to walk with you anyway?"* I slowed my pace. Whose voice was that? All I knew was at that moment it felt like someone walked alongside me.

Since my childhood, I always had a sense of God in my life. My mom and dad were both devoted Christians in their own faith: my mom a Southern Baptist and my dad a Roman Catholic, and all five children were raised Catholic. As a very young child, I saw God as the good shepherd, as expressed in Psalm 23: "The Lord is my shepherd…" I saw Jesus as my friend, one who comforts, loves, and supports. A framed painting of Jesus next to my bed calmed me.

But starting in my teenage years, the strict, rule-based, thou-shalt-not doctrines of the Catholic Church took over, and God became restrictive and punitive. As a natural rule-follower and the second youngest of five children, I toed the line and obeyed the rules. God became the Judge in the courtroom, and no matter how hard I tried, sin and guilt remained. Even after attending Mass every Sunday and going to confession regularly, I was never off the hook. I never saw myself as good enough or acceptable in God's eyes.

Yet I didn't question the church rules, regulations, and belief system, and had faith that Jesus the Good Shepherd was in there somehow. My faith was reinforced with moments of prayer when I felt connected to God and with an experience in my late college years when I felt God's loving presence in a deep and personal way.

For my entire adult life, I did my best to live a life of faith in God and be a good Catholic. I put my total trust in God during Annie's illness and dared to believe she would be healed. I fought back doubts with the biblical prayer of the man who pleaded with Jesus: "I do believe but help my unbelief!" (Mark 9:24).

But her death buried my faith in an avalanche of pain, betrayal, and loss. Any connection or relationship with God came to a grinding halt. With my back turned to God, I assumed God had turned His back on me.

Or maybe not. Did He still want to walk with me, despite my rejection of Him?

Something stirred inside and nudged me towards a small beam of daylight that pierced through the cave ceiling, just big enough to look through. I climbed up to the opening and stuck my head out. I saw a massive oak tree that had fallen to the ground—the tree of my faith.

How could something so strong and secure crack and fall? A lifetime of care, feeding, and growth—fallen. All the shelter, comfort, assurance, order, strength, stability, and security it provided over the decades—gone. All the trust and belief that went into each branch—gone. I saw words carved into them:

- Obey God/the Church and you will be protected.
- Disobey God/the Church and you will pay the consequences and suffer.
- You are dependent on the Church and its precepts and rituals.
- If you go to Mass and perform prescribed rituals, you will obtain healing graces.

And on the fallen tree trunk:

- Quid Pro Quo: If you obey, pray and believe hard enough, then God will reward you with blessings and miracles.

I stared at the wreckage, lost in confusion, until I couldn't look anymore. I climbed back down to the cave floor. I had to keep moving.

"Yes," I said. "You can walk with me. But just You."

"*Hope is being able to see that there is light despite all of the darkness.*"

—DESMOND TUTU

CHAPTER 15

THREE SINKHOLES

As the 6-month mark unfolded in October, I continued to attend GriefShare meetings and work through the sessions, but with a different set of eyes. I examined every scripture verse and faith concept to see if it applied to me or not. I no longer just accepted them at face value. My faith tree had fallen, but my faith wasn't dead. It continued in a new direction, an unknown direction. It was as if God and I were going through a separation. Trust had been broken between us. Could it be rebuilt?

I needed some time for deep and quiet reflection, but I wanted some company, so I searched for meditation groups and found one that met on Thursday nights. I had never attended a meditation group before but decided to give it a try. It had no religious affiliation, but it met at the same church where I had attended the VNA support group.

The meditation group consisted of about twelve friendly people, all around middle age. The facilitator opened the meeting in the center of our circle by ringing a bell bowl, which resonated with a calming, harmonic sound. The room lights dimmed as we sat quietly. She then read a brief excerpt from the Psalms and rang the bowl again to signify a ten-minute period of silence. My mind raced as the silence began, but eventually it rested in the quiet. At the ten-minute mark, the bowl rang again. This time, we stood up and walked slowly, in silence, around our circle a few times, and then sat back down. A second ten-minute period of silence followed, and then the meeting ended with a final reading.

During the time of silence, once my brain stopped spinning, the reality of how much I missed Annie surfaced. My soul groaned under the weight, and I just sat there with it. And yet, in the void and pain, I felt God's silent presence.

When my brain started to spin again, thoughts of Stephen arose: *Where is he? Is he still alive? Why haven't I heard from him in six months?* I started to panic. The next day I contacted a close friend and asked if they could search the Orange County Coroner's website for "John Doe" deaths. I had no means to contact him. No way to find him.

Then one day in late October I got a call from the Inmate Calling Service from the Orange County Jail. I knew exactly what it meant.

"Dad?" Stephen said.

"Steve! I'm so relieved to hear from you," I said. "But sorry you're in jail."

"Yeah, it's been rough," he said. "I've been going through a lot of shit." He went on to explain how he got into an altercation with a convenience store owner who called the police, and one thing led to another. He asked for money for the commissary, and neither of us had much more to say to each other.

"OK, love you, Dad."

"Love you, Steve. Hang in there."

Finally. At least I knew where he was—one less load to carry as the daunting holidays approached.

Thanksgiving, Christmas, and New Year's loomed ahead like three sinkholes. What used to be times of joy, love, fun, and family traditions now filled me with dread. To make matters worse, my GriefShare program ended just before Thanksgiving and wasn't going to start up again until January. But just before the break, I attended a special workshop called "Surviving the Holidays." About twenty people attended, and as I looked around the room, I took comfort from the fact that I wasn't in this nightmare alone. I came away with some good suggestions, such as:

- Make specific plans for each holiday; don't just wing it.
- Expect strong emotions to appear at any time; don't let them ambush you.
- Don't isolate; be with other people if possible.

✦ Don't feel pressured to do anything.

My approach boiled down to: stay as busy as possible through volunteer work and just make it to January 2, 2017.

But when I woke up on Thanksgiving morning, I could barely get out of bed. Sick with a cold-flu bug, I tried to take a shower and get dressed but couldn't. So much for my plan. I crawled back into bed, sick to my core and trapped with my demon. I had no choice but to endure the holiday in the worst way imaginable—alone in the torture chamber.

Over the four-day weekend, as families gathered to celebrate the holiday season, I just tried to hang on to sanity. I yearned for Monday morning to arrive so I could return to work.

I received several text messages from friends and family wishing me a happy Thanksgiving. They meant well, and I knew each was an expression of love and support, but they stung. How could I possibly have a happy Thanksgiving? For the first time in my life, I found myself on the outside looking in—the lost soul who stood outside the warm house looking through the window at the happy people inside. *Is this what some people have had to endure every holiday? Every day? Is this the agony so many people suffer year after year, while I took for granted the warmth and support of a loving family?* I never noticed the lonely souls, or even knew they existed. Now, an emptiness swallowed me. After six months my aloneness didn't get easier, it got worse.

I knew in my head that God somehow sustained me, but He felt no more personal than the force of gravity that held me to the ground. Empty and alone, I felt defective—someone to be pitied from a distance but avoided up close. I felt no sense of relationship, no sense of presence, no comfort, no companionship. I desperately needed human companionship and human interaction. I needed someone I could see, touch, smell, and hear. The fear of remaining alone crippled me and started to threaten my sanity.

I tried to find solace in research and awareness, so I downloaded an audiobook called *Loneliness: Making It Work for You* by Carole Riley, which offered ideas to accept and work with it. I pushed back. For me, loneliness was not a condition to accept, but a problem to overcome. But it helped me realize how many people suffer with this problem.

As the weekend came to a merciful close, I could hardly wait to escape from my prison cell and return to work. As I lay in bed Sunday night, I vowed to myself I would never forget the lonely souls of the world again.

I woke up Monday morning after the Thanksgiving weekend like a prisoner on release day. My cold-flu bug had passed, and energy surged in my body as I showered and got dressed. On my drive to work, my body settled into the driver seat. The warmth from the car air vents softened my face, fingers, and toes. The aroma of strong black coffee drifted out of my travel mug and filled my nostrils. I could finally breathe and relax. I got to rejoin the land of the living and interact with people. I got to talk and laugh. Thank God I made it through the first hole. One down, two more to go.

The monthlong stretch to Christmas looked impossible to cross, but I tried the same approach: stay busy, volunteer, and just get through it. And don't get sick!

Annie had always decorated the house for Christmas in the most elaborate and fun ways, but I couldn't move an inch in that direction. I couldn't put up a tree or the simplest of decorations. I couldn't open any of the Christmas storage boxes in the garage, which would destroy me with memories. All I could muster was to put up the exterior Christmas lights around the house, which I did every year anyway. At least from an outside perspective, the house looked "normal" for the season and served as a sign of life to the neighbors.

Although I couldn't decorate the house, I needed to change it. My life had forever changed, and the inside of the house needed to reflect it. I started to remove pictures of us from the walls and replace them with pictures that contained no emotional charge, like a generic scenery picture, or nothing at all. Then I decided to tackle something I dreaded: her clothes. It started through the annual warm coat and clothing drive sponsored by the local chapter of The Salvation Army.

I opened the closet door in the front hallway and looked at the hanging coats, most of them Annie's. Every single one had memories and images attached. The mid-length, red, wool London Fog coat she used to love to wear on cool nights. The full-length, brown, heavy coat with a hood she wore on cold nights. The thin windbreaker jacket and sweatshirts for walks around the neighborhood or beach.

I can't keep these. It makes no sense.

Someone could use them this winter.
But if I give them away, I'm giving away part of Annie.
I know, but she's gone. She's gone…and not coming back.
She doesn't need them anymore.
I can't keep them.
I don't need them.
Someone out there does.

One by one I pulled them off their coat hanger and started a pile on the floor. Each time I removed one, energy drained out of me. At the end, ten coats sat in a pile, and my internal battery dropped from 100 percent to 5 percent. I barely had enough energy to stand.

The same thing happened with pictures I removed from the wall. A single item could zap 50 percent of my energy, and anything else could leave me totally exhausted. At first, I couldn't figure out what was happening to me. I didn't do anything physically taxing, but the emotional exertion took its own toll.

It wasn't just a coat, a picture, or an item on a shelf. It was a life full of memories, emotions, hopes, dreams, attachments, and love. Every single item had an invisible string tied to an entire universe of meaning, and every time I decided to remove something, the string snapped. Another death. One after another.

I could have left everything alone, like Mom did after Dad died. Nothing of his in the house was removed. All his clothes remained in the closets. No pictures were replaced. Everything stayed the same. But I couldn't do that. I had to clear out the things that belonged to Annie. I had to work through them. They represented a contradiction in my mind: *Why are these things here? This is not reality. It hurts to look at them. I have to move forward.*

When I finally regained some energy, I loaded the items in my car and dropped them off at a donation center. It didn't seem real, and I tried not to think about it. When I returned home, I felt a bittersweet sense I had done the right thing—and I was heartsick.

As I fought through each battle with Annie's things, sleep started to elude me again. Each night I fell asleep from exhaustion but woke up a few hours later as my mind raced about the past, the future, and how long the pain and darkness would last. My friends at GriefShare helped me immensely, but I struggled through each day.

My pain had shifted from acute pain and shock to disoriented con-fusion. Each moment of each day, I stepped into the unknown. I had no idea what I was doing or where I was headed in life. Confusion and doubt filled my thoughts, but I disguised it well. I didn't mope or walk around with a sad look on my face—just the opposite. From the out-side, no one would notice or think anything was wrong. I became an expert on how to hide and fake my inner reality.

Late one night in early December 2016, I got a phone call from Ste-phen, still in jail. "Dad," he said, "I can't stay in here over Christmas. I can't do it. Can you post bail for me? Please? I'll pay you back, I swear. I have the name and number of a guy who can help. Please? I'm going fucking crazy in here. I've got to get out."

The heaviness that arrived every time Stephen called came rushing back. He always seemed to need something that only I could provide, and it always involved money. But this was something bigger. If I struggled on my Christmas alone, safe at home, how much worse must it be for him in jail?

During his childhood years, Stephen reveled in the magic of Christ-mas. He sang along with the Christmas carols, helped us decorate the tree, and picked out crazy ornaments (like Santa pulling Mrs. Claus on water skis behind a jet ski, a great white shark, or his favorite dinosaur ones). He loved to help Annie make Christmas cookies, which he sam-pled along the way. They called it the "great cookie adventure."

We loved to cuddle up on the couch under a warm blanket and watch TV Christmas shows like "A Charlie Brown Christmas" and "Rudolph the Red-Nosed Reindeer." He looked at everything about Christmas through the eyes of an innocent child, which sparkled with wonder.

"OK, Steve. I'll call the guy."

"Thank you, Dad. Thank you. And don't worry, I'll pay you back."

"Don't worry about that. Love you, dude," I said.

"Love you, Dad."

I rarely knew the right thing to do or not do for Stephen, but this was 100 percent clear. I couldn't see him in jail on the first Christmas after his mom died if I could do something about it. I was too wrapped up in my own struggle to think about his, but the level of desperation in his voice woke me up. Every request he made ripped my heart to shreds, which made it nearly impossible to say no, but this one went to his core. I spent the next hour in conversations and transactions with the bail bond company, along with that familiar knot in my stomach, but knew it was right.

The days leading up to Christmas contained a special brand of torture. Where did all the fun, joy, spirit, activities, warmth, and anticipation go? I never understood why some people hated Christmas, but now I got it. Every Christmas carol, every decoration, every Christmas tree, every Christmas card, every message of happiness and wonder, only amplified my pain, as if to say, "*Look what you lost. Listen to what you no longer have.*"

A single Christmas carol played in the grocery store would punch me in the gut, force burning tears from my eyes, and strangle me by the throat. A simple can of cranberry sauce or green beans could unleash a wave of sorrow. I had to keep my focus on the thin tightrope in front of me and just get to the other side each day—or fall into despair.

On Christmas Eve I took my mother-in-law, Germaine, to a 4:00 p.m. Mass. A faithful and devoted Catholic, she loved going to Mass with Annie, especially on Christmas Eve. But this time was agony for both of us. Germaine's body bent over her walker with sadness as her spirit sagged. I tried to act positive but just wanted the service to come to an end. We ate dinner together afterward, but still, I just wanted it to end.

When Christmas day finally arrived, I bolted out of the house at 8:00 a.m., drove to the Monterey County Fairgrounds, and walked into the 7,000-square-foot dining hall. Circular tables, each with eight to ten chairs, filled the main floor where hundreds of hungry families would enjoy a free turkey dinner. Some families had already gathered at the tables and enjoyed coffee and hot chocolate served by fellow volunteers.

I checked in with the volunteer coordinator, filled out my name tag and got busy. I started in the kitchen, which bustled with activities of joyful hard work. Loud voices, steam, and heat from the industrial-sized stove tops and ovens, and the smells of turkey, stuffing, and potatoes, filled the crowded space. Three chefs worked the kitchen in perfect unison, each one instructing groups of volunteers what to do. I joined an assembly line of volunteers who packed to-go meals, which would be driven to senior citizens who couldn't leave their homes. I stepped in wherever I saw a need—wash dishes, drain and mash the potatoes, slice loaves of bread, cut up vegetables, etc. All the while, smiles covered the faces of volunteers, and we all energized each other.

When the kitchen pace slowed down, I walked the large dining hall floor and helped clean tables or interacted with people. A spirit of joy and gratitude filled the entire space. As I looked at the hundreds of people all around me, I realized how many faced a much tougher road than me. I had a good job, a nice house, and plenty of food and clothing. How many of these people just struggled to survive each day?

The hours flew by. Before I knew it, the dining hall started to empty out, and the sounds of pots and pans being cleaned were all that filled the kitchen area. I felt exhaustion set in, just like I had hoped. I drove home, crawled into bed, and fell asleep. When the next morning arrived, I woke up, raised my arms into the air, and shouted: "I made it! I made it past Christmas!" Calmness filled me. I could breathe again. I felt the pressure release within and around me. Thanks be to God. One more to go—New Year's Eve and Day.

In the quiet days between Christmas and New Year's, I realized that, as a sojourner in the grief cave, I had been shackled with a burden to carry each moment of every day, like a backpack full of rocks. I had to walk my road with this backpack, which was locked on and couldn't be removed. The weight of the pack and the length of the road were unique and customized for me. And each day I had to decide: How will I deal with it today?

I just wanted to return to a "normal life," but as long as I was on this subterranean road, I couldn't. *How much longer? Will the load ever get lighter? Will the backpack ever come off?* All I knew is that I had to keep going.

When I looked ahead at the third sinkhole, New Year's Eve and Day, confidence bubbled inside me. It didn't have the emotional depth of the other two and was only a few days away. I couldn't wait to move from 2016 to 2017. Just the thought of a new year felt like a tangible sign of forward progress.

My confidence soared when a New Year's Eve gathering was organized by a few people from my grief support group. I wouldn't be alone! Five of us—three women and two men—met for an early dinner at a local restaurant, went to a movie afterward and then attended the festivities of First Night Monterey. The annual event in Monterey was a festive way to ring in the new year with the community and enjoy local performing arts.

One of the musical events was held inside a church, where I sat side-by-side with one of the women of our group, Nicole. Despite the fact she was a few years older than me and not a great match, she exuded warmth and friendliness. The physical sensation of our jacketed arms next to each other ignited my deep desire for female closeness. Just the feel of her next to me felt so simple and comforting. My body relaxed and soaked it in. So simple, so comforting, but so elusive.

Before the performance started, we talked with each other. She smiled. She laughed. When the music started, she nudged my arm with hers in response to the music. Like the hug in the brew pub, I relished the moment.

But when we all parted ways sometime after midnight, emptiness flooded back in. Instead of relief, sadness settled in. I drove back to the empty house, slumped into bed, and woke up early New Year's Day lost in a fog. Directionless. Hopeless. Stuck.

I took a walk with a friend later that day but couldn't shake the fog. I attended a church service that evening, but the hymns consisted of Christmas carols, which pummeled me. Happy couples and smiling families surrounded me. I sat there and forced my eyes closed. I took deep breaths to ground myself. I wanted to scream and run out, but just endured it to the end.

When New Year's Day came to a merciful end, I focused on one positive thing: my return to work the next day. Distraction. The mental engagement of work. Co-workers. Routine.

I made it past the three sinkholes only to enter a lonely swamp—surrounded by muck, slop, and penetrating wetness, where everything looked the same in all directions. I didn't want to short-circuit my road, but I needed relief. *O God, help me. Guide me. Show me the way.*

I wanted something to look forward to in 2017. Anything. I had to do something about my loneliness. I had to find someone more than just a friend or co-worker. Even more than a fellow grief support member. I needed a female companion. *Do I NEED companionship? Or do I WANT it? I don't know. I just don't want to be alone!*

But was I ready for a relationship? It had been eight months—a lifetime yet a mere flash in the grief dimension. I didn't want to jump into a relationship too soon, but the pull to move forward overpowered any brakes inside me. The time had come to act.

"*People label themselves with all sorts of adjectives. I can only pronounce myself as 'nauseatingly miserable beyond repair.'*"

—Franz Kafka, *Diaries*, 1910–1923

CHAPTER 16

THE DATING WORLD

I started 2017 equipped with an active radar for companionship. I dusted off the old radar from a forty-year hibernation, which still operated at full power like it did in my 1970s college days. But how does a sixty-year-old man use this thing? How do I navigate this entirely new world of women and dating?

It felt awkward to observe the world through this radar again. *What the heck am I doing?* But it also felt right and normal, like seeking food or water. I knew in my heart that I needed companionship, and despite how odd it felt, I told myself over and over: "Annie is gone, and she would want me to find someone to love. She told me so."

Despite its age, the radar wouldn't turn itself off. It would flash a message almost every time I saw a woman: *Is she available? What would it be like to go out with her? Is she a match?* But I had no clue how to approach someone, or where to begin. I had to start my search in the modern world—but online dating? No way. I had zero interest in social media, and I couldn't see myself navigating the dynamics. I had heard many horror stories about how people misrepresent themselves online, post fake photos to make them look good, etc. No thanks.

So I found a local matchmaker service that promised to set me up with only the most compatible matches "based on our extensive, mutual, personal profile system." It wasn't cheap, but I considered it my tuition. I also figured the cost would filter out any casual participants. The service included individual background checks, which worked both ways—the women would know I had been screened, and it reduced the chance I'd end up dating someone out of the *Fatal Attraction* movie.

So, one day after work in early January 2017, I drove to my 6:00 p.m. appointment in downtown Carmel. My breath quickened with eager anticipation as I stepped into the office and took a seat alone in one of the comfortable chairs inside a nicely appointed waiting room. At six o'clock, a professionally dressed woman in her mid-forties opened a door and greeted me. "Mr. McGuire?" she asked. "Welcome! Please come in."

She took a seat behind her desk and began the intake process. Almost immediately she pointed out a large three-ring binder on the desk, full of paper almost three inches thick.

"These are testimonials from many of our happy clients," she said. "Feel free to look through them. I'm actually a happy client myself. I met my husband through this company." Each page or two were letters written by people who had found their true love and gushed over the wonderful service the matchmaker company provided.

"Wow," I said as I flipped through the pages.

"Here's how it works," she said. "You fill out an extensive profile form that we provide—your likes, dislikes, preferences, activities you enjoy, what's important to you, etc. Then you select the kind of woman you're looking for—age, nationality, body type, etc., and the geographical area you're willing to travel. It could be local only, or you could expand up to the San Jose area or beyond. It's up to you. Then, once you clear the background check and we enter your exact profile in our system, we match you up with a compatible woman. You meet and go on a first date. If either of you don't think it's a match, you simply call us, and we notify the other person, which takes the pressure off you. Then we set you up with another potential match, for up to ten individual women. How does that sound to you?"

It sounded good enough for me to sign up, so I spent the next hour filling out a profile form full of checkboxes and fill-in-the-blanks about me and my preferences. As I plugged away, I couldn't believe how complex the world of dating had become. Forty years ago, if I saw an attractive young woman and she seemed even mildly interested, I would strike up a conversation and take it from there. Despite many crash-and-burns, it was simple. Now I found myself in a sci-fi movie filling out an order form for a Stepford wife.

"Mr. McGuire," the intake woman said. "Did you bring in the list of qualities we asked you to bring in when we set up your appointment?"

"Yes, I have it right here."

I handed her a sheet of paper with a printed list I created.

1. Understands loss—directly and personally—of the most important person in your life.
2. Believes in God and identifies as a Christian.
3. Works in a service field of some kind (or sees her work as a service, helping others—not just a paycheck).
4. Physically attractive—45 to 60 years old.
5. Takes care of herself—healthy eating and exercise habits.
6. Likes to laugh and have fun.
7. Enjoys long drives and deep conversations, but comfortable with silence.
8. Likes to walk, hike, go outdoors.
9. Would not freak out hiking in rain; might even like it.
10. Likes to travel but doesn't have to.
11. Likes to go out to dinner but doesn't have to; can cook and enjoy eating at home.
12. Likes and appreciates simple things in life—doesn't require extravagant things.
13. Likes music and going to musical events.
14. Would enjoy a day of: morning coffee, time at an outdoor health spa, lunch afterward, wine tasting, walk/hike, watch sunset, settle down with a movie at home and fall asleep with each other on the couch.
15. Understands the need for a spiritual retreat or visit to a monastery.
16. Understands and supports the importance of relationships with family and friends.
17. Not glued to her smartphone with constant activity. Doesn't "live inside" the social media world. Can have a good conversation without constantly checking for posts, photos, and text messages.

I watched as she read my list, nodding her head along the way. When she finished, she said, "Great! Very detailed list. It will be included with your profile form and given to your individually assigned relationship consultant, who will work directly with you to find the perfect match. I'm excited for you! There are many available women out there!"

As I drove home from the matchmaker appointment, I wondered what it would be like to have a woman in my life. I desperately wanted my loneliness to go away, but the thought of an intense relationship with someone made me nervous. Was I ready? Would it make things better or worse? It had only been nine months. The words of my grief support group echoed in my head: "No shortcuts. Don't move too fast."

But I stood on solid footing, ready to give it a try. My involvement with GriefShare had shifted from participant to volunteer team member, which strengthened my own grief recovery and kept me grounded. A new thirteen-week session had started, which helped reinforce the lessons.

I had also learned about a trap to avoid, in which I subconsciously remember only Annie's good qualities, and selectively forget anything less than positive. Eventually, she would become this perfect person to which no one could possibly measure up. I had to remember Annie wasn't perfect and had her shortcomings like everyone else.

One day I received a letter in my mailbox at home. It was from a woman I knew from church for many years. She knew Annie and me, but we were mere acquaintances who would say hello to each other and nothing more. The handwritten letter offered her condolences, moral support, and prayers. I read and reread the letter multiple times and couldn't help but think it contained a deeper message between the lines. Maybe this was an invitation. I had to find out, so I decided to call and ask if she would like to get together.

A few days later, I fidgeted nervously in my car before a Monday evening workout. My heart pounded as I dialed her number.

What the heck are you doing?

Calling a woman to ask her on a date.

Are you kidding me?

No, I'm not kidding.

Do you realize what you're doing?

She answered and sounded friendly and enthusiastic. The conflict between my head and heart bounced back and forth but I pressed ahead. I felt like an awkward teenager as our conversation struggled to gain traction. Finally, I asked if she would like to take a walk this coming weekend. She said she would get back to me later that night to firm up the timing.

The instant I hung up the phone, I felt elated. I did it! I made the call, asked her out, and she agreed. I broke the ice. I took a huge step forward. Hope surged within me.

But when I didn't hear back from her that night, hope turned to curiosity. Curiosity then turned to confusion when I didn't hear back the entire next day. Confusion then turned to anger when I didn't hear back the entire day after that. By the time I got a text message from her three days after my call, I felt like a complete fool.

We took our walk, but it was clear I had totally misread her letter. She expressed kindness and friendship, but nothing more. I tried to see something between the lines that wasn't there. Right off the bat, I fell flat on my face. *I'm such an idiot. How could I be so delusional? Am I that screwed up? Is this what the dating world is like?*

I licked my self-inflicted wounds and realized I had fallen into an old trap: I was too eager and too desperate. I fell hook, line, and sinker for the belief that I needed a female companion to make me and my life complete. I believed someone could take my pain away, as if by magic. I told myself I didn't want the helicopter rescue, but I really did—as if one even existed. Shame filled me.

In an attempt to regroup, I dug into the book *I Need Your Love—Is That True?* by Byron Katie. The book contained exercises to question two thoughts: "I need your love—is that true?" and "I need you—is that true?" But if those thoughts weren't true, why did they have so much power over me? In my head I knew that God was the only one I needed and the only one who could be with me 24/7/365. But why did the pull of female companionship have so much power?

My inner voice said, "*You have to become your own man, your own person, aside from anyone else. You have to be secure alone, before you can even think about a female companion. If you jump into a relationship too soon, it would be disastrous."* Yes, all true. But still, despite this and my initial humiliation, I pushed ahead with the matchmaker service.

Soon I got a call from my personal relationship consultant, Amber, who told me my background check had been completed and my profile had been entered and matched through their system. "Are you ready for your first date?" she asked. "Here's how it works. I give you her first name and phone number, and you call her to set up a place and time to meet. She has already agreed to meet with you based on your profile, so consider this a warm introduction."

"OK," I said. "I'm ready."

"Great!" Amber said. "The woman we have selected for your first date is named Liz. She's beautiful, smart, and has many of the same interests that you have. After you go on your first date, just call me back and let know how it went. If it goes well, we leave it up to the two of you to arrange your next date. If it doesn't go well for some reason, we will notify the other person and come up with another profile to try. Sometimes the process takes some tuning, but be patient—it will work!"

This time my heart rate stayed in the normal range when I called Liz and arranged to meet her for a walk in Monterey along the waterfront. Lesson learned; I had no expectations. We agreed on Saturday at 1:00 p.m. Because photographs were not part of the matchmaker service, we gave each other a general description and set up an exact location to meet.

It turned out to be a perfect February day for a walk—a clear blue sky with bright sun and a cool breeze in the mid-sixties. The sounds of seagulls and the occasional bark of sea lions filled the air. The Fisherman's Wharf buzzed with laughing children and tourists, some of whom stood and watched the street performers play their guitars and sing familiar tunes. Smells of caramel corn and clam chowder would occasionally drift past my nose.

As I approached our meeting spot, I felt more curious than nervous. What kind of woman would they match me up with? When I arrived, I looked around and noticed a woman also looking for someone among the crowd. I approached and confirmed she was my assigned match. The first-five-seconds-impression-test told me "not a match," and our walk confirmed it. With every step of the walk, the more awkward and out of place I felt. Other than our age, nothing between us matched up. I sensed a sad and negative energy from her, which made me cringe inside. As I calculated my exit, I tried to stay as friendly as possible.

Finally, I made up an excuse that I had to be somewhere, and we parted ways. Nauseous disappointment and worry filled me as I walked back to my car. *If this is the result of a professional matchmaker service, I've made a huge and expensive mistake. Nine more introductions to go.*

One week later I stood in the bright afternoon sunlight outside a local restaurant and waited for my next match to arrive. When she approached and we confirmed our identities, the five-second test pointed to a green light. And as we sat across from each other in the booth and talked, my interest grew. I sensed an upbeat, positive, and fun energy from her, and the conversation flowed naturally. Some of our interests lined up, like walks and outdoors, so we agreed to meet for a second date the following weekend.

I approached the second date with a feeling of optimism and positive expectations. When I asked if I could pick her up and drive her to our walking trail, however, she politely declined and said she would drive herself. Then it dawned on me. The world had changed—no one can trust anyone anymore. If I picked her up, I would know where she lived, which posed a modern-day risk. It made me realize how women must look at men in the dating world as potential threats to their safety. I never considered myself a threat to anyone, but that didn't matter—she did.

Despite the reality check downer, I pressed on and showed up at our prearranged meeting spot. From the moment I saw her, however, I noticed something had changed. The sparkle was gone. She was the same person but looked and acted different. After we walked on the trail for a while, we took a seat on a bench. The more she talked, the less attractive she became and the more confused I felt. The green light that had flashed on our first date had suddenly turned off.

We ended our walk with lunch at a local restaurant and then parted ways. Neither of us mentioned another get together. I drove away full of confusion and disappointment. *How could someone change so drastically from one meeting to the next? Did I imagine it all? How could I see two completely different people on only two dates?*

Although my matchmaker setup process had just begun, foreboding discouragement started to set in. *This was supposed to be easy! There are so many eligible matches out there, but so far, it's not even close.*

I pressed ahead with my third date. We met in the evening at a busy coffee shop in the Monterey mall. We located each other quickly and found a corner high table to sit and talk. The five-second test again pointed to a green light, but the more we talked, the more it faded. She checked her cell phone every few minutes.

"Excuse me," she said. "I have to reply to my daughter's text and let her know I'm OK."

"Excuse me. I just have to reply to this."

As she focused on her phone, I felt like asking if she wanted her daughter to join us, but bit my tongue.

At the end of our conversation, however, I found myself intrigued and wondered if the second date experience would work in reverse. Maybe the light would revert to green. I asked if she would like to meet again, she said yes, and we parted ways. An hour later, I received a text from her: *"I'm sorry. I'm not ready for this. I'm going to chicken out. Sorry."*

The entire matchmaker process had started with enthusiastic expectation but turned into one disappointment after another. Over February and March, I received multiple introductions from the matchmaker service, but none of them led to a second date or any mutual interest.

On the other hand, I appreciated the efforts of friends who arranged outings and introductions to single friends of theirs. Some friendships developed, like with Debbie, who I could talk to and spend comfortable time with. Comfortable but confusing. Are we dating or something else? It didn't matter. I was grateful for the companionship.

But April 25 appeared on the horizon, the one-year anniversary of Annie's death. As I approached it, a jumble of emotions poured in:

* Anguish and sorrow: New waves of grief crashed into me.

My cell phone photo app popped up daily reminders of what

happened a "year ago today"—vivid reminders of Annie's final weeks, events and places that stung me.

* Relief: The first year of sheer agony was almost over. I had heard the first year is the toughest, and each year after gets easier.
* Hope: Once I break through the one-year barrier, things will change for the better. I heeded the advice: "Don't make any major decisions the first year." But afterward...
* Proud and grateful: I survived the worst eleven-plus months of my life, one step at a time. I commemorated the passage of each month like a prisoner who etches a mark on his cell wall. Each mark represented an achievement milestone. And the next one would be number twelve—an entire year.

I called the matchmaker service and told them to put my account on hold. I had to shed any distractions and focus my attention on the one-year mark. I had learned to make a definite plan for the one-year anniversary. *"Don't let it slam into you like a truck."*

Around this time, my dear friends Tim and Alice invited me over for dinner at their house, as they had so many times before. Friends for more than twenty-five years, they walked every step of Annie's brain cancer road with us, from the initial onset to the very end. And they supported me as I tried to navigate my new road. I always felt safe with them.

As we got caught up with each other over drinks and appetizers, Alice said, "Bob, I don't want to butt into your business, but I have a question: Would you be interested in meeting Susan's sister, Lauren? You know Rob and Susan, next door? Lauren lives in Los Angeles and comes here to visit their mom every so often. She's also a widow. She lost her husband a year before Annie passed. Would you like to come over for dinner on her next visit? Here's a photo."

Alice smiled and handed me a photo of a small group of people. "That's her, there on the right," she said.

I looked at the photo and saw an attractive woman. "Sure," I said. "I'd love to."

As we continued with our evening, Tim and Alice listened to me tell my matchmaker tales of woe, and my ups and downs with grief recovery. I updated them on my plan for the one-year mark. "I'm going to take two days off from work and retrace some steps," I said. "I'm going to drive up to Chico where we met, and then to Visalia where we got married. I just want to spend some time at each place. When I get back here, I have a few activities planned for the actual anniversary day."

"Sounds like a good plan," Tim said. Alice smiled as she listened.

"Thank you both," I said. "And thank you for always being there for me. You have no idea how much your friendship means to me."

Several weeks later, in late March 2017, I arrived around 6 o'clock on a Friday evening at Rob and Susan's house. I knew Rob from some computer training work we had done many years prior but had only briefly met Susan.

I went into the evening preoccupied by the upcoming anniversary and with zero hopes or expectations based on my matchmaker dating experiences. After I parked in their driveway and opened the car door, I heard sounds of music and laughter behind a six-foot wooden fence. I opened the gate and stepped into the backyard area.

An open-air patio with a four-post, square-shaped gazebo covered a blazing firepit surrounded by couches and chairs. Classic 70s rock music played in the background as Rob greeted me. "Hey, Bob! Great to see you! Come on in! Have a glass of wine!"

"Hi, Rob." I said. "Hi, everyone. Thanks for having me."

After the hello hugs ended, Lauren and I were formally introduced.

I stepped forward to greet her with a safe hello-hug: "Hi, Lauren, nice to meet you."

"Nice to meet you," she said, smiling.

Soon, the six of us took seats around the warm fire pit. I sat next to Lauren, but we didn't talk much—conversations jumped like popcorn in all directions. Music, wine, food, laughter, and conversation flowed easily in the early evening sunlight.

When the song "Don't Rock the Boat" by the Hues Corporation band started to play, Lauren started to chair dance. "I love this song!" she said as she moved to the rhythm and sang along. Her spontaneous playfulness was a joy to witness.

In between verses, I asked, "So what year did you graduate from high school?"

"74," Lauren said, smiling.

"Wow, same here," I said. "What high school?"

"Costa Mesa High."

"Cool. I went to Foothill High in Tustin."

When the song ended, another classic rock song followed, and we all got up and began to dance on the patio. Spontaneous laughter and sing-along voices filled the air as each of us moved to the groove. The scene could have been straight out of another 70s classic: "Dancing in the Moonlight" by King Harvest.

Without realizing it, I found myself having fun, something I hadn't experienced for years. It felt so strange and awkward, yet vaguely familiar.

Eventually we moved into the house for dinner and gathered around a rectangular table. Again, I sat next to Lauren, but group conversations prevailed. As the gathering drew to a close, no thoughts crossed my mind about any follow-up with Lauren. She was attractive, fun, friendly, and my age, but she lived in LA—way too far away. I had enough trouble getting started with someone locally, so how could I possibly manage a long-distance thing? We all hugged and said our good-byes.

It had been a great evening—simple, fun, easy, and refreshing—an oasis. But I had to get back to the business at hand. The one-year mark loomed directly in front of me, and I had to take it head on. I had to focus. Everything else had to take a back seat.

"And the day came when the risk to remain tight in a bud was more painful than the risk it took to blossom."

—Anais Nin

CHAPTER 17

THE CALL TO THE CAMINO

Saturday morning, April 22, 2017, I loaded my overnight suitcase into my car and headed north, through the Bay Area, past Sacramento, and into the wide-open country surrounding Highway 5. My mind and body relaxed as I looked around at the once-familiar vistas from my college years at Cal State Chico, from 1976 to 1980.

The warm, late-April sun and blue sky surrounded me on the open road as I wondered what lay in store for me on this trek. I needed to do something out of the ordinary to honor the one-year anniversary of Annie's death. Somehow, a revisit to the places where our relationship started made sense to me. I also hoped the trip would help me get some perspective on where to go from here.

When I arrived in Chico, the natural beauty of the small town gently welcomed me, just like it did in 1976. Then I was nineteen years old, didn't know jack, and had no idea where I was going in life. Now sixty, I had come full circle. I knew a few things, but once again, had no idea where I was going.

I parked my car along the street next to the campus and started my stroll. Immediately I recognized the wide walkways surrounded by green grass, the old buildings, and the sheer beauty of the grounds. The green ivy–covered brick buildings and the myriad of trees that graced the campus all registered in my memory banks. I retraced old familiar routes between buildings and stopped midway across one of the concrete and metal pedestrian bridges. I gazed down at the sight and sounds of the clear rushing creek below. Birds chirped, flew, and hopped among the creek-side vegetation. I inhaled the clean air that smelled like spring.

For the next hour, I strolled past every familiar corner of the campus and soaked it in. *This was such a long time ago.*

Next, I needed to revisit a special place across town, so I got in my car and drove to Craig Hall, the off-campus, co-ed dorm where Annie and I first met. Located eight blocks away from the main campus, Craig Hall was situated in a more rural, peaceful side of town, away from all the action. Compared to the on-campus dorms, which at times resembled scenes out of the movie *Animal House*, Craig Hall was a somewhat calmer refuge. Quiet streets, residential homes, and rows of almond tree orchards surrounded the two-story building.

But a co-ed dorm full of wild and crazy teenagers, many of them freshman away from home for the first time, was far from a quiet place to live. As a junior, I had already sowed my wild party oats in my freshman and sophomore years, and now it was time to get serious. I would shake my head in disgust at their drunken antics and found any way I could to escape the noise and stupidity. One of my favorite escapes was the nearby almond tree orchards.

I drove past the two-story dorm building, which still looked familiar forty years later. Soon the road turned into a narrow country road bordered by almond trees. The sight of the orchards rang a distant bell. I slowed down and found a place to pull over on the dirt shoulder and turned off the engine.

I stepped out of the car into the warm afternoon sunlight, ten-feet away from the rows of identical trees. I took a long breath and looked deep into the quiet orchard. I had just missed the annual bloom, but some white blossom remnants remained on the dirt rows below. Each tree had a green canopy about twenty feet high and ten feet wide with a trunk eight to ten inches in diameter. Each tree lined up perfectly with the ones in front, behind, and next to it, which created a sense of order and peace. No surprises.

For a moment I was nineteen again, in late September 1976. Red-brown tree leaves covered the perfect dirt rows as far as I could see in all directions. In the quiet, crisp autumn air, I walked alongside Annie who listened to every single word that flooded out of me. We had only known each other for just over a month, but I opened my heart and soul to her and felt amazingly safe doing so. She listened to every thought and emotion my mixed-up nineteen-year-old head and heart had to say—and accepted it all. She accepted me when I couldn't accept myself.

I heard a distant rumble, which slowly got louder and louder until it was right on top of me. A large pickup truck with thick-tread tires rolled past a few feet behind me. I snapped back to the present moment and saw the orchard in front of me. Emptiness. Other than memories of long ago, nothing was there for me. I stood for a few minutes more, then got back in my car and drove away.

I revisited some more of our old, familiar spots, but each one made me aware of the painful present, not the pleasance-filtered moments of the past. Each location—a park, a walking path, a tree grove, a particular section of campus—reminded me that the past is gone, and I couldn't go back.

The next day I drove five hours south to Visalia, Annie's hometown. I drove past the house where she grew up and I first met her mom and dad. I spent time with some of her closest friends. We talked, laughed, cried, and connected over her life that ended too soon. I drove to St. Mary's, the church where we got married in 1980, only to discover the gates closed and doors locked. The only thing missing was a sign that read: *"Move forward, Bob. Don't try to go back. It's OK to honor the past, but you need to live now in the present moment."*

As I drove back home, the final leg of my road trip, words from one of the grief books came to mind: "Thank you" and "Good-bye."

The one-year anniversary trip gave me a clear message: *"Be grateful for the time you had together but know that your life is in front of you, not behind you."*

But soon after I returned to my weekly work routine and tried to resume my altered life, a sense of panic surged inside: *Is this my life now? Is this all there is? If I just keep going to work, day after day, week after week, month after month, year after year—just playing it safe—then I'll wake up one day, look back and realize I threw it all away. I can't do that! I won't do that!*

I suddenly identified with Ebenezer Scrooge at the cemetery with the angel of death, who showed him a vision of a future yet to come—the end, with no more chances. Or was another future possible? Could there be a different ending? Could I get a second chance to live?

My old life was gone, forever gone. I had to do something to force myself into a brand-new orbit, to force change in my life. Something completely out of character, completely off script, and completely out of my comfort zone. I had to find a new way forward. But how? What?

Another thought, one that had been brewing for some time, bubbled to the surface: *Walk the Camino de Santiago.*

Many years prior I had watched *The Way*, a movie that planted the seed. And now as my grief journey entered the second year, that seed broke through the soil. The more I thought about it and researched it, the more it made sense. I talked to a friend who had walked the Camino and strongly encouraged me to go.

And even though the Camino seemed like the best move, I had something to do first. I had to return to the most solid anchor point I knew: upstate New York, where I grew up. Our family moved to California when I was twelve years old, but part of me—and part of my family—never left. What better place to decide on how to move forward with my life?

I booked the trip for late May and planned multiple stops to see family: my sister Ann in North Carolina, Aunt Betty in New York City, Aunt Dolly in New Jersey, Aunt Virginia in Long Island, and then my other sister, Mary, in upstate New York.

My first revelation came as I talked with my sister Ann. The late afternoon sunlight filtered through the tall trees in eastern North Carolina as we walked along a dirt trail in a forested park. "How are you doing, Bob, really?" she asked.

"I don't know," I said. "I'm trying to move forward, but I don't know how." My eyes started to burn. "I've always done what was expected of me. I've always followed the rules. I went to college right out of high school. After college I got a job and got married. I've always tried to be reliable and dependable. I always tried to do my job the best I could.

I've always devoted myself to my family—but now I don't know which way to turn."

I suddenly realized that I no longer had a set of rules to follow. I had no script. No map. Nothing to follow. What was my job now? Everything I knew—the entire structure on which I had built my life—was gone. I had no sense of family. No sense of home. No sense of direction. I had two choices: I could step into the unknown, or I could return to my job at the county and "play out the season." Fake it; a thought that made me sick to my stomach. I had to find a new way, a new path. I had to discover a new vision forward. I needed a pilgrimage.

After a couple days, I hugged my sister good-bye and boarded a train bound for Penn Station in New York City, where I started the next leg of visits: Aunt Betty in New York City, Aunt Dolly in New Jersey, and Aunt Ginny in Long Island. All young-at-heart sisters of my dad in their eighties and nineties, they welcomed me with warm hearts and open arms.

With each visit I felt the grounding effect of family and a sense of belonging that replaced my sense of loneliness. I was, in fact, part of a big and loving family. I just had to reach out. My heart and soul settled down.

When I reached Aunt Ginny's classic country home on the northern tip of Long Island, a surprise awaited me. As I walked around the four-acre property, the beauty of nature—the green grass, the old trees, the birds, the flowers, the smells, the buzzing sounds—everything—connected me back to my childhood home in the little town of Scottsville in upstate New York.

As I explored the grounds, I spotted a large wooden garden shed. I opened the double barn doors and stepped inside. The mixture of smells—dry grass, dry leaves, old wood, and the gasoline engine of the lawn mower—immediately transported me back to my childhood.

I climbed up and into the seat of the ride-along lawn mower and remembered the red Toro mower I rode as a kid. That instant, a revelation hit me. I practically ran back to the house.

"Aunt Ginny, would you mind if I mowed the lawn?" I asked.

"Bobby, you're here on vacation. You don't need to do any chores for me," she said.

"I know it sounds crazy, but there's nothing I would love more."

"Sure, if you insist. Have fun," she said as she shook her head in disbelief.

Straight out of the H. G. Wells novel *The Time Machine*, the lawn mower contained magical power. From the instant I started the engine and heard that sound and smelled the exhaust, it catapulted me back to my ten-year-old self. I was a kid again!

As I rode the mower over the green lawn in a rhythmic pattern of ever smaller loops, curving around tree trunks and flower beds, my youth returned. Not a care in the world. The smell of the freshly cut grass intoxicated me as the orange-chested robins hopped around the grass in my wake—just like in Scottsville.

After I finished and put the mower back in the shed, I sat down in a far corner of the lawn to stay in the moment. The sun warmed my body, a gentle breeze caressed my face as the green leaves in the trees above me softly fluttered. I soaked in the sweet fragrance of the purple lilacs that hung from tree branches. Every piece of grass, every weed, every dandelion—whether closed-up green bud, bright yellow flower, or delicate white puff—took me back.

I lay back onto the grass and looked up to the blue sky, spotted with white clouds. The warm grass on my back and the sun on my face and body felt like a loving, intimate embrace. Tears of relief flowed out as I realized the gift I had been given: the renewal and comfort of my youth—and the strength to move forward.

By the time I arrived in upstate New York to see my sister Mary, my decision to walk the Camino was all but voiced out loud. I drove back to my old neighborhood, saw my old elementary school, walked along the old railroad tracks down near the open, flat fields, and visited the grounds of our old house. My soul settled with a peaceful grin on its face.

After I mowed the lawn at my nephew John's house, I returned to Mary's for dinner. Right before we dug into the pizza and beer, I looked at her and said, "Well, Mary, I've made a decision. I'm going to walk the Camino this fall."

"Wow, Bob, that's so cool!"

PART 2

THE CAMINO

"My Lord God, I have no idea where I am going.
I do not see the road ahead of me.
I cannot know for certain where it will end.
Nor do I really know myself, and the fact that I think
that I am following your will does not mean
that I am actually doing so."

—THOMAS MERTON, *THOUGHTS IN SOLITUDE*

CHAPTER 18

CLEAR THE RUNWAY

With my decision to walk the Camino made, I couldn't stop thinking about it. *Now what? I have a million things to do and don't know where to start.*

I fidgeted at the boarding gate in the Rochester, New York, airport as I awaited my flight back to California. A group of forty to fifty young adults with identical red jackets mingled, laughed, and talked in front of me, all waiting for the same flight.

An announcement sounded: "Good morning, ladies and gentlemen. Our flight is currently oversold, and we are looking for volunteers to exchange their flight from this one to another one today. We are offering a $200 travel voucher to the first six people willing to adjust their travel plans. Please see us at the desk if you are interested. Thank you." I perked up and thought about it.

Five minutes later, the same announcement sounded, this time offering $400. A few minutes later, $600. When the amount reached $800, I jumped up to the counter. I asked the airline agent: "Is the voucher good for travel overseas, like France or Spain?"

"Yes, it is," she replied. "We have regular flights to Paris and Madrid."

"Great," I said. "I'll take it."

Within thirty minutes, I found myself seated in a taxicab, traveling from Rochester to Buffalo to catch my alternate flight back to San Jose. *What just happened?* I reached inside my jacket pocket and pulled out my $800 travel voucher. I couldn't take my eyes off it.

After I returned to my daily work routine, I knew what I had to do next: get approval for a big chunk of time off. Not a one- or two-week vacation, but a two-month leave of absence. I decided on two months after doing some basic research and chose September and October—two of my favorite months. That gave me three months to prepare: June, July, and August.

I scheduled a lunch meeting with my boss to make my request known. It was a big ask. A two-month absence for a team manager would create disruption and require a significant adjustment within the department, including a temporary assignment for someone to fill in at my position. My boss, the director of the IT Department, possessed an intense, hard-driving approach to work, but I also knew him as a thoughtful and perceptive man. As we sat across from one another at a local restaurant over turkey sandwiches and iced tea, I laid it all out and told him why I needed this time off. He listened, nodded, and when I finished, looked at me and said, "Bob, you have to do this. No problem from me. Is two months enough time?"

Within two weeks, my leave of absence paperwork was approved and I picked a departure date of Saturday, September 2, 2017, Labor Day weekend. Now I could focus all my energy on preparation. Every day after work, I took long hikes within the Fort Ord Natural Reserve until darkness fell. With each hike, I settled into my new purpose: Just walk. Nothing else. Just walk.

> *Will I be able to handle the Camino?* Don't worry about it; just walk.
> *Where am I going in life?* Don't worry about it; just walk.
> *How do I prepare for my future?* Don't worry about it; just walk.

Day after day, mile after mile, my sixty-year-old body started to remember the feel of my backpacking days many decades ago. Mountain climbs. Desert hikes. Forest hikes. Like rediscovering old treasures in the attic, a long-dormant part of me started to wake up inside. The simple act of walking connected me to the earth below the ground. It plugged me into my most basic elements—my breath, my body, my thoughts, and my very existence.

I researched the Camino, learning about various Camino routes throughout Europe that all converge in the city of Santiago. I chose the most common and well known, the Camino Francés (French Way): an 800-kilometer (500-mile) trek starting from southern France, over the Pyrenees mountain range into northern Spain, and across the entire country to the city of Santiago. My enthusiasm grew daily as I consumed books, movies, documentaries, YouTube videos, and podcasts.

I learned that *Camino de Santiago* translates to "The Way of Saint James"—one of the original twelve disciples of Jesus. The legend of James begins after his execution by King Herod in AD 44, and his body was transported from Jerusalem and buried in Spain. Eventually pilgrimages to the site in Santiago gained traction between the 12th and 14th centuries. The history of the Camino fascinated me, like the fact that Saint Francis of Assisi himself made a pilgrimage walk to Santiago in the year 1214.

Simply the words *pilgrim* and *pilgrimage* intrigued me. I identified with the concept of a seeker—someone on a mission to find something. I knew the basic concept of the "vision quest" tradition in some Native American cultures, when a young man separates from the tribe and goes alone into the wilderness to find his identity and way forward. I needed to find or rediscover my own identity and way forward, apart from every distraction of daily life. I needed my own vision quest, my own spiritual odyssey.

A longtime friend, Michael, had walked the Camino the previous year and called me regularly to give me encouragement and insights. My close friend, Father Patrick, told me stories of one of his buddies who walked the Camino several times and even created podcasts about his experiences.

The local REI store became my go-to place for all the hiking gear I needed. Everything had to be carefully selected to keep the maximum weight of my new backpack to approximately twenty pounds. My new hiking boots took the longest to figure out—I tested three different pairs before I found the right ones. Every item was essential: socks, shirts, underwear, minitowel, headlamp, waterproof gear, sun hat, cold weather cap, sleeping bag, alternate shoes, warm layers, drinking water bladder/tube, foot blister kit, trekking poles, etc.

I purchased a Camino guidebook, applied for my Camino passport, made flight reservations through a travel agent friend, made my initial hotel reservations in France, bought a Eurail pass, and planned two pre-Camino days in France.

One thing I knew for sure: Before I took my first step of the Camino from the village of St.-Jean-Pied-de-Port, I had to spend one day and night in the town of Lourdes in southern France. I wanted to go back and revisit the place that meant so much to Annie, despite the fact no healing miracle happened. *But did something happen, in some other way?*

Somewhere beneath the physical and mental preparations that now consumed me, I felt an unmistakable pull to the Camino. I didn't know exactly what was behind the pull, but I knew it was much deeper than a desire to take a long hike.

On one of my phone calls with Stephen, I informed him of my plans.

"Wow, Dad," he said. "That sounds awesome. Maybe I should do that someday."

My Camino preparation took center stage and occupied all my thoughts and attention, except for one thing: the elusive woman in my life. I wanted so badly to find a companion—a woman to walk with me on the road of life. I didn't want to go it alone.

My dating experiences provided little hope. I had exhausted all ten of my introductions through the matchmaker service, with nothing to show for it except disappointment and frustration. How would I ever find someone? Even worse, despite my grief recovery work, I still didn't feel ready to commit to a new, long-term relationship. How would I know if or when I was ready? How long would it take? I had zero answers. All I knew was that all love and goodness started with God.

During one of my training hikes, I sensed a God nudge inside: *"Give this relationship thing to Me. Let go of it. Don't reach for it or for anyone. Leave it with Me. I know what you want, but you do not need a woman to live. You must stand on your own first. Stand in Me. Live in Me. Trust Me. I'll guide you."* Easier said than done. I wanted so badly to find someone and start a new life together. What could be more natural? And more difficult? I felt like the rope in a tug of war: One side pulled and said, "Wait, rebuild, let it unfold," and the other side pulled and said, "Jump!"

Was the Camino part of my internal rebuilding process? Was it the prerequisite to a new relationship in my life? Again, I had no clue. But I knew I had to follow the pull to this trek to find out. I made my decision: Trust God. Wait. Rebuild. Walk.

By early August, after two months of constant hiking, pain and stiffness started to scream in my feet, ankles, and lower legs. Panicked, I immediately consulted a physical therapist.

"I'm leaving for the Camino in three weeks," I said. "But I can't go into it with this pain."

"How much stretching do you do?" he asked.

"Stretching? None. I'm only hiking, not running. Why do I need to stretch?"

Over the next three weeks, he worked with me twice a week until my muscles loosened, and my pain faded. I shook my head in relief and gratitude for the expertise of this physical therapist who helped me dodge a bullet. With only four days to go before my departure, however, I had to consult another type of therapist.

Late one night I sat alone in the silence of my bedroom. My stomach twisted. My chest tightened. I grabbed my cell phone and the "Employee Assistance" brochure from work and nervously dialed the number for the 24-hour therapist support line. *Do I really need to do this? Am I so messed up that I need to make this call?*

An operator answered the phone, asked me a few screening questions, and then connected me to the next available therapist. My heart pounded. *Too late now.*

"Hello, is this Robert?" a female voice asked.

"Yes," I responded.

"So how can I help you? What's happening?"

I took a deep breath. "I'm struggling with anxiety. I can't eat. I can't sleep. I shouldn't be feeling this way, but I am. I'm on my way to Europe in four days, and I should be happy and excited. But I'm more afraid than anything. Is it normal to feel like this?"

"Well, it could be. Is there a big change happening in your life?" the therapist asked.

"Yes. My wife of thirty-five years passed away last year—sixteen months ago. But I've been going to grief support groups and making good progress. But now I feel like I'm right back at square one."

"So where do you think the anxiety is coming from?" she asked.

I thought for a moment. "Maybe it's the change itself. I don't want this change. I don't want this to be happening. But it is. I don't have a choice."

As we continued to talk, my boiling anxiety slowly subsided. Eventually, I thanked her, said goodbye and hung up.

My life had changed forever, against my will. And now I was about to step into an unknown future. Something beyond me. I saw the Camino as my final good-bye to my old life. Like undergoing a new birth, I was getting pushed out. I had to go.

Another final good-bye happened in 1968 when I was twelve years old and our family moved across the country from upstate New York to San Mateo, California. The move shook me to the core and coincided with my departure from childhood. I knew life would never be the same and wrote these words in a school essay titled "My Home in New York":

My home in New York was the best house I have ever lived in in my life. It was a very big house and it had tons of land. You wouldn't believe how it looked and how it felt to live in a great place like that. We lived in it eight years, and when we had to leave it was like saying goodbye to your own life. I stay up about every night just thinking about it and many good times we had.

The last night I stayed in it was the saddest night in my life. I stayed up looking at the house thinking about all the good times we had. It was so good to us, and we loved it so much. I keep on saying to myself, Why, why did we have to leave? I really don't know to this day. I'll just say this—If you lived there as long as I did, and had to leave so sudden, you would never, never want to be happy again.

A few nights before my departure, my phone rang. It was my dear friend Alice. "Hi, Bob. I know you're busy getting ready to go, so I'll keep this short," she said.

"OK, no problem," I said.

"Well," she said, "I wanted to check your calendar for Friday, November 3rd. Lauren—you remember—will be up here visiting again, and I wanted to see if you were free for another dinner get together." A calendar date in November—two months away—seemed so far and distant that it didn't even register. I couldn't see more than 5 minutes in front of me.

"I have no idea, but I'm sure I'm free," I said. "I'll put it on my calendar. Thanks, Alice."

"OK, great," she said. "Have a wonderful trip. Please keep us posted. You're in our prayers!"

I entered the event in my phone calendar and didn't give it another thought.

The next night, the final night before lift-off, I sat on my bedroom floor, surrounded by my backpack and everything that would go inside it. I mentally checked off my preparations: My work life was now 100 percent on hold. My bills were all set to autopay. I had arranged for a friend to house-sit. I had my passport, my tickets, my reservations, my international cell phone plan, my European electrical converter adapter. I checked and rechecked every single item that would go in my backpack. I had trained and prepared my body. For the next sixty days I would live overseas on what I wore and carried. My phone buzzed several times with text messages from friends or calls with variations of "farewell," "good luck," and "see you when you get back."

I tried to get some sleep, but my racing mind and pounding heart wouldn't allow it. I lay awake in bed and took deep breaths as I tried to relax. Finally, late into the night, I fell asleep.

Early Saturday morning, my pounding heart and racing mind returned to wake me. After a shower, coffee, and a granola bar, I initiated the call for a ride to a shuttle bus in downtown Monterey that would take me to the San Francisco airport. Full backpack in hand, I closed and locked the house front door. Blue sky and morning sunshine greeted me, along with the cool, clean morning air against my face and inside my lungs. The neighborhood sat quiet—no cars, no one walking their dog, no open garage doors. I stood on the front porch, alongside my backpack, my sole companion for the next two months, and waited for my ride. *This is it. No turning back now.*

My fingers shook as I tried to line up each nail inside the thin slit on the tiny clipper. *Shake…clip. Shake…clip. Shake…clip.* Soon, the sound of an approaching car signaled the moment had arrived. I watched the driver pull up in front of the house. I took a final look back at the house and climbed inside.

The driver, a middle-aged woman, glanced at me and my backpack, smiled, and said, "Wow. Where are you headed?"

After the fifteen-minute ride to downtown Monterey, she dropped me off and wished me luck. A few other people waited for the same bus and mingled around the area. I stood there with my backpack and wondered if this is how astronauts felt before their launch. I rechecked the essentials: cell phone, boarding pass, passport, wallet with ID and credit card.

Thirty minutes later, I climbed aboard the fifteen-passenger mini-bus, took an open window seat, put on my music headphones, and looked out the window. The very moment the bus pulled onto the road and started rolling, a tidal wave of emotion crashed into me. The bus had instantly and physically transported me to a new orbit, where I could look back and see my old life from a distance.

As the bus rolled north on Highway 1 through Seaside, with the blue, green, and white waters of Monterey Bay on my left, the bus window became a transparent screen on which I saw past scenes from the life now gone. I saw the Seaside neighborhood where we moved into our new home on Labor Day weekend in 2004, exactly thirteen years earlier. Annie and I stood on the porch in front of the locked front door. She jumped up and down with excitement as she pulled the key out of the eight-by-ten-inch manilla envelope. She turned the key in the lock and opened the door wide.

"Yay!" she shouted as she bounded inside. "Our new home!"

The bus continued to roll north, past the San Miguel Canyon Road exit on Highway 101 to the home where we first lived when we moved to the area in January 1986. I saw Annie holding a five-month-old Stephen as the movers unloaded the huge truck. Then I saw Stephen inside the baby-backpack as we explored the yard and trees—with his breath and little baby sounds in my ear.

Scenes continued to unfold as the bus rolled on. Despite my awareness of other passengers, silent tears flowed out uncontrollably. Finally, thankfully, the tidal wave receded, and I caught my breath and regrouped. The song "Only in God" by John Michael Talbott played on my headphones and reminded me that only God accompanied me on this pilgrimage. Me and God. Even though I felt alone, I kept telling myself I wasn't.

God's presence. Not physical, tangible, or audible, but noticeable. It landed me safely that first and darkest night when I tumbled into the abyss. And when I crawled through the cave, the sense something was there—an invisible, good, and peaceful energy—enough to make me stop, look around, and say, "Who's there?"

And that Presence remained with me no matter what I did or didn't do. Whether I prayed or not. Whether I attended church or not. I didn't have to earn it, deserve it, or be worthy of it. I didn't even have to acknowledge it. But when I did, I felt great comfort and assurance. And now, God's presence was my one and only companion as I launched into the unknown. *I have no idea what I'm doing. I have no idea where I'm really going. But at least God is with me. The real God, my true companion God. I can start over from here.*

An hour later, the bus pulled up to the International Terminal at SFO. After getting through TSA security with my backpack intact, I arrived at the Air France departure gate in plenty of time for the flight. Over the next hour, the boarding area swelled with people talking, laughing, and mingling. Everyone seemed to belong to a family, a couple, or a group. I felt conspicuous in my singleness. But it didn't matter. Let me be conspicuous. Let me stand out. I was on a mission. Nothing else mattered.

An announcement sounded: "Welcome, ladies and gentlemen, to flight number 1003 to Paris. We will begin boarding shortly."

"You have to leave the city of your comfort and go into the wilderness of your intuition. What you'll discover will be wonderful. What you'll discover is yourself."

—ALAN ALDA

CHAPTER 19

ARRIVAL

The overnight flight to Paris was memorable, thanks to the great food and beverage service, but also due to the sudden turbulence somewhere along the way. The peace and quiet of a darkened jetliner full of sleeping passengers was suddenly shattered by a violent drop in the plane's altitude. The drop was so intense that my breathing instantly stopped, my stomach tightened, and the sound of people screaming and babies crying filled the cabin. I felt a grip of fear I had never experienced on an airplane before. I prayed and tried to breathe during the chaos.

Thankfully, the turbulence subsided, the pilot made a reassuring announcement that everything was OK, and everyone slowly quieted down. Several hours later, morning sunlight drifted into the cabin, along with the smell of coffee and breakfast.

After the plane landed in Paris and I got through customs, my goal was to find the train platform to my first destination, Bordeaux. I planned one night to adjust to the new time zone before I traveled to Lourdes for one night, and then St.-Jean to start the Camino. I stopped to ask directions at least five times, and eventually arrived at the train boarding area with a few minutes to spare. *So far, so good.*

When the train pulled up and opened its doors, I guessed on which one to enter and found an open seat. After the train slowly pulled out of the station and reached the open tracks, the conductor opened up the throttle. The acceleration force gently pulled me back into my seat as the train sped southwest through the open French countryside. I sat back and soaked in the feel of silky-smooth speed as I listened to the nearby melodic sound of conversational French and gazed out the panoramic window. *You made it. Relax. Try to enjoy this.*

I arrived in Bordeaux around 2:00 p.m. and began my search for the hotel I had booked for the night. Blue sky and warm sunshine welcomed me as I walked out of the train station into the buzzing city. I stood there, jet lagged, and tried to get my bearings. *Which way do I go? What's the address again? What does my phone GPS show?* Suddenly, a loud horn blasted in my right ear. A train barreled down on me—I didn't realize I stood right in the tracks! I jumped out of the way just in time, heart pounding. *My God, Bob. You could have been killed!*

Rattled and disoriented, I walked in circles for an hour around the city looking for my hotel. I finally found it, directly across the street from the train station. How could I have missed something right in front of my face? When I checked in at the front desk, the attendant confirmed my reservation and handed me the key to my room. My entire body exhaled in relief.

Unaccustomed to cramped European hotel rooms, I did a double take when I stepped into the room and realized it barely had enough space for a twin bed and a bathroom. But it was my room. I immediately pulled the electrical adapter from my backpack to charge my cell phone. Success! Then a wave of fatigue hit me, and all I wanted to do was sleep. But I resisted the urge and forced myself to walk around the city for the rest of the afternoon. I found a casual street-side café near the hotel, sat down at an empty table, and enjoyed a quiet dinner. I kept fighting the urge to sleep and told myself I had to make it to 8:00 p.m. before I returned to the hotel.

After dinner I walked back to the train station and located the platform for the next morning's trip to Lourdes. The smell of cigarette smoke and sounds of people mingling filled the interior. Nausea and fatigue set in. I took a seat on a wooden bench and tried to stay awake. Finally, when I could no longer keep my eyes open, I returned to my hotel room and passed out.

I woke up the next morning ready to roll. My first stop was the hotel's breakfast room, where I loaded up on eggs, cereal, yogurt, fresh coffee, French bread and butter, and warm French madeleines, which tasted so good that I stuffed my jacket pocket with a handful more. I checked out of the hotel and walked across the street to the train station and platform gate. As the train rolled southeast to Lourdes, I soaked in the beauty of the French countryside: acre after acre of brown remnants of sunflower fields, green trees that dotted rolling hills and clear blue skies.

Two hours later, as the train pulled into the Lourdes station around noon, I snapped out of my daze to remember the reason for my visit. I walked through the town with my backpack, found the hotel I had booked, and checked in early. My room was located on the fourth and top floor of the old, quaint hotel. The wooden stairs lined with a red, patterned carpet runner creaked as I ascended the narrow stairway.

A clean twin bed greeted me as I entered my room, which had a rooftop window overlooking the city, a wooden floor, and a low, angled ceiling. I set down my backpack in the corner and immediately headed back out. I walked through the narrow streets to the sanctuary site of Lourdes that Annie and I visited in May 2015, nearly two-and-a-half years earlier—a lifetime ago.

I had to go back and visit the grotto, the baths, and the entire space. As I entered the grounds, instead of sadness, anger, or grief, I felt a sense of peace—the exact thing Annie prayed for herself. When I walked up to the grotto tucked in the rocky hillside, I joined a group of about a hundred people gathered there in silent prayer.

I took a seat in one of the back rows of wooden benches and took a deep breath. I saw the ten-foot-high, triangular shaped metal structure, full of burning white candles, a hundred feet or so in front of me. Behind the candles on the left side lay the dark, cave-like opening of the grotto, the source of the spring water that Bernadette discovered in 1858. On the right side of the candles, about twenty feet above the ground inside the gray and black hillside, a six-foot-tall, white marble statue of Mary stood inside a small opening. Her face gazed out toward the people gathered, with her hands joined together in prayer.

The sounds of shuffling feet, camera clicks, soft conversations, and recited prayers filled the area. I looked at the people gathered around me and wondered what miracle they were hoping and praying for.

But now it all looked and felt different. I sat there with no hopes or expectations, and no sense of dependency. All of it had lost its meaning: the prayers, the rituals, the water, and the candles. I let go of it all. No more holding my breath for a miracle. But one thing prevailed as I sat there: an overriding sense of God's peace, God's presence.

I nodded a good-bye to the grotto and moved over to the baths, a short walk away. Unlike the swarms of people that filled the waiting areas in 2015, on this day it was mostly empty. I just stood there in limbo, outside a waist-high metal barrier. I didn't know what to do, so I just stood and remembered. After a few minutes, a man approached me. "Would you like to go into the baths?" he said with an Italian accent.

I looked up and saw an older man with gray hair and kind eyes. His face didn't look familiar, but I wondered if he was the same man I once talked with. I thought for a few seconds. "Sure, I'll go."

He ushered me into the waiting area directly in front of the curtained-off entrance to the baths. I sat alongside a small group of six men who waited to go in. As I sat and listened, the men all talked loudly with each other in a language I didn't recognize. Russian? Ukrainian? They were a tough-looking bunch—large in stature, tattooed, and exuding a dominating presence. *What are they doing here?* I wondered. The Italian volunteer, unintimidated, kept telling them to quiet down.

"Shhh! Be quiet!" he said. "This is a holy place. Put away your cell phones! Show some respect." They all complied in silence.

Within fifteen minutes the volunteer escorted us past the curtain into the bath area, where we each got undressed and wrapped a white towel around our waists. One by one we were escorted by a separate group of volunteers into our individual bath. Just like before, I descended the three stairs into the clear, cold water. I stood waist deep in the water with one volunteer on my left and another on my right. And just like before, one of them looked at me and spoke in a German accent: "Dear brother, would you like to say a prayer first?"

I nodded and silently prayed for Stephen, peace, healing, and a good Camino. I nodded again, and they lowered me backward into the water—cold, clean, and sharp but incredibly comforting. The next instant, they lifted me back to my feet, where I stood for a few seconds. After I dried off, redressed, and exited the baths, I noticed the peace that filled me. I felt lighter and calmer.

But I noticed something else as I walked the grounds of the Lourdes sanctuary. The externals didn't have the pull on me they once did. Here I was, immersed in a mecca of Catholic religious elements: towering church steeples, chapels, prayer stations adorned with glowing candles, rosary walks, and statues of saints everywhere. But now I felt a strange detachment from them, as if they didn't apply to me anymore.

I had to face the reality that countless prayers for healing and deliverance didn't prevent Annie's death or help with Stephen's addiction. Decades of obedience and observances didn't. Devotions didn't. Lit candles didn't. Anointings didn't. Immersion into Lourdes water didn't. Begging and pleading didn't. Not a single ritual or ceremony did.

Did they do something I didn't notice or couldn't see? Or had I falsely believed in a fantasy god all these years? A magician god or Wizard of Oz god who granted wishes if I followed all the rules and delivered the broomstick like an obedient servant?

I also knew in my heart that everything was done with love and the best of intentions. No one tried to deceive anyone—just the opposite— everyone tried to help. Everyone expressed their love in amazing ways and stood with us. It was no one's fault. *So where do I go from here? How do I move forward?*

God's loving presence was all that remained. I could let go of everything else: the observance of religious requirements and obligations, clinging to hope and expectations for miracles to happen if certain rituals are followed, and the endless prayers for specific outcomes.

I continued to walk and reflect, walk and reflect. Finally, I looked at the time: 7:00 p.m. I had to leave, find dinner, get back to the hotel, get some sleep, and get ready to go.

Tomorrow was day one of my Camino, but in reality it had already started.

"There is a journey you must take.
It is a journey without destination. There is no map.
Your soul will lead you. And you can take nothing with you."

—Meister Eckhart

CHAPTER 20

THE ROAD BEGINS

I opened my eyes to the morning light in my tiny hotel room in Lourdes. I felt an overriding sense of God's peace after a great night's sleep. The moment had arrived. After breakfast at the hotel, I hiked back to the Lourdes train station for a stop in Bayonne, where I would transfer to a final train that would take me to the starting point of the Camino Francés, St. Jean Pied de Port. As the train pulled away from Lourdes, I looked out the window and silently said good-bye.

Thoughts raced through my mind: *What would the Camino be like? Will I make it all the way? Will I make it over the Pyrenees trail on Day 1? Who will I meet? What will I encounter? How will I change? Remember, Bob, just walk.*

For all my anxious thoughts, I didn't have a single doubt that I was doing the right thing. I knew deep in my soul that this trek had my name on it. The peace inside confirmed it, despite the whirlwind of competing thoughts. Somehow, I felt a sense of recognition—the call to do this came from a familiar voice, one that I trusted. It would have felt wrong *not* to go.

When the train pulled into Bayonne, I stepped off, walked through the small station, and stood in the bright midmorning sunshine. I had a few hours to kill before boarding the final train, so I decided to walk around the city. People, cars, motor scooters, and the bustle of the city whirred around me.

As I walked alone in the crowded streets, I felt changes already happening inside me. With every move and decision, no matter how small, I rediscovered a muscle long forgotten—my self-direction muscle. Which way to turn on this street. Which shop to go inside. Which ones to skip. Where to go for a bite to eat. What to do at every moment. So simple, yet so profound.

I started to realize that I had lived most of my life in response to other people's wishes, expectations, or directions. They led and I followed. But now, here I was, alone in a foreign country where no one knew me, and everything was up to me. Everything. No one told me where to go or what to do. The raw freedom confused and startled me.

I tuned into an inside voice connected to my comfort compass. Was it God's voice, my own, or some combination? I wasn't sure, but all I knew was that God and I were in this together.

One decision was so automatic it pulled me in like a magnet: a French bakery on a street corner. I stood paralyzed in front of an L-shaped glass display loaded with golden-brown and multicolored pastries, madeleines, cookies, pies, cakes, and breads. The smell of fresh bread, vanilla, fresh fruit, and confectioners' sugar filled my nostrils with all the lure of a seductress. After I snapped out of my trance, I asked the busy young woman for two almond croissants—one for now and one for the road.

I found an open bench, sat down, and bit into one. The taste of the white powdered sugar and shaved almonds on top of the warm, flattened flaky croissant filled with butter-infused almond paste almost knocked me out.

By the time I returned to the Bayonne train station two hours later, many more fellow backpack-carrying travelers had arrived and gathered on the concrete platform next to the train tracks. The next train to arrive would take me to St. Jean Pied de Port ("Saint John [at the] Foot of [the] Pass"), the Camino Francés starting point.

I saw gray-haired men and women, young twenty-somethings, and people in between. Everyone had a backpack. Some had bicycles. The crowd of approximately seventy-five people dressed in T-shirts and light clothes for the warm September afternoon.

Fifteen minutes before departure time, the entire group edged slowly toward the tracks. When the train pulled up, the mass squeezed together and jockeyed for position. The train looked way too small to handle everyone. When the sliding doors opened, everyone crushed together to board, and a crazy game of musical chairs ensued.

Elbow to elbow, chest to backpack, backpack to chest, we shuffled into the sardine can. When I entered the jam-packed train, I squeezed past seated passengers and headed to the rear where I managed to find an opening. Without hesitation, I shoe-horned myself between two others, who welcomed me with a smile. I smiled back and watched the crush continue until all seats were taken. The heat inside the stuffy train rose by the minute until the conductor asked everyone who didn't have a seat to disembark. They would have to wait for another train. For all the intensity, no tempers flared.

This is it. I made it. I'm on my way to the starting point.

As the train rumbled south to St.-Jean, I must have heard at least five different languages in conversations. I sat quietly and listened. Here I was, on a train loaded with fellow travelers to the Camino—fellow pilgrims. When we arrived an hour later, everyone squeezed out of the train and walked en masse toward the town. I had no idea where we were going, so I just followed the crowd. Soon, I found myself walking alongside a young woman who looked to be in her late twenties.

"Do you know where we're going?" I asked.

"I have no clue," she said in perfect English.

English! It sounded so…normal. She had blond hair, a smiling face, and introduced herself as "Molly from Alaska." I introduced myself as "Bob from California," my new nickname. We chatted as we walked along with the group.

Ten minutes later, the crowd entered the town and took a left turn down a narrow street. The whole feel of the place—the narrow, cobbled streets, the old buildings with white walls and red shutters, the brown-stone church tower, the stone bridges and red tile rooftops—transported me back in time.

After a few minutes, we arrived at the Pilgrim Welcome Office, where we all stood in a line that stretched well outside the front entrance. This is where everyone registers and gets their Camino Passport or Credential, which is used to document a pilgrim's starting point, their (hopeful) finish in Santiago, and their myriad stops along the way.

The office also had maps and the next day's weather forecast for the trail over the Pyrenees.

When my turn finally came, I approached the long registration table and sat in front of one of the staff members. She recorded my name and country from my U.S. Passport and asked me a few questions:

"Are you traveling on foot, by bicycle, or on horseback?" she asked.

"On foot," I replied.

"Your reason for walking the Camino? Religious, cultural, other?" she asked.

"Religious, spiritual, and other."

She smiled and said, "Buen Camino"—have a good Camino.

I looked at my three-and-a-half-inch-wide, six-inch-high Camino Passport with the words *Credencial del Peregrino* printed above a brown-ink image of an ancient stone bridge. I opened the accordion-folded heavy paper credential and saw my name and U.S. Passport number, my start date of 05-09-2017 (day-month-year), and a blank space at the bottom for the "Arrived in Santiago" date. I unfolded the entire passport, which stretched more than two feet wide, and saw my first Camino stamp in black ink: a coat-of-arms, a medieval-era pilgrim, tall mountain peaks, and small-lettered banner "St. Jean Pied de Port." The single stamp looked lonely on the upper left corner of the empty passport.

I needed to find a place to stay for the night. A few doors down the same street, I saw a sign advertising ten euros per night, which looked as good as any other. I entered the open front door, walked down a narrow hallway that led to the inside living room area. A middle-aged woman with black hair and a raspy voice greeted me. A few other pilgrims, including Molly, stood in front of the check-in desk-table as the proprietress collected everyone's payment. The house smelled like an animal shelter, and soon I counted five cats and two dogs. After everyone paid their 10€, she gathered us all together for a lecture—which she repeated several times—on the "rules of the house."

"One thing I require," she said in a grouchy schoolteacher voice, "is time alone each night. That means you all need to be out of the house—yes, completely out of the house—from 6 to 8 p.m. No exceptions. And lights out by 10 p.m. Are there any questions?"

An awkward silence prevailed as we all fidgeted and avoided eye contact. Finally, she concluded, "I'll take you upstairs to your room. Follow me. Remember, lights out at 10 p.m."

As we followed her up the wooden stairs, some of us exchanged glances that said: "Can you believe this? What really goes on each night for two hours?" She opened a door to a room with four bunk beds squeezed inside. Close accommodations for eight adults, four men and four women. No matter, we claimed beds, got settled, pulled items from our backpacks, and began introductions. Other than Molly, everyone was from another country, but knew enough English to carry on basic conversation.

When the 6:00 p.m. hour arrived, we all vacated the house and went in search of dinner. A small group of us walked into the town, past the old church, to a restaurant with an outdoor eating area. Soon I found myself at a table eating dinner with six people I didn't know from Adam, all from various parts of the world. I felt a surprising connection with these familiar strangers. Each one of us here on our own, each one of us on our quest.

After dinner I roamed around St. Jean on my own to soak in where I was and what I was doing here. Tomorrow would be huge—up at the crack of dawn for an early start. I needed to carry my own breakfast, lunch, and water, and then hike twenty-five kilometers through the Pyrenees to a large hostel in Roncesvalles—the first stop in Spain. Anxiety filled my stomach, but I also had confidence I could make it. I was as ready as I would ever be.

I returned to the animal shelter mystery house for a quick shower and dry-off with my minimalist microfiber towel, which felt funky but worked. Then I joined my bunk mates for a bit of conversation before lights out at 10:00 p.m. My nerves, my bladder, and constant snoring in the room kept me awake all night. Daylight couldn't come soon enough, but when it did, I wasted no time exiting the house. I had a full water pouch in my backpack, a banana, an apple, some sliced salami, and a couple of candy bars.

When I stepped out the front door onto the cobbled street around 7:00 a.m., the raw energy of the launch surged inside me. This was it—the first steps of my own journey.

Coming from my right, people were making their way to the edge of town and the Camino trailhead. The sounds of people talking, laughing, and the clack-clack-clack of trekking poles on the narrow street filled the air. I entered the procession. As I passed by the old church, I whispered a prayer for my feet and gave a final surrender to whatever awaited me in the days and weeks ahead. My adrenaline powered me forward, despite the lack of sleep. This is what I came to do.

Soon the road came to a fork where the two routes to Roncesvalles diverged: the Valcarlos route and the Napoleón route. The guidebook listed Valcarlos as the one to take "in poor weather" and the Napoleón "in good weather." The damp, early morning gray sky signaled rain was coming, but I had my heart set on the Napoleón route regardless. I wanted to travel over the same ground Napoleon's troops took to cross into Spain. A wooden post pointed the way, 24.3 kilometers away through the Pyrenees.

Soft blankets of foggy mist hung over the green hills and pastures, obscuring the mountainous terrain ahead. A slightly inclined asphalt road led away from town, up into the misty mountains. Fellow pilgrims greeted one another and chatted happily. I walked past a group of three women from Ireland who gave me a dose of their top-of-the-morning Irish energy and cheer.

Then I encountered a solo female hiker, who I guessed to be in her forties, average height and weight, with dirty-blond hair spilled out behind her wool cap.

"Hello," I said as I pulled up alongside her. "I'm Bob from California."

"Hi," she said. "I'll Jill from Seattle."

We chatted for a few moments on basics like the weather, work, and career. Then I asked her, "So, what brings you to the Camino?"

"I need to start a new phase in my life," she said. "I had to get away from it all. It's kind of like the ancient rite of passage, where the person separates from the tribe in order to find their true self. You know that expression about losing sight of the shore? You have to lose sight of the familiar shore before you can sail to a new land. That's what I need to do. It scares me, but it's what I need to do."

Then she looked over at me and said, "How about you? Why are you here?"

"Wow, I couldn't have said it better," I said as I shook my head in disbelief. "I lost my wife last year to brain cancer. We were married thirty-five years. I'm here to try to find my way forward."

"I'm sorry."

We talked for a while longer until I realized I wanted to walk at a slightly faster pace. No offense, and none taken. We wished each other well, and I slowly pulled ahead. It wasn't long before I couldn't see anyone in front of me, partially due to low visibility and also the transition of the paved road into a narrow, rocky, and steep dirt trail. I was on my own now. Just me and my thoughts.

Just walk, Bob. Just walk.

Soon the mist turned into a light rain shower, which then turned into a steady rain. I could only see the immediate path ahead of me for each step, which became increasingly slippery and muddy. Deep breaths of cold, wet air invigorated my lungs. My backpack felt snug and stable on my back and waist, and my entire body felt strong. Every choice of hiking gear proved nearly perfect: My wool socks and boots kept my feet dry and firm on the trail. My brim hat kept the rain off my face and neck. My hiking pants repelled the water and allowed free movement of my legs, and my skin to breathe. My upper long-sleeve layers made of high-tech fabric kept me warm and dry.

But when I reached the seven kilometer mark at Orisson, a pit stop with a small *albergue* (Spanish for hostel) and a restaurant-bar, the rain got so heavy that I had to regroup. Pilgrims and backpacks jammed the restaurant and bar areas, but I decided to prepare myself for the intense climb ahead.

Under the cover of an overhang, I tucked my cell phone inside a waterproof pouch (no more photos for now), covered my backpack with its waterproof cover, put on my rain jacket, and pulled the hood over my soaking wet brim hat. My pants, socks, and boots were waterproof enough to move on. I settled into the reality that today would be a sopping wet slog and got back on the trail.

The next few hours of solo walking immersed me in a spiritual realm that overpowered the physical elements around me. Despite the driving rain, cold wind, and exertion of the climb, I felt an avalanche of emotions break loose inside me. I found myself openly weeping as my lungs and muscles pushed forward. My friend Grief had reappeared in a big way. But I didn't mind. We were going to work together through whatever we needed to. A mixture of pain and peace filled me with each step I took.

At the same time, I sensed God's voice whispering to me over and over: *"I love you, no matter what. You don't have to do anything to earn it. I love you, no matter what."*

I kept my focus on the muddy next step in front of me as the path traversed upward. My hiking poles helped keep my body balanced and in control. The wind, rain, and clouds kept coming. I couldn't see more than two hundred feet in front of me. So much for the spectacular Pyrenees mountain views mentioned in the guidebook.

Then it hit me. This wasn't just a hike over the mountains; it was an initiation! An initiation to the Camino and to my new life. I laughed out loud in the wind and rain. *Welcome to the Camino, Bob! Welcome to the beginning of your new life!*

An hour or so later, the muddy trail opened onto a section of paved road, still climbing upward. The change from slippery mud to solid pavement felt stable under my boots, and my body relaxed. Up ahead I saw a lone figure walking. The wind played havoc with the pilgrim's rain poncho, which flailed in every direction. As I got closer, I could tell it was a man—stocky and medium height. He held a wooden hiking stick in his right hand and trudged slowly along with a distinct limp. I felt sorry for the guy and pulled up alongside him, thinking he could use some encouragement.

"Hello, how are you doing?" I said. "I'm Bob from California."

He looked over at me through his hooded poncho. His brown, rounded face looked middle-aged with heavy, dark eyebrows and a stubbled black and gray beard.

"Hello, my name is Jesús (hey-Zeus)...from Mexico...I'm doing OK," he said with a distinct Spanish accent in-between deep breaths of air.

"Is this your first Camino?" I asked.

"No...it's my fifth."

Stunned, I didn't know what to say, and then he told me his story. As we walked through the wind and rain, he told me he walked his first Camino six years prior.

"I came to my first Camino stuck in life. I didn't know what to do. But by the time I finished, I got the clarity I needed. So I returned to Mexico, made the necessary changes, and moved on with my life. But I keep getting stuck," he said as he shook his head and smiled under his rain hood, "so I keep coming back."

Keep coming back. Keep trying. Keep seeking. Don't give up, even if you have to limp along. He's not ashamed, doesn't pretend, and doesn't hide. It's OK to struggle. I felt so humbled next to him. I didn't want to accept my struggle; I wanted to get through it, get to the other side, and get it over with. I wanted to conquer and overcome, not keep coming back. I wanted resolution, not struggle.

Through the wind and rain, he listened to every word as I told him my story. When I finished, he looked over at me and said, "Well, I can tell you this: If you're seeking something—an answer, some direction, some guidance—you will find it on the Camino. It may happen somewhere along the way, or at the end, or even afterwards—but you will find it."

"Thank you," I said.

"Thank you for sharing your story."

We wished each other well, and I went back to my own pace, deep in thought. I recalled excerpts from the Bible where Jesus would often go off by himself to be alone and pray. Why did he keep going back for space and solitude? Did he struggle to find clarity?

Wow, I walked with Jesus today. Alone. Just me and him. We both talked. We both struggle. We walked and shared our true selves with each other. No pretenses. No posturing. We connected with each other. We thanked each other. Jesús from Mexico. Thank you, God, for sending him my way.

Soon, the wide, paved section of the trail turned back into a narrow path of mud and rocks, and I turned all my energy back to navigating the slippery trail. Somewhere near the 4,700-foot plateau, I reached an open area with a small hut-like building. I walked to the side away from the driving rain to take a short break, where I bumped into five or six other pilgrims who had the same idea. We all huddled against the brick wall. No one spoke, but we all nodded in comradery with each other and just shook our heads at the crazy weather conditions.

The moment I stopped, I realized how wet and cold my entire body felt, despite the rain gear. I took out a candy bar from my rain jacket pocket—a European version of a Kit-Kat bar—and fumbled with the wet wrapper to get it open. When I took a bite, the chocolate felt like cold wax in my mouth. I stuffed it in anyway and nodded a farewell to the group. I had to get moving. I wanted to get this day over with sooner than later.

The climb soon started to descend, and the trail became a slippery, muddy mess. Downhill proved trickier than uphill, and I lost my footing and fell twice onto my side and back, thankfully unhurt. Somewhere along the trail a fellow pilgrim told me we had crossed the border into Spain, and the finish line for the day drew closer. Each time I encountered rain-soaked pilgrims, we encouraged each other forward.

Toward the late afternoon, the trail entered a quiet forest of tall trees as the rain started to ease up. The peaceful grove felt like an indoor refuge away from the driving wind and rain outside. Not long after the grove ended—hungry, exhausted, wet, cold, and exuberant—I walked into the small Spanish village of Roncevalles. My body melted in relief.

Around 4:00 p.m. I walked up to the finish line—a large albergue with a crowd of over one-hundred pilgrims who had already arrived. Friendly chatter in multiple languages filled the air as we stood in line outside, awaiting admittance. Patches of clear sky could be seen through the clouds. The rain had finally relented, as if to say, "OK, that's enough for today. You made it. I'm going to back off now."

When my turn came at the registration table, I paid my lodging fee and presented my clean, dry Credential, which was stamped and dated 06-09-2017 (September 6, 2017). The blue-ink stamp had an exotic look—a pointed oval filled with symbols and Spanish words. I smiled inside when I thought of what was behind my first hard-earned passport stamp.

The woman handed back my Camino passport and a piece of paper with a number written on it. "This is your room assignment," she said. "Dinner is not served here at the albergue, but there are several restaurants close by."

I thanked her and started my way through the ancient building. The old hallways hummed with the energy of fellow pilgrims who made the Day 1 trek. Muddy boot tracks covered the concrete floor. Soaking wet backpacks of all colors and trekking poles leaned against the walls. After a turn or two, at the far end of the hallway, I saw the number of my assigned room and stepped inside. The long rectangular room with a wooden floor had ten double bunks, five along each wall. A few room-mates sat or lay on their beds and greeted me warmly. A young couple with their infant child in tow smiled at me.

After a gloriously warm shower and a change into dry clothes from my backpack, I teamed up with a few others for a short walk into town. We found a booming restaurant and enjoyed a rousing happy hour and dinner. With more familiar strangers and fellow pilgrims, we celebrated our Day 1 victories.

After dinner, nourished and tired, we wished each other well and went our separate ways. I walked around the village and explored some of the old buildings and historical markers. A road sign along the near-by highway read: "Santiago de Compostela 790 (km)"—490 miles to reach Santiago.

That evening, as I settled into my bunk bed and sleeping bag, I thought about my check-in a few hours earlier. It wasn't just my Credential that got stamped; I myself got stamped at that table. Validated. Officially admitted to my spiritual odyssey. I passed my first Camino test. There was no way out now except through. No turning back. I could practical-ly hear the door to my previous life slam shut behind me.

I celebrated the magnitude and thrill of Day 1, but tomorrow would bring Day 2, and then Day 3, and God knows how many days after that. What would they bring? Would I make it? I couldn't look too far ahead. I just had to take one day at a time. I was on my way, and God was with me.

Just walk, Bob, just walk.

"Hiking—I don't like either the word or the thing. People ought to saunter in the mountains—not 'hike'! Do you know the origin of that word 'saunter'? It's a beautiful word. Away back in the Middle Ages people used to go on pilgrimages to the Holy Land, and when people in the villages through which they passed asked where they were going, they would reply, 'A la sainte terre,' 'To the Holy Land.' And so they became known as sainte-terre-ers or saunterers. Now these mountains are our Holy Land, and we ought to saunter through them reverently, not 'hike' through them."

—John Muir

CHAPTER 21

BACK TO SCHOOL

Despite my fatigue from the Day 1 marathon, I couldn't sleep for the second night in a row. Another snore-filled room, accented by occasional cries from the infant child, made it impossible. I kicked myself for not bringing earplugs. Exhausted and angry, I laced up my muddy wet boots and got ready to hit the early morning trail. I vowed to find a quiet hotel room for my third night. I had to get some sleep.

Around 7:00 a.m. I strapped on my backpack, grabbed my trekking poles, and stepped outside into the cold morning air. The sky greeted me without a rain cloud in sight. I followed a few scattered pilgrims to the six-foot-wide dirt trail and took a deep breath. Within minutes I found myself walking through a green forest of trees and countless types of foliage.

The sheer natural beauty hugged me in a long embrace, as if to say: *"Forget about the madness of yesterday's trail. That's over. Just relax today and soak in the peace and beauty all around you."* My irritation and anxiety slowly fell away with each step on the solitary dirt trail.

My destination was the town of Zubiri, twenty-one kilometers away, but I felt no pressure to get there. Like Dorothy who had just arrived in the Land of Oz, I gawked and marveled at the world around me. I, too, had come from a black and white world. But today, colors surrounded me: multiple shades of greens, browns, and yellows. The trail continued to unfurl a gentle path through groves of lush trees and vegetation. In some spots, the natural growth created living tunnels to walk through. I walked past brown-and-white-spotted horses that grazed or lounged in rolling hills of tall grass.

The trail crossed small creeks of clear running water, past weathered fence posts, pink wildflowers, and bushes of wild berries. I walked through old groves of stalwart trees anchored with large, worn trunks. I walked through young groves of trees close together with their small, clean trunks. How could any place on Earth be more magical? Calmness filled me.

I practically had the trail to myself, and leisurely took photos along the way. I settled into a slow pace and relished the quiet reflection and solitude. Sometime midmorning, I walked into my second Spanish village and stopped at a cafe for my first *peregrino* (pilgrim) breakfast: cafe con leche (coffee with milk), fresh orange juice (from an orange-crushing machine), a piece of French bread, and a large slice of a Spanish tortilla (a cross between a two-egg omelet and a quiche).

The rest of the day followed the same pattern: solitude on a nearly empty trail that traversed through stunning natural landscapes interspersed between small, ancient villages. It occurred to me at some point: *Where am I? What am I doing? What an odd and wonderful thing: I'm walking alone in a foreign land on a trail that leads to a promised destination some five hundred miles away. And I have no idea what I'm doing.*

Then I encountered my first sighting of the Camino's telltale symbol: a dark blue, eight-inch square tile etched with a bright yellow scallop shell symbol, shaped like a hand with nine fingers. The tile was embedded near the top of a three-foot-high, tapered concrete signpost, which reassured me I was on the right path. I had seen actual scallop shells tied to the rear of many backpacks already, but this was my first assurance from the trail itself. Something else caught my eye: a bright yellow arrow, spray-painted like graffiti, just below the blue tile on the concrete post. It pointed in the direction to travel. I felt more like Dorothy all the time: I had a far-off destination, some faith, some hope, and a path to follow.

Hope—for a new life. Was it an illusion? Maybe. All I knew was that I had a simple job to do: walk the trail each day. That's it. Nothing else. Just keep going, one step at a time. Leave the rest in God's hands. Walk and trust. I could handle that. For the first time in a long time, something made sense.

By the time I reached the town of Zubiri in the late afternoon, I walked straight past every albergue in search of an actual hotel. At the first one I saw, I stepped inside and nearly kissed the woman behind the front desk when she said she had one room left. As I unlocked the door, entered the room, saw a large, clean bed and a private shower, and heard nothing but peace and quiet, I leaped into a virtual backflip. I laid out my wet clothes to dry, soaked in the hot shower for twenty luxurious minutes and flopped on the bed for a short rest before dinner. Pure heaven.

Near 6:00 p.m. I walked into town, spotted a busy restaurant with tables outside, and saw people I recognized after only two days. When I walked up, I was greeted and welcomed to sit with my new friends, which transformed a simple dinner into something extraordinary. The Camino had already taught me there are no strangers on the way. We are all fellow pilgrims—fellow peregrinos—and we are in it together. *Wow. I've sat in many restaurants and felt so alone, but not here.*

The next morning, after a glorious eight-plus hours of sleep, I felt like a new man. My destination was the famous city of Pamplona, listed as Stage 3 in the Camino guidebook. A twenty-one kilometer hike on a relatively flat trail, it looked like no problem. My body felt strong and ready.

The morning sunshine warmed my face and soul as I started out on the trail. Nature's beauty blew me away again. It bathed me in its colors, hills, wide open fields, grazing horses, running creeks, and open vistas.

I bumped into the young couple with their infant son, who was fast asleep in his dad's backpack. We chatted for a few minutes and formally introduced ourselves. They were from Hamburg, Germany, and had decided to walk the Camino as a young family. We shared a laugh about the youngest pilgrim on the Camino. I took their picture and then resumed my solo pace. Soon, the trail took me past a mural painted on the side of a barn that welcomed me to Basque country.

Everything was going well until the early afternoon, when a blister on my left foot started to yell, and then scream. I had another eight to ten kilometers to go before the goal of Pamplona, but the blister had other plans. When I walked into the tiny village of Zuriain, I ran into my new friend, Ryan from Canada. We met on the first crazy day over the Pyrenees and bunked in the same room in Roncesvalles. I told him about my blister problem, and he suggested an option I didn't even know about—a little albergue-church named San Esteban just up ahead. "I thought about stopping there myself," he said. "But I've decided to push on to Pamplona."

We walked together until we reached a fork in the trail. The blister had spoken, and I listened. I thanked Ryan, said good-bye, and reluctantly headed up the trail to San Esteban. I felt like a failure. A weakling. At the top of the short trail, a large grass lawn opened in front of me. A few fellow pilgrims sat there, resting and talking.

I also noticed an old church building with open wooden doors, which beckoned me inside. I removed my backpack, leaned it against the stone wall, and stepped through the old doorway onto the rustic wooden floor. I immediately felt a sense of peace and quiet. The empty wooden pews faced the front altar, which was unlike any I had ever seen.

A looming display of multicolored, three-foot-tall, three-dimensional carvings of saints covered the thirty-foot-high arched wall behind the altar. Bright sunlight flooded through a high circular window, illuminating the colorful figures. I sat down to gather my thoughts and soak it in. Mounted on the wall next to me, at eye level, was a three-dimensional figure of the crucified Christ, with hundreds of bright green sticky-notes covering the wooden mounting surface. I looked closer and noticed they were prayer requests of all kinds. After I added my own—for a good Camino and for Stephen—I noticed a prayer card display and picked one up titled "El Camino." The last line read: "The Camino calls you to contemplate, to be amazed, to welcome, to interiorize, to stop, to be quiet, to listen, to admire, to bless...Nature, our companions on the journey, our own selves, God."

The message was clear: Today wasn't about achieving my goal for the day and making it to Pamplona. It wasn't about pushing through pain like I'm in a rush, a race, or a competition. I needed to let go of my goal and accept the unexpected change in my plans. To allow myself to accept some humility and say no to my proud ego that thinks I'm tougher and better than everyone else. I needed to stop for the day. To listen. To release my self-applied pressure. To let the Camino teach me. I could sense my mind, body, and soul start to calibrate to the Way of St. James.

As I got up to exit the church, an older woman approached and welcomed me. She stood about five feet tall, had thick, neat white-gray hair that covered her ears, and kind eyes behind clear glasses. Her black vest highlighted a silver crucifix at the end of a long silver chain. She introduced herself as one of the sisters (Catholic nuns) who lived and served there. She pointed out a door leading to an old stone, spiral stairway that went up to the ancient belfry.

"You're welcome to climb the stairs to the top and ring the bell. Just keep it to a minimum so you don't wake the neighbors," she said with a smile. "Also, if you plan to stay here this evening, you can check in at the albergue next door. After dinner, we hold a little prayer service in the loft upstairs," she said as she pointed to the choir loft in the rear of the church. "It starts at 8:00 p.m. Hope to see you then."

I thanked her, and she went about her way. I opened the old wooden door to the bell tower and climbed up fifty to sixty feet inside the cramped stone stairway spiraling to the top landing. As I gazed out the open-air tower to the world below, I realized I stood inside a centuries-old space. I wondered what stories it could tell, and who had stood here so many years before me.

I looked up at the large church bell supported by thick wooden beams ten feet above my head, with a long and tattered rope that hung down to my level. I stepped onto some old wooden boards to reach the rope, which slightly bowed beneath my body weight. I looked down at the gaps between the boards and wondered if they would hold. I reached out and grabbed onto the bristly weathered rope and pulled downward. Nothing. I pulled again, a little harder. Still nothing. I pulled a third time and heard the clear voice of the weathered bell speak. The sound of vibrating thick metal echoed through the tower and through my body.

I climbed down, gathered my backpack, and walked over to the adjoining albergue to check in. When I entered the front door, it was like walking into someone's welcoming home. Instead of a registration table occupied by an attendant, a small wooden box sat on a shelf with an open slot and a sign that read "Donativo"—Donation. The cost was up to each pilgrim—whatever amount I wanted to donate.

An open living room had couches, chairs, and magazines, creating a welcome rest area. The large kitchen-dining area buzzed with friendly volunteers who invited me to help prepare dinner for the evening meal at 6:00 p.m. A total of twenty chairs sat alongside a long, communal dinner table. The clean sleeping area upstairs was filled with perfectly made twin and bunk beds in a sunlit room.

The afternoon gently drifted into the early evening. *Here I am, surrounded by fellow pilgrims from around the world—perfect strangers, but new friends.* We gathered in the kitchen to help prepare dinner, a vegetarian soup-stew of some kind. We laughed, talked, and got to know each other as we chopped, peeled, and sliced. When dinnertime came, we all filled the chairs at the long table, and one of the albergue volunteers welcomed us and poured the vino tinto—red wine. Conversation, laughter, and joyful fellowship flowed for the next two hours.

After dinner, I gathered in a circle with a group of ten other pilgrims on a pillowed floor in the church loft for the prayer service. A gentle mood was set with soft lighting and low-volume background music. Three of the Sisters of the Sacred Heart, including the one who first greeted me, introduced themselves and began the service with a short prayer. For the next thirty minutes, I listened to music and scripture excerpts read in multiple languages. At the end, one of the sisters said, "If you would like to, please tell us what brought you to the Camino. We'll go around the circle. Feel free to pass or share."

When my turn came, I spoke from my heart and didn't try to hide my struggle or pain. Afterward, a young man in his twenties with super-short blond hair told his story. "I lost my mother to cancer in March 2016," he said in a Scandinavian accent through tears. "I have suffered with depression, drugs, and darkness ever since. I came to the Camino to try to find some peace." As he shared his pain, I saw Stephen in him. My eyes burned with tears as he described how damaged and distant his relationship with his dad had become—just like me and Stephen.

After the service ended, without either of us saying a word, we found and hugged each other. For that few seconds, I hugged Stephen. He introduced himself as Jannik from Denmark. As we talked, a tall young woman with long blond hair in her thirties approached us. "Hello," she said with a foreign accent. "My name is Hana, from Czech Republic. I heard your stories, and my heart broke. Can I give each of you a hug?"

When she hugged me, my initial sense of shock was instantly replaced with grateful acceptance of loving care from a total stranger. I sensed a special warmth from her and a genuine concern as I felt her arms hug me and felt her hair on the side of my face. Boosted by a surge of energy, I let go and thanked her.

Then the sister who welcomed me came up and said, "I know it is not your blistered feet that have the most pain, but your heart. God bless you on your Camino." Another sister encouraged me with a Bible verse about how God makes all things new.

Jannik and I talked late into the night and provided some hope and healing as surrogates for each other—me as his widowed dad and he as my motherless son. As he talked, I looked at him with the pride of a surrogate father. He's here. He's doing something. He's taking on his pain head on. He's trying. *Why can't Stephen do something like this? Why don't I see him trying? Maybe he is.*

I lay in bed that night stunned by what had happened over the last twelve hours, how God had led me to this time and place to meet these people—all through the pain of a blister.

The next morning, after another night of minimal albergue sleep, a small group of us, including Jannik and Hana, headed back on the trail to Pamplona. My blister was pain-free as we walked and talked through the gray, drizzly morning. I talked for a while with Jannik, then with Hana, then with Patrick from Ireland, then with Tatianna and Sasha from Russia. I couldn't believe how many people knew enough English to carry on a conversation.

Before I knew it, we arrived around noon on the outskirts of the big city. As we entered the densely packed streets, the group split up in different directions, and I soon found myself alone. No problem, I'll just find a hotel where I can get some sleep. The first one I tried had no vacancy, and I struggled to navigate the streets of Pamplona to find another one.

Something felt off. My internal compass clearly registered Uncomfortable. Unsettled anxiety had rudely replaced the peace and serenity I felt on the trail for the past few days. I stood on a street, surrounded by vehicle exhaust fumes, engine noises, and sounds of city commotion, and decided to keep walking until I reached the next small town.

The instant I made the decision, I felt a strange and wonderful sense of empowerment. Rather than follow the pack, or the guidebook, or something external—which I had done all my life—I decided to listen to that unfamiliar and quiet voice inside me.

As I walked through the streets of Pamplona, heading out to my own destination, I stood a little taller. Suddenly I heard someone call my name. It was Tatianna and Sasha. They joined me as we walked through the large city. We spotted a small cafe with some outdoor tables and decided to stop and get some lunch. After we took a seat and placed our orders, we spotted Hana on the crowded street, walking in our direction. We flagged her down and asked her to join us, and soon the four of us proceeded to enjoy an impromptu meal with lively conversation.

In the span of one hour, I had weaved from one ad-hoc group to being alone, and then to another random group. I was learning the two alternating modes of the Camino: Alone time and together time. Alone together.

After lunch I told the group of my plan to hike to the next small town, and we said farewell to each other. To my pleasant surprise, Hana said she was also headed to the next town, so we decided to walk together. I couldn't believe my luck. Hana was warm, expressive, friendly, about five feet, ten inches tall, attractive, and had a deep spirituality and positive energy. She was far too young for me, but I felt so relaxed and comfortable with her. And I sensed the feeling was mutual.

As we followed the scattered Camino scallop symbols out of the city, I felt a sense of elated confusion. *Wow, this is amazing, but why on Earth would a young woman like this want to walk with a sixty-year-old lost and struggling man like me?*

She spoke with a distinct Czech accent, but thanks to her excellent English, our conversation flowed naturally. We each wanted to know more about the other one's story. When I asked what brought her to the Camino, she said, "I needed to gain more independence and courage in my life, so I decided to walk the Camino starting from my home in Czech Republic."

I looked at her in shock. "Wait," I said. "You mean you walked from your home—across Europe—just to get to the Camino? And now you're walking it?"

She nodded, and said, "Yes. My parents, my dog, and a friend walked with me for the first ten kilometers, from my home to the edge of town. We cried when we waved good-bye to each other, but I knew I had to do this."

She told me how she slept outside or in churches, and sometimes relied on the kindness of strangers. She figured everything out along the way—and covered more than one thousand miles. Completely alone. "Wow. I'd say you accomplished your goal," I said smiling.

Time flew as we walked and talked in the warm afternoon sun, and we arrived in the small town of Cizur Menor around 3:00 p.m. We checked into an albergue and claimed two available twin beds on different sides of the room, which held roughly fifteen pilgrims. People sat, rested, or chatted on their beds. I talked with a husband and wife from Iceland who bunked next to me.

Soon, to my pleasant surprise, Hana and I resumed hanging out together as we strolled through the lush green gardens and grounds. More elated confusion. *OK, we've arrived, but neither one of us wants to go off on our own. Is she just being polite?*

Then we made a spontaneous decision to take a metro bus back into Pamplona to see the sights. Now I was seriously in a state of happy shock. Our time together started to feel like an actual date, to which my brain kept shouting, *"No you idiot! You're NOT on a date!"*

We sat side-by-side on the bus as it rolled along for the fifteen-minute ride. We laughed and talked and looked around at the open scenery. Her physical and energetic presence next to me took me back to my teenage years, as if I sat on a school bus next to the fun and mysterious girl from Algebra class.

A photo montage could have been made from the sights and sounds we experienced together as we explored the vibrant city of Pamplona. We saw statues and monuments related to the annual bull run, the Plaza de Toros stadium, the Hemingway references, and toured inside the towering cathedral, Santa Maria. We looked at little shops along the narrow streets and alleys, ate cookies, drank coffee, and watched the swarms of people and activities in the bustling city center. We bumped into Patrick from Ireland and the young German couple with their infant son. The six of us decided to sit together for a fun dinner of tapas and drinks.

Afterward we watched a crazy uproar on the streets. A wild-looking troupe of ten men and women gathered, draped in medieval leather-fur dress and boots, horned helmets, and painted faces. They waved flags, banged leather drums, played rustic bagpipes and time-period clarinets. Tourists and visitors formed a wide circle around them and clapped and cheered on the merry band of ancient revelers.

At the end of the evening, exhausted but energized, Hana and I took the metro bus back to join our fellow pilgrims in the albergue snoring room. We said a very simple good-night to each other and retired to our respective beds.

Once I crawled into my sleeping bag on top of the bed, I shook my head in wonder at the incredible day. For the first time since Annie's death, I felt I could see myself with someone. Actually be with someone. Until that day with Hana, it seemed the world had changed so much that it had completely passed me by. My futile matchmaker dates had left me more hopeless than anything, and made me wonder if I was an outdated, defective puzzle piece that no longer fit with anyone. *Wow, maybe I'm not defective after all. Maybe I'm OK as I am. Maybe there's someone out there who will fit. This young woman actually wanted to spend time with me and get to know me, and vice versa. There's hope!*

I drifted off thinking that even if our paths never crossed again, Hana had given me a priceless gift.

When I woke up the next morning, after getting some actual albergue sleep thanks to the earplugs I bought the day before, most everyone had already left, including Hana. When I realized she was gone, I couldn't deny my disappointment. But soon it gave way to another lesson from the Camino: *Let it go. Keep your hands and heart open. Don't grab or hold on. Learn something alone today.*

My morning walk out of Cizur Menor reminded me of Day 1—rain, mud, and a mountain climb—but I walked with so much more confidence. Solitude, my trusty companion, returned to settle me down, especially after a day like yesterday. It gave me a chance to think. To process. To ponder. And just be present to myself.

I entered a village, stopped at a small church, and went inside. The sacred and quiet space gave me another refuge of peace and reflection.

But as I sat there, I realized the church building didn't contain God, as if that were even possible. I felt God's presence everywhere, especially in the beauty of the natural world that surrounded me.

As I walked along, the day's lesson started to sink in. The things I wanted in life—peace of mind, acceptance, love, a life companion—were all wonderful, but it didn't help to obsess over them. They weren't objects to grab and possess, like external things. They were internal states of being and had to unfold in their own time, like a plant or a flower. I couldn't force them into existence. I had to let them go. I had to let everything go, to let things come and go freely. No pressure, no force, no control, no conditions, no possession. Just keep walking, stay open, and pay attention to God's guidance.

A few hours later I entered another village, walked past an outdoor cafe, and heard a familiar voice.

"Bob!"

Hana ran up from behind and hugged me. My spirits instantly soared, and I joined her for lunch. As we talked, it shocked me how much our unexpected reunion energized me. She finished her lunch and gathered her backpack to resume her solo walk, and I wasn't about to intrude. But before she left, realizing I may never see her again, I had to let her know. "Thank you so much for our time yesterday," I said. "You may not believe this, but it healed a part of me. Thank you."

She smiled, nodded, and said, "I enjoyed our time together too." With that, she turned and walked away.

I finished the day in the town of Puente La Reina when the blisters on my feet said *stop*—a repeat of a recurring lesson: *Listen to my feet and body—even if my mind and ego want to push on.* I checked into the Jakue Hotel, and couldn't wait for my rendezvous with delicious sleep, only a few hours away.

After a fun dinner with fellow pilgrims in the hotel's dining room, I dove into bed early to relish the peace and solitude. I had only been on the trail five days and learned so much already. But as I drifted off, I had the sense this was only the beginning. How many more lessons awaited me? And how difficult would they be? Would they teach me or break me?

Just walk.

"Have patience with all things, but first of all with yourself."

—St. Francis de Sales

CHAPTER 22

SHUT DOWN

Over the next several days, the path continued to work its magic. The beauty and vastness of nature seeped into my soul with every step. As I merged into the rhythm of the solitary trail, I slowly discovered a hidden realm inside me. External elements like my image and persona fell to the ground, allowing the real me underneath to emerge. Tears flowed as the armor dropped off.

I walked past rows and rows of lush vineyards and groves of mature olive trees. I watched an old farmer painstakingly hold a twenty-foot-long wooden stick to knock olives high in the tree down to a spread-out, black collection net on the ground. I wondered how many thousands of years this harvest technique had been used.

On the outskirts of the city Estella, I drank red wine in the mid-morning hours from an open spigot at the Bodegas Irache winery. Set up specifically for the pilgrims who pass by, the free wine flowed from one of two handle-operated spigots built into a towering stone wall with an image of a medieval pilgrim directly overhead.

My sleep remained marginal, but enough to keep me going. For dinner, I loaded up on carbohydrates, protein, and beer from the three-course meals offered on the ever-present pilgrim menus.

Whenever I encountered a river, I studied the solid, hand-built, arched stone bridge that spanned it. Each stone, each rock, was laid by hand, one at a time. How and when did they do it? And here it is today, still standing strong.

The flow between wide-open vistas of nature and old villages created a rhythm that now felt comfortable and familiar. Each little village held its own ancient signature: narrow, brick-lined streets, old buildings on both sides with flowered window boxes, ornate architecture, weathered doors, stone water fountains, and the always-visible bell tower and crucifix of the local church at the highest point. The sounds of church bells often echoed through the air. Their soothing tones anchored me, perhaps as they did for generations long ago.

On the outskirts of one village, I walked along a path of large stones embedded in the ground and saw a signpost that read "Roman Road / Calzada Romana." I realized that my boots stood directly on top of a time machine. *Who laid these stones how many hundreds of years ago? What were their names? How did the Roman soldiers treat them? How did they even survive day after day?*

The trail even provided occasional entertainment. I walked past an elderly couple who I assumed to be husband and wife. They each sat on stools alongside the trail, under the shade of a tree, next to a Camino trail marker. Dressed in casual clothes, she played the accordion, he the violin. Donations accepted in the open violin case on the ground. Their music and smiles lifted the spirits of all who passed by.

But then everything changed. On Day 10, close to 8:00 a.m., instead of walking the trail, I sat alone on a bench outside a bar-cafe in the village of Nájera. A cold morning breeze chilled me under the gray, cloudy sky. Twenty minutes earlier, I had to wave a sad farewell to my new friends, Joseph from India and Sean from England. They headed west on the trail to Santiago without me. I couldn't go on.

Knee pain—sharp and stabbing, under each kneecap—had built up over the past several days and had finally gotten so painful that I had to do what I feared most: stop walking. Far worse than a blister, it meant I had to stop for an entire day, or maybe longer. I heard stories from other pilgrims of people who had to stop for one reason or another, but I didn't think it would happen to me. *What if I can't go on? What if I have to end my Camino here? What if my odyssey completely blows up in my face? How could I face everyone back home? How could I face myself? This can't be happening!*

For the prior two days, I fought off blister and knee pain with everything I could muster—knee braces, blister patches, doses of 600 mg ibuprofen tablets (dubbed "the morphine of the Camino"), and even use of a backpack transport service to lighten my load—all to no avail. Joseph and Sean encouraged and helped me along and made the pain bearable. They exemplified the Bill Withers song "Lean on Me" and did everything except physically carry me.

But I didn't want to lean on anyone for anything. I didn't want to confess to or show my pain. And God knows I didn't want to transfer my backpack and carry a lighter daypack, even for a single day.

I felt the sting of the chisel and hammer of the Camino as it broke away chunks of my ego and pride. Joseph and Sean didn't mock, judge, or condemn me. They supported me with deep conversation and encouragement. Without hesitation, Joseph lent me his own knee braces. Then he helped me navigate a *farmacia* (pharmacy) in the next village, using his Spanish-language skills, so I could purchase my own.

But it was no use. The intense pain in my knees left me no other choice but to face it and surrender to it. Like wrestling a stronger opponent, I kept trying to escape its grip, but it wouldn't let me go. Finally, it locked me in its arms, flipped me over onto my back and pinned both shoulders to the mat. No matter how hard I kicked, squirmed, and fought, I couldn't escape. The referee slammed his hand on the mat signaling it was over. I lost.

I had to admit I was powerless over my pain—and once I did, a landmine of self-doubt and self-condemnation detonated inside me. I felt like a failure, a loser, a reject, an outsider, a nonparticipant, an outcast. I had to stop and stay behind.

I was now the sick child who has to stay at home in bed while everyone else goes about their day. Or the high school kid who breaks his ankle in football practice and has to sit on the sidelines all season when all he wanted was to prove himself. *What good am I if I can't perform, deliver, or DO something? What's my worth if I merely exist?*

Joseph, Sean, and Hana (who had also stayed in Nájera) all had sad faces as we hugged good-bye. "Hang in there, Bob," Joseph said. "You're doing the right thing. Rest and take care of your body. Hopefully you'll be back on the trail soon, and maybe we'll see you down the road." I watched them walk away and felt sick to my core.

To top it off, the possibility that I may never see them again dev-astated me. I had only known them for a matter of days, but somehow, days on the Camino are like months or years elsewhere. I had connect-ed on a deep spiritual level with these beautiful souls. They had become part of me.

Back to Camino 101: *Let it go, keep your heart and hands open.* Another verse of the "alone together" theme. They couldn't tend to me any more than they already had. They needed to move on. I had to learn that while I needed people, I also had to be able to function on my own. I had to grow past my tendency to get overly dependent on others. I had to learn a balance between attachment and detachment.

Feeling lost, alone, afraid, and despondent, I checked into a nearby albergue to rest my knees. They hurt so bad I could barely climb the stairs up to the third-floor bedroom. Humiliated, I felt like a crippled old man. The room had four clean beds and a bathroom, and a large skylight in the ceiling. For now, I was the only occupant, so I picked out a bed and flopped down to think and regroup.

As I gazed out through the skylight to the cloudy sky above, I real-ized how frail my human body was and how much I took it for granted. I was reminded that everything I am comes from God—every single muscle, nerve, cell, and molecule inside me—all a gift from God. He holds me together and makes everything in my body work. I can't take credit for my heartbeats, my oxygen-exchange process, and the thou-sands of other things happening inside me. It's all a gift.

Over the next few hours, as I rested in solitude, I eventually stopped feeling sorry for myself and accepted my situation. Whatever happens, happens. I'd figure it out with God's help. It could be worse. I could be sick or have a broken bone. As I relaxed on the bed and took slow, deep breaths, my body slowly uncoiled from the inner tension, and I dozed off into a quiet afternoon nap.

After I awoke, I hobbled down the stairs, out the front door, and into the village. I washed my clothes at a public laundromat. I toured the local church and museum, hung out in the bustling city square, and soaked in the crowd's energy. By sheer luck it was a major Spanish holi-day, and the Nájera residents left no doubt. The entire city rocked with happy people, large family groups with young and old, stage bands, ad hoc musical troupes parading through the streets, costumes, streamers, balloons, and fireworks after dark.

When I returned to my albergue later that night, I was greeted by my new roommate, Vitor from Brazil. A young man in his late twenties or early thirties with trimmed black hair and a short black beard. He spoke excellent English, and we talked for the next thirty minutes or so until we each admitted we needed sleep. I climbed into my sleeping bag on top of the twin bed and looked through the skylight at the night sky above. Patches of moonlit clouds floated above. Sounds of festival music and revelers continued to fill the air. As I fell asleep with my earplugs snugly inserted, I sent up a prayer that I could return to the trail in the morning. I would at least give it a try.

The instant my eyes opened to the morning light, I climbed out of my sleeping bag atop the bed and stood up. I still felt knee pain, but much less than yesterday. I decided to go for it but take it slow. The guidebook showed three places I could stop along this stage: one at five kilometers, one at fifteen, and another at twenty. In an act of faith or stupidity or both, I arranged for my backpack to be delivered to a hotel at the twenty-kilometer distance.

I inhaled the morning air as I walked out of the village onto the open trail. It had only been a single day, but it felt like a reunion with a long-lost friend who joyfully greeted me. As I breathed in the crisp, clean air, I vowed to never take another single step for granted. I walked slower and more deliberately than ever and celebrated every step.

Sometime midmorning, I encountered a man and woman on the trail. The woman, who I guessed to be in her forties, had dark hair, an athletic build, and a kind smile. She introduced herself as Gabriella from Brazil and the man as Paulo, her seventy-five-year-old father. Paulo stood tall, proud, and fit.

She said that for well over ten years Paulo had been telling his family that he wanted to walk the Camino, but no one took him seriously until a few months ago when he made flight reservations and arrangements. "None of us thought it would be safe for him to walk alone, especially at his age," Gabriella said. "Somebody needed to go with him, and the job fell to me." Then she said, "But I've been with him on the trail for over a week now, and he's fine. Totally fine. And safe. I've decided to go back to Brazil in a few days and leave him to his journey." Paulo, who wore a bright fluorescent-green windbreaker, smiled from ear to ear under his blue floppy hat.

Suddenly a voice called from behind us: "Hello, hello! Does anyone want a beer?" A group of four hikers approached—two women and two men, all thirtyish. The man with the beer introduced himself as San from South Korea. "This beer is getting heavy. I could really use some help," he said, smiling.

Gabriella, Paulo, and I obliged, and each took a can. As the warm beer foamed inside my mouth and traveled down my throat, I smiled at how morning alcohol consumption could become a Camino tradition. We all introduced ourselves—Dora and Carla—two smiling, energetic friends from Croatia, and Nicholas—a tall, blond-haired, reserved young man from Switzerland.

The seven of us walked along together and got acquainted until we reached the next village, where we all said farewell and drifted back into our group or solo mode, Camino-style. *Open heart, open hands. Let everything unfold naturally.*

Thankfully, my knees felt good enough to keep going—helped by the ibuprofen, the braces, and the positive spirit of my fellow pilgrims, especially Paulo. Just the gleam in his seventy-five-year-old eyes inspired and strengthened me.

Each person I met, each interaction, each conversation, registered with an especially strong signal, either positive, negative, or neutral. It was like the Camino had given me a precision people-vibe radar. An interaction on the trail with someone positive—like my newfound friends—would boost my spirits for the entire day. The level of connection amazed me.

Conversely, on the rare occasions when I found myself with someone with whom I felt a negative energy, I would politely extricate myself from a detailed discussion by saying, "I'm just here to reboot my life. Buen Camino." I also avoided those who were driven or competitive. Some people would jump out of bed at 5:30 a.m., rustle all their stuff together, and hit the dark trail by 6:15 a.m., driven to achieve their distance and destination goal for the day. Or those who had an itemized itinerary for every day of their Camino—where to be and when—which reminded me of a frenzied work grind back home, exactly what I wanted to leave behind.

Sometimes my competitive side would kick in and I'd try to keep pace with someone or try to prove how fast I could climb a hill. But with each passing day, I settled into a more relaxed mode and allowed myself to notice things inside me and around me. I reminded myself this was a spiritual quest, not a physical one.

One day I met Jim, a man in his late fifties or early sixties, six-feet-tall with receding red hair and a flushed, expressive face with light blue eyes. A retired policeman from Northern Ireland, he was on his second Camino. "On my first Camino," he said in a classic Irish accent, "it was all about the destination. I had to get there, to arrive in Santiago. I pushed myself every day to get there, to arrive. But afterwards, I realized I had missed everything along the way. So this time, I'm here for the journey. I'm taking my sweet time. And I'm seeing everything for the first time. It's all about the journey, not the destination."

With every pain-free step I took that day, I soaked in the absolute gift it was. I didn't take a single step for granted. I walked with the total gratitude of someone who has been given another chance.

Midafternoon I arrived in the village of Santo Domingo de la Calzada—the twenty-kilometer distance I hoped to reach—practically jumping for joy. I picked up my backpack from the hotel I had selected for delivery, but no rooms were available. No matter. No problem. Today was not the day to be alone in a hotel room.

I checked into a large, old albergue down the street called the Abadia Cisterciense (Cistercian Abbey) run by Catholic nuns. After I checked in and got my room assignment, I walked inside and admired how it resembled the architecture of the California Missions. Heavy, dark-brown ceiling and support beams contrasted against pure white walls and ceilings, along with stone and concrete exterior walls. One entire room was dedicated to peregrinos' boots and trekking poles—rows upon rows of weathered wooden shelves filled with pairs of dirty boots.

I ascended a narrow stairway and found my "room": a seven-foot-wide and fifteen-foot-long, pantry-sized area, which barely had enough room for three single beds—two of them side by side at the far end with twelve inches in between, and one next to the door. My two roommates had already been here and claimed the two at the far end, so I put my backpack on the one remaining bed and went back downstairs.

I walked into the dining area, which had five or six rectangular tables covered with blue and white–checkered plastic tablecloths. Ten or twelve fellow pilgrims sat and talked, scattered around the room on benches and chairs. The roomy space had a rustic feel and a positive energy.

I sat down at one of the tables and joined in a conversation. We all shared our names and countries of origin, although "Bob from California" always sufficed. The conversation then spilled over to others in the room, and soon we made a collective decision to eat dinner together. A small group of us walked to a local market to gather dinner provisions that we brought back to share.

And there we sat—ten complete strangers but fellow pilgrims from all over the world—together enjoying an ad hoc dinner accented with wine, laughter, and fun conversation.

Afterward I went out alone to explore the town. A towering cathedral stood above every other building at the far end of the narrow, crowded street. As I walked along, I bumped into Vitor from Brazil, who was on his way to a restaurant for dinner. I joined him for conversation over a bottle of Spanish Rioja red wine, and we said our farewells.

By the time I returned to the albergue, it was after 9:00 p.m. I entered the miniroom and met my two jolly roommates—Natalie and Frank from Germany. Laughter and conversation flowed past the standard ten o'clock lights-out limit until fellow pilgrims from across the hall objected. "Do you mind?" said an irritated voice from across the hall. "We're trying to sleep." Busted, the three of us laughed and said good-night.

I flipped off the light switch and settled into my sleeping bag on top of the red and black–checkered bedspread and marveled at what happened that day: In the early morning I held my breath as I took one cautious step after another on the trail as if on thin ice, just waiting for the crippling pain to reappear. But it didn't. Gradually—with every step and every encounter—the trail under my feet and knees felt more solid, and I started to breathe again. By the time my Credencial del Peregrino passport received its sixteenth stamp at the abbey-albergue, alongside fifteen others of different shapes, sizes, and colors, it felt like the glorious ending of Day 1 all over again.

Joy and gratitude filled me. My knees had held up. Even my blisters cooperated. I had a new lease on Camino life. Earplugs in, eyes closed, I couldn't wait to get back on the trail. My odyssey had been saved. So much still awaited me.

"My advice is: Go outside...enjoy nature and the sunshine, and try to recapture the happiness in yourself and in God. Think of all the beauty that is still left in you and around you and be happy."

—ANNE FRANK

CHAPTER 23

ROLLER COASTER

The next day, I crossed over from the wine region of Rioja into the wide-open region of León, which gave me a preview of the upcoming desolate section of the Camino called the Meseta (plateau). As the early morning sun rose behind my back, with clear blue sky above me, I took a photo of the trail ahead. My long, dark shadow stretched out in front of me on top of the twelve-foot-wide, light-brown dirt trail that stretched out into a tiny string that connected me to the distant horizon.

The joy of pain-free knees and feet carried me along. With no rush, no hurry, and no pain, I soaked-in the trail and the vast display of boundless brown fields accented with occasional clumps of green trees or rectangular piles of haystacks as large as semi-truck trailers.

I walked for a while with a young woman in her early thirties from Japan who was in between jobs and was trying to figure out her next move in life. She related to the story of Jesús on Day 1 who kept seeking clarity.

After I arrived and checked in at an albergue in the town of Belorado, I strolled the area to look around. I sat near a wall painted with a mural of Alfonso I de Aragon (1073–1134), a Spanish king. He looked like the classic warrior-king figure with a crown on his head, medieval chainmail chest armor, a strong bearded face and chin, and his battle sword in hand. I stood lost in thought over the history of Spain, which seemed like something out of the *Lord of the Rings* movie.

Then my phone buzzed. I didn't recognize the number but answered anyway.

"Hi, Dad?" Stephen said.

"Hi, Steve," I said as the heavy weight fell on me. We talked for a few minutes before he told me he needed some money transferred as soon as possible.

"Sorry to bug you about this, Dad, especially now," he said, "but could you help me out?"

After we hung up, I used my phone to transfer some money. When I finished, I felt sick inside. I didn't want to groan, or feel sick, or feel like Stephen just crashed my Camino—but I did. I didn't want to be so distant from him, but I was. I didn't want to see him engulfed inside his addiction, but he was. I wanted to help him more than anything, but other than enable him, what could I do? The main message from my own recovery work was to "release him to his higher power" and to "detach with love" from him—things I tried to do and often failed.

What am I supposed to do? How do I do this?

Just keep going. Keep walking.

Over the next couple days, my knees and feet remained pain-free, but grief tugged at me, as if to say, "Enough distractions. You need to pay attention to me now." A dull ache in the pit of my stomach confirmed my invisible companion's presence. As I walked along in solitude, a wave would pass through me and burn my eyes with tears. When it subsided, my aloneness showed up to taunt me.

Everyone I saw seemed to be with someone else—husbands-wives, friends-companions, families, or groups. When a husband-wife couple smiled at me and said "Buen Camino!" I returned the greeting with a forced smile, but in reality, I groaned and burned inside. I reminded myself that God walked with me, and that many other solo pilgrims walked alone, but the pain still ate away at me. When I heard other people carry on conversations in languages I couldn't understand, I felt even more lonely and isolated.

Being alone was the last thing on Earth I wanted. I didn't ask for this. But now, the Camino paired me up with it, like an unwelcome walking companion, just as it was about to lead me into the Meseta—a long, flat, desertlike section of the trail.

I heard the expression many times already: The Camino was one-third physical, one-third mental, and one-third spiritual. Maybe I had gone through the physical third, and now the other two awaited me. But they all felt intertwined; on any given day I had experienced all three. Maybe it had to do with intensity. Maybe the real fire awaited me.

But before any of that, I had to pass through Burgos, my second big city, which would put me five hundred kilometers, about three hundred miles, away from Santiago. I walked with Jim from Ireland, who helped me through the long, hot slog into the city with his engaging conversation and wit. Unlike Pamploma, I decided to stay in Burgos, mostly due to exhaustion. I found a clean hotel room, where I showered and rested before I headed out to explore the bustling city.

I walked around the towering Burgos cathedral and marveled at the intricate thirteenth-century gothic architecture. But what most impressed me was the energy that buzzed within the city square— the Plaza Mayor—a large, open, brick-paved area where everyone gathered. Kids laughed and screamed as they ran around, kicked soccer balls, and pushed little scooters. Their parents and grandparents watched from the cafe-lined edges of the square, where they sat at open air tables enjoying conversation over coffee, beer, or wine. Every generation was represented: babies in carriages, young and old married couples, groups of giggling teenage girls and energetic teenage boys, and families of all sizes.

For an American like me who barely knew his neighbors and lived so far away from family that get-togethers often involved a wedding or funeral, the sight of Spanish family life in the city square blew me away. It looked so natural, joyful, and simple, yet seemed so radical and unfamiliar. The more I watched, the more I realized my yearning to belong.

The next morning, I navigated the streets of Burgos, following the Camino arrows and symbols, which sometimes hid in plain sight. For a large city, Burgos had a positive vibe, and I didn't feel the need to flee. As I walked past the university on the outskirts of town, a group of young college students noticed me, waved, and wished me a "Buen Camino!" I waved back, smiled, and thanked them, gladly accepting the energy from the surprise power boost.

Once on the open trail outside of the city, I decided to make it a short day, just because. My knees and feet felt fine. I just wanted to stop and slow things down. Maybe the words of wisdom from Jim about the journey had sunk in. I walked less than fifteen kilometers, stopped at a tiny village called Rabé de las Calzadas, and called it a day. *Slow down. Take everything in. Breathe.*

The soul-anchoring sounds of church bells echoed through the village. I walked up to a small albergue and entered, which immediately felt welcoming and comfortable. I relaxed and got acquainted with my fellow peregrinos as we sat in chairs and enjoyed the warmth of the afternoon sunshine.

Among them was a devout Catholic woman, Dominique (forty-ish) from France, who told of her plans to attend a prayer service that evening at a local nun's convent. A few of us expressed interest, and a couple hours later, we set out through the narrow streets and cryptic addresses and found it. We entered the unlocked door, walked down a hallway, and sat in a small chapel with about ten other people—some peregrinos, some locals.

At the top of the hour, a few older nuns entered, took their seats, and began the service with a recited prayer and song. The service progressed with deep reverence and sense of tradition. Afterward I walked back to the albergue with Dominique, and despite our language gap, we were able to relate to each other on a spiritual-faith level. She spoke with a thick French accent and chose her English words carefully. "God… guides…me…each day. Always," she said, smiling.

The next day, the trail took me into the wide-open space of the Meseta, which felt like I had stepped into another dimension. Everything fell away and slowed down. The trail stretched out in front of me like an endless path through the desert, with nothing to see but empty brown fields, rocks, and open, dry pastures. I didn't see anyone else on the trail—zero distractions. As I walked along under the hot sun, hour after hour, nothing seemed to change, like I wasn't even moving. I bit down onto the mouthpiece of my drinking tube and tasted warm, bland water, even though I filled it that morning. Each time I took a small sip into my dry mouth, I hoped it would be enough to last the day.

This was "the mystical path" referred to in the guidebook, and it enveloped me. I was still shackled to aloneness, but I also felt God's invisible presence. Soon I started to notice things around me. Up on a distant hill, camouflaged by the endless brown landscape, I spotted a flock of sheep shepherded by a man and his dog. I felt the hot sun press against my head, legs, and body. I noticed the hot air that filled my mouth and throat with every breath. The weight of the backpack on my shoulders and back and the feel of the cork handles on my walking poles grounded me in the here and now. At that moment they were my only physical possessions.

I tuned into the sound of my boots and trekking poles on the crunchy rock-dirt path, which created a hypnotic rhythm that pulled me into a peaceful place where I could just be. I could just be with my aloneness. With myself. With God. As I walked through the desolation, I relaxed into an unexpected sense of peace.

Eventually, a tiny village appeared on the horizon, like a scene out of the movie *High Plains Drifter*. Hot, tired, and ready for company, I decided to stop for the day. After I checked into an albergue and claimed a lower bunk bed, I consulted the guidebook. Hontanas, a village with a population of seventy.

I joined the crowd gathered in the outdoor patio for a spirited happy hour. The cold beer tasted divine as I chatted with fellow pilgrims. I met a man in his fifties with receding, short gray hair, black-rim glasses, and a big smile. When he said he was from Spain, I looked at him in shock. "Wow," I said, "you're on your home field. You're the first Spaniard I've met so far."

He laughed, smiled, and said, "The Camino is our country's pride and treasure. All Spaniards are encouraged to walk the Camino, as early as teenagers. Some just take a little longer to go, like me."

Another man, from Australia, who looked to be in his seventies with a full head of white hair, sat at the same table and listened to our conversation as he strummed his guitar. Someone asked him how he managed to bring his guitar on the Camino. "It's a custom folding guitar," he said, and demonstrated how the guitar could fold up and fit in his backpack, and then resumed playing. "When I decided to walk the Camino, I had to figure out a way to bring my guitar. No guitar, no Camino. I have to play it every day."

A few minutes later, the Spaniard stood up, slipped away, and returned with a guitar from the albergue bar. The two of them sat directly across from each other, knee to knee, and began to weave their music together. Everyone gathered around to watch the show.

But soon I felt the tug to be alone again, to reenter the solitary space I left a few hours earlier. I walked around the tiny village and soaked in the age of the old buildings—the worn bricks, the gray stones, and the weathered wooden beams. With a tiny population in the middle of nowhere, I wondered who lived here and what kind of life they lived. After a while, I heard the echoing sound of the church bell and decided to attend the service.

When I walked into the church, I immediately recognized the calmness of a sacred space. A reflection-prayer area greeted me on the left, adorned with burning candles, seat cushions, an open Bible, and images of worldwide spiritual leaders. In addition to Jesus Christ, images of Gandhi, Desmond Tutu, Martin Luther, Martin Luther King Jr., Saint Francis, Malala Yousafzai, and others hung on the wall. On the right side sat a table of pamphlet-sized paper worship guides in every possible language. I found the English one, which had the words "Mass for Pilgrims" on the cover.

I took a seat in one of the wooden pews, which were soon filled with fellow peregrinos. A young priest with a full head of dark hair entered, welcomed everyone, and presided over the Mass. We recited prayers and sang hymns, each in our own language. What should have sounded like chaos sounded beautiful. We smiled and extended our hands to each other at the moment in Mass called the "sign of peace."

It didn't matter that we didn't know each other; we all belonged to the same universal family. At the end, the priest invited anyone who wanted a pilgrim's blessing to come forward. A group of us stood shoulder to shoulder in front of the altar as the priest outstretched his hands and prayed for our safety, guidance, wisdom, and a closer walk with God on our Camino. Afterward we all disbanded, but I hung around the prayer area a little longer to absorb the peace.

The rest of the evening continued to feed my body and soul, including a family-style dinner at a village restaurant, until it was time to turn in for the night. The twelve-person bunk room became an impossible place to sleep, despite ear plugs. The hot and stuffy snoring chamber was bad enough, but the amorous adventures of a couple only three feet away from me put it over the top. With nowhere to escape, I endured the night and counted the minutes until morning arrived.

The darkness of the early morning trail didn't matter; I had to get out of the hot box and on my way. After I laced up my boots and ate a quick breakfast at the albergue cafe-bar, I walked out the front door into the dark morning. An older woman I met the day before at happy hour, Anne from England, greeted me and asked if we could walk together. I was happy to oblige, and we both strapped our headlamps to our foreheads, found the yellow arrow, and got on the trail.

We walked single file in the dark along a skinny dirt trail through tall, dry grass. Mostly silent, we focused our attention more on the trail than conversation. But as the morning light slowly overtook the darkness and the trail widened, I asked what brought her to the Camino. She told me she wanted to go on an adventure alone and decided this was the perfect one—at seventy-five years old.

"Wow. What do your friends and family think about you doing this alone?" I asked her.

In her proper British accent, she responded, "They all think I've gone quite mad. But I haven't. I'm not ready to call it quits. I have a lot of life to live. Just keep moving—that's my motto."

She asked what brought me here, and I told her my story. When I finished, she said, "I know exactly what you're talking about. My husband died of brain cancer—an astrocytoma—over fifteen years ago. He was fifty-seven years old."

For the next few hours we talked in detail about what each of us had gone through. I asked if she had remarried, and she hadn't, but had a long-term relationship with a man she met through work. When she asked me about my relationships, I said, "I've dated, but so far nothing serious. I don't know. I'm trying to figure it out."

My internal compass told me I needed to return to solo walking mode, so I thanked Anne and we wished each other a Buen Camino.

Another messenger. This one named Anne who had walked the same road. Keep moving.

The Meseta still beckoned, and I didn't want to miss what it had to say. Just the sheer expanse of land spoke to me. After I climbed to the top of one hill in the barren landscape, I gazed out at the serpentine trail ahead, which spilled out to the distant horizon like an endless line. Like eternity.

I walked in solitude and soaked up the peace and quiet. It confused me how time alone could be comforting at times and torturous at others. In the midafternoon, the trail took me directly past an old building in the middle of nowhere, surrounded by a clump of trees like a little oasis. Some pilgrims gathered around the front doorway, just a few feet off the trail, so I stopped to investigate.

I recognized one of them, Daniel from Italy. A young man in his thirties, Daniel's slender build stood about five-feet, ten-inches tall. He had jet-black short hair, black eyebrows, and a short black beard. We had met several days earlier at an albergue and walked together the next day. Daniel had a natural warmth, kindness, and depth about him. One of our main topics was the concept of God, church, spirituality, and how differently the generations look at them. "My generation doesn't look at God and religion the way our parents and grandparents do," he said. "It's different for us, and not even relevant in many ways."

Daniel waved and greeted me at the arched, stone entrance of the old building in front of a dark-brown wooden door. "Hey, Bob! How you doing?" he said in his Italian accent. "This place is awesome. It used to be an old monastery, but now it's an albergue run by Italian volunteers. It has no heat, electricity, or Wi-Fi service. I've already checked in. You should stay the night!"

He then told me most of the twelve beds had already been taken, so I had to make up my mind quickly. One other detail: The volunteers put on a great pasta dinner for the pilgrims. Sold. I had planned to press forward to the next village, but this was too good to pass up. I checked in, claimed one of the few beds left, and settled in.

The pure simplicity of the dwelling calmed me. Dedicated to Saint Nicolas, the thirteenth-century, two-story stone structure was built in a basic rectangular shape, roughly two hundred feet long and thirty feet wide. Inside, sunlight from the few window openings illuminated the long, narrow space, which had an altar cove on one end, a dinner table with chairs down the middle, bunk beds on the other end, a wooden stairway to an upper loft, and rustic wooden beams overhead.

As I walked around the grounds, I saw Dora from the "beer brigade" sitting on a bench. She waved me over. The late afternoon sunshine lit up her short red hair. We greeted each other with a friendly hug and got caught up over bread and cheese. When I asked about the others, she told me they wanted to press onward, but she wanted to stay here. Soon, the conversation turned to why we were on the Camino.

"My boyfriend was killed in a motorcycle accident," she said, "and I came to the Camino to process everything. To regroup." I listened as she opened up about her struggle, marveling at her calmness and depth. She then listened as I told her my story. Afterward we just sat together in silence.

I heard solitude knock, so I thanked Dora and walked into the open countryside that surrounded the hermitage. Several hundred yards away, I heard the sound of running water. I walked over to a stream about twenty feet wide and sat down on the brown grass slope. The late afternoon sun warmed my back and neck as I sat and watched the water flow by. The sound of the water transported me back to a stream in upstate New York where I walked barefoot as a little kid in the ankle-deep water and explored what was around each bend. Simple, peaceful solitude.

As the daylight faded and dusk arrived, I returned to the albergue. When I stepped inside, the only light came from burning candles and the last of the dim sunlight, which cast a gentle illumination on the darkening space. For some reason, everyone spoke in soft voices and hushed tones, as if in sync with the fading light.

A short while later, the four volunteers gathered us together for an evening prayer service in the altar cove. The twelve of us sat side by side on wooden chairs arranged in a semicircle. One of the volunteers read a prayer of thanksgiving for the day, followed by a group recital of the Lord's Prayer.

We were then asked to remove our boots and socks. A young man who looked to be in his thirties with blond hair knelt on the hard floor in front of me and gently poured water over each foot, which trickled down into a shallow basin. He then took a white towel and carefully dried off each foot. Then, one at a time, he took each foot in his hands, kissed it on top, and lowered it back to the ground.

I knew of the ritual, established by Jesus at the Last Supper, and had participated in it before at church services. But this was different. No one had ever kissed my feet before. I felt raw and naked—but loved and accepted. I squirmed inside as I sat there and tried to accept his act of divine kindness. My heart overflowed with a mixture of shame, gratitude, sorrow, and love.

When the foot washing concluded, a reverent hush filled the cove. No one spoke, but a spirit of unity and peace hovered over us. A closing song ended the service. We were invited to move over to the table for dinner, where red wine and conversation flowed freely.

Darkness filled the sanctuary, but the warm glow of candlelight provided all the light we needed. The hearty pasta dinner fed our bodies as the fellowship fed our souls. I raised my glass to Daniel across the table, and we shared a good laugh.

Bedtime came early that night, which I welcomed. Without the usual distractions of modern life—something as basic as electric lights—a natural cycle took over. Darkness meant time to sleep. The sound of reverent silence surprised me, as if we all recognized the same thing.

But in the early hours of the morning, another form of nature called, and I had to use the restroom located behind the old building. Pitch black and stone quiet except for light snoring sounds, I crawled out of my top bunk with my headlamp, quietly made my way to the heavy wooden front door, and slowly opened it. When I stepped outside, my eyes looked up into the night sky. The sight of the Milky Way jumped out at me like I had never seen it before. It looked like a cosmic brush-stroke across the heavens, surrounded by billions of other stars. The sight almost knocked me over. The infinite majesty of God's creation held its arms wide open in a grand display as if to say, "I'm here. I'm always here. I love you. I've got you. Don't worry, she's safe with me."

Something else hit me. I'm not on the sidelines of the universe—I'm inside of it all. If someone or something was out there somewhere looking in my direction, they would see what I'm seeing. My location would look to them as wonderous as the majesty that now filled my eyes. I'm a living being inside this beyond-belief universe, and I'm looking in a gigantic, galactic mirror.

Just before sunrise, still surrounded by silent darkness in my upper bunk, I awakened to the sounds of Gregorian chant that echoed through the chamber. As we all started to stir and climb out of their beds, the song "Imagine" by John Lennon played. A short while later, we gathered for a simple breakfast, then stepped outside into the early morning light and prayed the Lord's Prayer. The hosts gave each of us a farewell hug for the journey ahead.

I knew I was brought here for a reason, like it was part of a plan. I hugged and thanked Daniel, and then we each said our good-byes. As I walked westward on the trail, I turned back to capture a final photo of San Nicolas: the old stone monastery oasis in the middle of nowhere, surrounded by a clump of trees and open, brown fields, the pale morning sky, and the golden morning sun rising on the eastern horizon.

"Life is a journey, not a destination."

—Ralph Waldo Emerson

CHAPTER 24

THE REAL DESTINATION

After leaving San Nicolas, I walked alone for most of the day, just what my soul needed to take stock. Eighteen days into my odyssey, I had grown in my ability to look inward instead of outward for guidance and direction. My internal radar muscles had gotten stronger. I had a long way to go, but it was a start. Grief tugged at me but didn't drag me under. With each step, God strengthened me.

Where am I really going in life? Do I return to my daily work grind when I get back, or make a bolder move? Maybe it's time to pull the plug on work and move into retirement. Look at this, I'm on the other side of the globe doing something I never would have imagined. The world has opened to me—people, places, experiences. How much longer can I stay in my IT job, sitting in front of a computer screen under fluorescent lights?

One idea that kept rolling around in my head was to set up an educational foundation in Annie's name for people who want to become therapists in the field of addiction recovery—to help carry on the work she yearned to do more than anything. I didn't know what to do about it, but the concept made sense.

Two days later, September 25, marked the seventeen-month anniversary of Annie's passing. I spent most of the day walking with two sisters-in-law (in their late fifties) from France, both named Anne. They were on their annual, two-week Camino getaway walk, which they had started many years earlier. Each year, they picked up where they left off.

"At our pace, we might reach Santiago by the time we're eighty," they said laughing.

We stopped at the tiny village of Ledigos for a late lunch, and I decided to stay. It was the end of their two weeks, so they called for a taxi to take them to a bus station and eventually back home. We hugged farewell and exchanged contact info. It was a strange sight to see a taxi pull up, load their backpacks in the trunk, and drive them away. But taxis were used whenever needed on the Camino—for injured, sick, or tired pilgrims, or to begin the journey home.

I checked into the albergue connected to the restaurant and was relieved to see only a handful of people had checked in. I desperately needed sleep after getting little to none the previous night in another overcrowded, stuffy snore room. But the lack of sleep was a small price to pay. The Santa Maria albergue, Carrión de los Condes, was managed by a group of Catholic sisters associated with Saint Augustine. The albergue itself could sleep over fifty people in large rooms with bunk beds—the bittersweet bane of my Camino existence.

First, they extended their hospitality by inviting us to attend their Vespers (Latin for evening) prayer service at the adjoining Santa Maria church at 5:30 p.m. The meditative music, singing, and prayers from the young nuns in the darkened church soothed my soul. Afterward they asked us to join them in the albergue for a communal singalong. About fifty of us crammed into the lobby area as four nuns sat together in a row up front and led us in song. The acoustic guitar chords and uplifting voices reminded me of the folk music played at church during my college years.

When the singalong ended, they asked each of us to tell the group where we were from and what brought us to the Camino. My heart rate beat faster and faster as my turn approached, and I debated whether I should gloss over my reason or put the truth out there. I decided to go with the truth. When I finished, the room got a little quieter. When everyone had finished and the final song ended, the group disbanded, and everyone went about their way.

After I claimed a bunk bed and started to get settled, a woman with blond hair who looked to be in her fifties approached and gave me a gentle hug. "I'm sorry for your loss," she said in an Australian accent. "I've also lost someone, my son, who was killed in an automobile accident a few months ago." She introduced herself as Ruth, and we proceeded to connect on a heart-and-soul level for a few minutes about our respective grief journeys, and how we were doing on the Camino. Afterward, I thanked her for her kindness, and we hugged farewell.

Many of us then attended the Pilgrim's Mass at 7:00 p.m., which concluded with a pilgrim's blessing from the priest, and an individual blessing from one of the nuns. When my turn came, I stood face to face with a young nun whose piercing and kind eyes connected briefly with mine. She then laid her hands gently on top of my bowed head, whispered a short prayer, and traced the sign of the cross on my forehead. Before I walked away, she handed me a little paper star. When we had all been blessed, we gathered side by side in the quiet, darkened church accented with soft flickering candlelight.

One of the sisters stood in front of us and said, "The star we gave you represents God's light in our lives—and reminds us that we can be lights for each other. We ask you to carry this light inside you as you go forward on your Camino, and always. And remember, your destination goal is not to reach Santiago, but to reach God. God is the goal."

These were the moments that recharged me and confirmed at a soul level that I was on the right path—like internal yellow arrows guiding my way. Santiago was my physical destination but not my real, inner destination. That was unknown, which both frightened and excited me. Every step I took contained a tiny part of a complete cleansing process, but where would it take me?

Fear, uncertainty, anxiety, confusion, and exhaustion—interlaced with moments of relief, clarity, and recharge—were my constant companions. Each step brought a discovery about myself and the world around me. Every person, every village, every tree, every hillside, every bend in the road—all were brand-new, and all were leading me somewhere.

The next day I crossed the halfway point of the Camino, marked by a fifteen-foot-high stone monument that resembled the image of King Aragon I saw ten days earlier. The ancient warrior-king stood tall and strong, with right hand resting on the handle top of his battle sword, his left handing holding a scroll, and his crowned head turned toward Santiago.

On September 28 I entered the huge city of León with Blake from South Africa—a tall and hearty man in his late forties with brown hair, a round face, and a gentle soul. Both solo walkers, we met at the albergue in Ledigos, walked at the same pace, and enjoyed the company and conversation. What brought him to the Camino was the adventure aspect, and he was always on the lookout for a "proper" breakfast and dinner.

When he told me about the posh hotel where he had booked a room in León, I scoffed. "Are you kidding me? That's crazy!" But the more I thought about it, the more I convinced myself to find out if they had a vacancy. *Look, Bob, this is your one and only Camino. When will you ever have a chance to do this again? You've got to go for it. Do it!*

I called, and sure enough, they did—the ritzy Parador de León hotel, which appeared in *The Way* movie. I booked a room.

On our walk into Leon, Blake suggested we take a public bus to cut through the traffic and congestion of the large city. I wasn't thrilled with the idea but went along. When we disembarked and walked to the spacious courtyard in front of the sprawling hotel, it looked something like Buckingham Palace. As I stepped into the front lobby, it reminded me of an art museum. The soaring architecture, the enormous chandelier, the classic paintings, the majestic stairway, and the overall ambiance all told me I had entered a new world. When I unlocked the door to my 150€ per night room and walked inside, I laughed out loud at the accommodations—the complete opposite universe of an albergue. After a luxuriously long shower, I wrapped myself in a thick cotton towel to dry off, took a short nap on the soft bed, and then went out to explore León.

As I walked along a crowded street lined with restaurants and shops, I heard someone yell, "Hey, Bob! Bob!" It was the beer brigade—all of them—including a new recruit, Lucas from Czech Republic. We hugged and high-fived each other, and then decided to get a table and get caught up. We enjoyed the warm afternoon sun with beer, food, and laughter.

"How was your walk into Leon, and where are you staying, Bob?" Dora asked. "We're at the albergue down the road."

"Uhhh, well..." I said, feeling guilty I had committed a Camino crime. "I took a bus into the city and have a room at the Parador Hotel."

Their initial look of shock flipped into hysterical laughter and roasting. All I could do was hang my head and take it, defenseless.

Eventually, they let me off the hook and invited me to Carla's farewell party that evening outside their albergue. She had to return home to Croatia the next day, so a mojito party would help take the sad edge off. I told them I wouldn't miss it and headed toward the cathedral.

The massive León Cathedral, built in the thirteenth-century, took my breath away. It stood like a proud giant, strong and solid, with two imposing towers that jutted skyward. The inside space felt surreal, with impossibly high stained-glass sides that reached up to join the criss-crossed, domed ceiling. I felt so tiny, so small, but so blessed and grateful.

I also sensed a detachment from the concept of "God's house" and from the other religious symbols that adorned the cathedral, like I felt in Lourdes. Everything exuded beauty and awe, but it didn't pull me into a connection with God like it used to. I sensed God all around me and felt His presence as powerfully in nature—even more so—than I did in a building made by human hands.

After my cathedral tour, I walked around León to take in the sights, sounds, and culture. I realized I wasn't irritated by the city atmosphere anymore. I actually enjoyed the energy and sensory overload. Maybe I had grown to accept the yin and yang of the Camino.

Late in the afternoon, I found the mojito party just under way in an open courtyard area outside their albergue. Nicholas mixed and served the mojitos, while the beer brigade made sure Carla's cup stayed full. Fellow peregrinos (most in their twenties or thirties) mingled around the central water fountain, played music from a small boombox, and smoked cigarettes.

Local children played nearby and curiously looked on. Carla's eyes looked both sad and happy, but her energetic spirit prevailed. Conversations, laughter, music, and mojitos flowed, but after a while, the time came to take my leave. I found Carla, wished her well, and we hugged good-bye. As I walked away, sadness and gratitude arrived. I couldn't imagine leaving the Camino at this point, and thankfully didn't have to.

After a guilt-free sound sleep at the Taj Mahal, I enjoyed the best five-star breakfast spread I could recall. I saw Blake through the stacks of plates covered with eggs benedict, omelets, bacon, and pastries, and thanked him for the over-the-top hotel suggestion. He smiled from ear to ear and raved about the most "proper" of breakfasts. He had finished and was on his way out, and we said our farewells.

A short while later, as I checked out, I felt the urge to run full speed away from the lap of luxury before it ruined me. I had to get back to the solo trail and reconnect with the raw essence of the Camino.

I didn't have to wait long. The hike out of León provided a gradual transition from the bustle of the city to the solitude of the trail. I relaxed into my solo rhythm as the trail welcomed me back without judgment. My knees and feet continued to cooperate, and my thoughts focused on the Cruz de Ferro, only a few days away. After about twenty kilometers, I stopped on the outskirts of the small village of Villadangos del Páramo and checked into a basic hotel alongside a busy roadway.

I didn't see or hear any other guests at the roadside hotel. The strange emptiness threw me off balance, like I had landed into an episode of the *Twilight Zone*. I walked into town for dinner, but everything felt strange and unwelcome. Maybe it was Camino karma for my León indulgence. Whatever it was, I couldn't wait to hit the trail the next morning.

The Cruz de Ferro awaited.

"Grief is like a drunken house guest, always coming back for one more goodbye hug."

—STEPHEN KING, BAG OF BONES

CHAPTER 25

NO MORE GOOD-BYES

I set my focus on my arrival at the Cruz de Ferro—the "Iron Cross" which held immense significance. An iron crucifix mounted on top of a tall wooden pole in the center of a rockpile didn't sound like much, but I simultaneously anticipated and dreaded it. As a place of reflection, prayer, intention, dedication, blessing, and love, it carried a lot of weight. Over the centuries, pilgrims had deposited their tokens—a stone, a rock, a message wrapped around a stick, a letter, a photo, or a tangible symbol of some kind—onto the ever-growing mound. The tokens represented any intention or loved one inside the pilgrim's heart.

Months before I left, I looked at the Cruz de Ferro as a key element in my Camino journey. I saw it as a place where I would say a final good-bye to Annie, release my burden of grief, and dedicate a prayer for Stephen's recovery.

Midafternoon on the first day of October, my favorite month of the year, I arrived in the tiny village of Foncebadón, a lonely outpost situated among desolate rolling hills. Located a short walk away from the Iron Cross, it was a perfect spot to spend the night and then arrive early the next morning. I checked into one of the few albergues that sat alongside the main dirt-rock road. The proprietor reminded me of the first one I encountered in St.-Jean: eccentric, strange, and overbearing, but tolerant enough to roll with the constant influx of pilgrims.

All the beds were taken in the main bunk room, so he showed me an adjoining church building as an alternative place to sleep. The stark room had no heat or beds, but it looked superior to another snoring sauna, so I eagerly accepted. Soon, a few other peregrinos joined me, and we each set up our spots on the floor with sleeping cushions.

I returned to the main albergue to hang out with others while dinner was prepared. A friendly group of about twenty mingled around, including a group of six lively Italians (three men and three women in their thirties), who set the tone for happy hour. Plenty of beer, wine, conversation, and laughter flowed as happy hour rolled into dinner. As we all dug in, I looked up and down the rowdy table, which resembled a ragtag family.

Where else but the Camino would this happen? Twenty strangers from all over the world connected to each other through this journey, having a blast at the dinner table. The party moved into the cramped kitchen after dinner, where everyone who could squeeze in helped do dishes and clean up.

Many of the young peregrinos then took the party to a bar down the street, but the time had come for me to settle in for the night and get prepared for an early start the next morning. I planned to be on the trail for Cruz de Ferro well before daylight so I could arrive for sunrise.

I sat on the floor in the darkened church building, on my sleeping bag and cushion, and dug through my backpack to find the two items I carried for this moment. The first was a walnut-sized granite rock from Skellig Michael Island off Ireland's southern coast, which I visited with my brothers in 2006. It represented my life and rock-solid marriage with Annie, a part of me and my Irish heritage. The other was a sobriety coin from NA (Narcotics Anonymous) that belonged to Stephen, which read "Higher Power" on one side and "If God brings you to it, He will bring you through it" on the other.

The next morning, I left the albergue with Dora and San from the beer brigade in the predawn darkness, with headlamps attached. When we arrived at the site, I saw the Cruz de Ferro in the predawn light. It stood high above the apex of a massive mound of rocks and stones, connected to the top of a thirty-foot-high wooden utility pole.

The early morning blue-gray sky waited patiently for the sun to rise. Even at this hour, ten to fifteen pilgrims lingered at the top of the pile, so I decided to wait for the crowd to thin out.

I walked back a hundred yards or so and joined a small group who gathered on a hillside to watch the sunrise. Words can't adequately describe the glorious display that followed. The sun first colored the horizon and low clouds in blazing orange, and then illuminated the vertical streaks of falling rain from a distant black and gray cloud. Soon the entire clouded sky glowed in orange fire as we watched in silent reverence.

Inspired and strengthened, I returned to the cross, where the pilgrims had thinned out to a handful, and slowly climbed the rocky hill. I noticed all kinds of devotionals—painted rocks, plain rocks, photos, notes wrapped around stones with twine, tiny scrolls of paper—each one representing a prayer, desire, hope, or intention. Rocks against rocks under boots were the only sounds. With each step, my stomach tightened, until I reached the top and stood near the center pole.

I took the half-dollar-sized coin in my hand, said a prayer for Stephen, and watched it disappear inside the pile along with the ting sound of metal against rock. I lost sight of it like I had lost sight of Stephen. No matter what we tried, he disappeared from us, and from the vibrant, full-of-life young man he once was. He could turn it around, but that was up to him. *You can live a life of recovery, Stephen, but it's up to you.*

Then I took the rock in my hand, kissed it, and tossed it gently on the pile. I watched as it also disappeared in between the mass of other gray stones. I whispered a broken-record-repeat prayer of "thank you" and "good-bye." I took some photos of the exact spot but didn't know what else to say or do. I stood there in anticipation as absolutely nothing happened. No release from my burden of grief. No lightening of the load. Nothing.

I descended the pile in confusion and defeat. The rock and the coin I selected so carefully had been swallowed up. My hopes, prayers, and intentions fell flat. I've come all this way—for this? I stood at the bottom of the pile and looked up at the others still on the pile in quiet devotion. *Look at them. They're having the experience I didn't. Did I do something wrong? Now what?*

I couldn't rewind or do it over. I couldn't linger. What choice did I have but to get back on the trail? As I walked away from the Iron Cross, my twenty-pound backpack turned into a two-hundred-pound rock that pulled me into the ground. *Wasn't this supposed to be liberating? Why do I feel this way?*

For the next few hours, despite the clear blue sky and bright morning sunshine, I trudged along lost in a fog. Then, out of nowhere, I heard an inner voice, loud and clear:

"Bob, it's time to stop saying good-bye. You've said good-bye enough. You don't have to say good-bye anymore. I'm OK. Don't worry about me. It's time for you to say HELLO to your new life. Don't stay stuck. You need to move forward. You need to live your life. Find someone. Share your life with someone. Live. Love. Go! Develop a new life. You can do it. Do whatever you need to do—but live your life. Say hello. No more good-byes."

If I had looked over that moment and seen Annie walking next to me, it wouldn't have shocked me in the least. It rang so true to her voice as something she would say to me. Did she? All I knew for sure was that mid-stride, the two hundred pounds lifted off my shoulders and stomach. My entire body eased and straightened. I could breathe again.

Right then and there, I realized that my continual good-byes were my way of hanging on to my life with Annie. Deep down I didn't want to let go. If I did, what would I have left? What would I do? Who would I be? How could I let go of an entire lifetime and start completely over?

But now I had no excuse. I knew what I had to do. *OK, but how? How do I do this? I don't know, but I'll figure it out.*

I loosened my grip on my old life. The mere thought confused and excited me—like a prisoner who, strangely accustomed and oddly comfortable in his jail cell, looks up and sees the cell door cracked open.

"You cannot hold onto the old all the while declaring that you want something new. The old will defy the new; the old will deny the new; the old will decry the new. There is only one way to bring in the new. You must make room for it."

—Neale Donald Walsch

CHAPTER 26

<hr>

THE FINAL APPROACH

The next day I walked along with a new and thoughtful spring in my step at the possibility of a brand-new life. I started to look around at the world as a set of possibilities instead of a never-ending connection to the past. On top of my newfound revelation, each day brought me closer to Santiago, now just over two hundred kilometers away.

On the morning of October 3, I walked with Dora and San as we entered the large city of Ponferrada. When we stopped for a late morning coffee at a cafe, I bumped into Dominique.

"Hi, Dominique! How are you?" I asked.

"Fine," she said, but then tears filled her eyes. She sobbed out in broken English about her knee pain. "I am afraid...I have...to stop—quit—my Camino," she said as tears flowed.

She cried into my shoulder as I held onto her shaking body. Dora and a few others surrounded Dominique to offer support. My heart broke as I instantly identified with her crippling pain and fear. More than anything, she wanted to keep walking, but the pain stopped her. Even worse pain came from the possibility of not being able to continue. The same daggers that stabbed me a few weeks earlier had found Dominique—the damaged pride, the wounded ego, the frailty of the body connected to a determined spirit, the overpowering fear, the sudden crack in seemingly solid faith. The painful side of the Camino.

Everyone offered Dominique moral support and our best advice: Stop and take a rest day or two, get a knee brace, and take "Camino morphine"—the 600 mg of ibuprofen. I gave her a packet of the painkillers,

Dora gave her a pastry, and everyone gave her hugs and encouragement. As we said good-bye to resume our journeys, I thought back to that exact moment with Joseph, Hana, and Sean. She managed to smile at us through her tears and say, "Merci beaucoup."

By midafternoon, the heavy October heat convinced me to end the day at a winery-hotel in the village of Cacabelos, where I enjoyed an evening of solitude and sound sleep.

The next morning, October 4, I left the hotel at my normal time of around 7 a.m., in predawn darkness. My headlamp became a fixture of the autumn mornings, which signaled the forward march of time and seasons. I walked alone on the silent, deserted road that led out of town. After thirty long minutes in the dark, my circular light beam finally revealed a yellow arrow spray-painted on the asphalt. After a short while, the path turned into a dirt-rock road, leading who knows where. Had I missed a sign or turn? I continued to walk in the dark and trust the beam of light ten feet in front of me.

At first I could barely make out the outline of rolling hills and trees against the dark-gray horizon. About twenty minutes later, I saw my surroundings: acre after acre of sprawling vineyards that lined the rolling hills. Slowly, the vineyards came alive with colors—muted at first—then shades of red, yellow, and green leaves appeared. Then I noticed little farmhouses scattered among the hills, and tall trees with green and golden leaves—all against the backdrop of the pale, multi-colored sky.

When the sunrise extravaganza finished, the bright yellow sun took center stage. The whole morning walk was a message: *"Just trust in Me like the yellow arrow and the light beam. Focus on the next step in front of you, and I'll take care of the rest."*

The day marked what would have been our thirty-seventh wedding anniversary. I observed it, thought about it, blessed it, and released it. It didn't fill me with sorrow. No tears fell. It didn't throw me into despair. I stood tall. *No more good-byes, Bob. No more good-byes.* I now turned my focus on the present moment and my forward direction.

A strong tailwind pushed me toward Santiago. The thought of arriving on my sixty-first birthday, only seven days away, made my heart pound with anticipation. I thanked God my feet and knees continued to hold up and prayed I would make it.

As the day progressed, I noticed with a growing sense of disdain that the trail had become more and more crowded with fresh hikers who had arrived just to walk the final stretch of the Camino. I judged the newcomers with an attitude of superiority, as if they were somehow inferior—not "true" pilgrims. As my arrogance grew stronger with each step, I came to a fork in the trail. I didn't see an arrow marker, so I had to guess which way to go. With total confidence, I chose the downhill path to the right.

After thirty minutes or so, I sensed something was wrong. I didn't see a single soul or any arrow markers. At first I felt conspicuous in my solitude, then the doubt hit me. Had I taken the wrong turn? No way. Not possible. But now, completely alone on a mountain road, I stopped and waited to see if anyone would appear. No one did. I finally had to admit I made a wrong turn, and retraced my steps, kicking myself the whole way. Sure enough, when I got back to the fork, I noticed a yellow arrow that pointed up the hill—the way I didn't take. How could I have missed something so obvious?

Camino karma had humbled me once again and taught me another lesson: Stay humble and don't judge. My arrogance had literally blinded me and added four to five kilometers to an already long and difficult day. A wave of shame and embarrassment flooded in. *I'm such an ass. Who am I to think I'm better than everyone else?*

When I crested the top of the hill and saw a group of people gathered outside a small café, I smiled and shook my head in relief. I was back on track. And these were my people—my fellow pilgrims—no matter when they arrived. We are all equal in value, and we are all in this journey together.

By the time I arrived late in the day at my destination, my body ached from thirst and exhaustion. To make matters worse, every place I attempted to stay was full—*completo*. My heart pounded faster and faster as panic started to set in on top of my fatigue. At that point, I didn't care if I had to sleep in a barn.

Finally, I found an albergue with a vacancy, which perfectly fit my nightmare criteria, but I didn't care: a large room with about thirty people, bunk beds, hot, stuffy, and noisy. Later that evening, I practically begged a husband and wife near the window to open it for some air, but they refused because she was afraid of bugs. During the night, frustrated and hot, I took my sleeping bag to a small couch near the front door. The bright lights and noise from the vending machines next to me made for a sleepless night after one of my worst and longest days on the Camino.

Frazzled and exhausted as I staggered out onto the early morning trail, I promised myself two things: From this point on to Santiago, I would call ahead and make reservations at hotels only—no more albergues— and I would never judge another fellow pilgrim again.

That day, October 6, the Camino delivered exactly what I needed. As daylight slowly emerged under a gray sky, I saw trees and rolling green pastures covered with soft blankets of morning fog all around me. I walked past pumpkin patches on scattered farms. The morning solitude, the silence, and the splendor of nature whispered to me: *"Today is a new day, Bob. Soak it in. Forget about yesterday."*

Suddenly, from behind, loud voices and the sound of marching boots shattered the silence. Two young men charged past me as if I was standing still. I watched as they sped past me while talking to each other at the top of their lungs, and then disappeared down the trail. Rattled by the broken peace, I heard an inner voice that said, *"Let it go. Let it go. Stay inside your hula hoop. That's them, not you. Don't judge. Stay within yourself. Stay on your path, at your own pace."*

Distractions and solitude, like yin and yang, took turns as the day unfolded. I encountered pilgrims on foot and on bikes who talked away on their cell phones, and an hour later I found myself inside a silent forest path surrounded by trees and beauty.

I approached a small village and noticed an old woman in front of me on the trail. I could tell she was a local—no backpack, no boots, simple clothes. *How cool. A local out for a stroll, living a simple, uncomplicated life in a tiny village in northern Spain. I wonder what it's like to live so detached from the crazy, modern world.* But as I came up behind her and got a few feet away, I noticed she held a smartphone in her hands crossed behind her back as she ambled along. So much for a detached life.

I couldn't do anything about the distractions except to stay within myself. If anything, the bombardment of the modern world and distractions in the final days of my Camino journey made me refocus and rededicate myself to why I came in the first place. I refused to allow anything or anyone to get in the way of everything the Camino had to teach me. I only had a handful of days left before Santiago, where my journey would end, and I didn't want to miss a single lesson.

Santiago—now less than 150 kilometers away. The end. The finish line. Several fellow pilgrims told me they didn't want to see it come to an end. A few dreaded it. Not me. I looked forward to the end of the daily grind, which slowly but surely wore me down. I didn't want it to end early, but when the time came, I wanted it to be over.

By early afternoon, I arrived at my destination for the day and checked into a small, simple, quiet, and glorious hotel room. After a quick nap, I set out to explore the city and saw several familiar faces seated outside a local bar. Positive anticipation filled our conversation as we discussed the ever-closer Santiago over a glass of wine.

After a while, I bid my fellow pilgrims farewell and walked around, where I noticed a mural painted on a concrete wall that grabbed my attention. It showed a group of medieval-era pilgrims on their way to Santiago. An old man, with a wooden staff in one hand, pointed with his other in the direction to travel—no yellow arrows to follow back then. Another figure, a cloaked woman, held the hand of a hunched-over elder, maybe her father, and helped guide him along. Perhaps it was his lifetime dream to make this pilgrimage, like Paulo. Another cloaked figure, a younger father, held a wooden staff in one hand and rested his other on the shoulder of a toddler, possibly his child. They were on their way together, and they would arrive together, no matter how long it took.

The crazy thing was, the early pilgrims had to walk both ways—to and from Santiago. I had the luxury of walking a one-way ticket to Santiago and could travel back home in modern comfort. They had to walk round trip. How on Earth did they do it? How many even made it back? I walked away from the mural struck by the contrast between the true Camino pilgrims of old and the Johnny-come-lately ones like me.

That night I fell asleep before my head hit the pillow and woke up ready to go. If all went well, I had only four hotel stays left.

I made my way through the darkened, early morning village toward the edge of town. The stillness was so complete that the sound of my boots against the stone pavement echoed in the narrow alleys. The abandoned streets, lit by the hazy glow of streetlamps in the predawn mist, created a mystical walkway, in stark contrast to the hustle and bustle the night before.

Once I got on the solo dirt trail, surrounded by the morning's gray fog, I did something I hadn't done for years: I started to pray the Rosary using my fingers to keep track. I avoided it for a few reasons: It wasn't my style of prayer, and it was way too near and dear to Annie's heart. She prayed it daily until she physically and mentally couldn't. But now, I let the meditative rhythm of the prayer sink into me as I walked along. Instead of sadness, a calmness settled over my soul.

As much as I looked forward to the end of the Camino, I knew I would sorely miss my daily immersion in nature's unsurpassed beauty, especially my early morning solo walks like this one. I saw new sights around each bend. I felt the cold, damp air against my face, listened to the sound of chirping birds, and saw sheep and cows grazing in lush green fields. I was surrounded by rolling hills, old trees laced with climbing vines, and the morning fog-mist.

I felt connected and at one with it all. Nature had become my daily companion. I experienced an ancient form of prayer that connected me to everyone who ever walked the Earth. But it would all end in a few days.

As I walked along the solitary morning trail, I realized that a strange peace had settled over me in a realm of my life where, up until now, confusion and angst had reigned supreme: a life companion. Someone to share my life with. Somehow an inner assurance emerged that it was going to happen. It shifted from *if* to *when*. Like spring cleaning, the clutter inside me was getting moved out, making room for something new.

Could this person already be in my life? My thoughts shifted to Lauren and the upcoming dinner on November 3 that Alice had arranged before I left—a lifetime ago. What would happen? What would our second meeting be like?

Near midday I heard the distant sound of a lone bagpipe, which got louder and louder as I approached. Then I saw a solo bagpiper who stood and played alongside the wooded trail. He wore a ceremonial uniform—a black brim hat, a white coat and shirt, red pants, and knee-high boots. The distinctive tones from the lone piper touched a nerve inside me that caused a flood of sadness and tears to pour out. Maybe it was the fact my journey's end was near. Maybe it reminded me of the bagpipe that played at my dad's funeral. Maybe it connected me to the end of my own life. Or maybe a combination of everything.

When I arrived midafternoon at my destination, less than one hundred kilometers remained. I checked into my hotel room and went about what had become a pattern: venture into the city for the evening, explore, talk with fellow pilgrims, attend an evening Mass, and enjoy a late dinner.

A Spanish Catholic Mass grounded me with something familiar when nothing in my life felt familiar. Even though I didn't understand Spanish, I recognized every part of the hourlong ritual, which allowed me to rest and breathe. I didn't go out of any sense of obligation like I used to. I didn't believe I would gain special power or grace like I used to. I just went to rest and reflect.

I returned to my hotel room and lay in bed as my mind wandered. I had only three hotel stays left before I arrived in Santiago. I had become so accustomed to the sense that God guided me along—through every person I met, through every mistake I made, through every yellow arrow, through every step I took. Like the GPS system in my car that gives constant guidance and redirects me when I take the wrong turn, I had an inner assurance that whatever happened on the Camino, God guided me.

Slowly but surely, the Camino had taught me to trust the path I walked—my own, unique path.

But what about afterward, now only a few days away? How could I learn to trust my post-Camino path back in the real world? Someone I met along the way summed it up: "What are we going to do without the yellow arrows when we get back home?"

"Come to me, all you who are weary and burdened, and I will give you rest. Take my yoke upon you and learn from me, for I am gentle and humble in heart, and you will find rest for your souls. For my yoke is easy and my burden is light."

—MATTHEW 11:28-30

CHAPTER 27

THE ONE WHO WALKS ALONGSIDE

I left the city of Portomarín early in the morning of October 8 and walked twenty-five kilometers to Palas de Rei, where I checked into a tiny but nice hotel room. The trail had been surprisingly uncrowded, like I somehow got out in front of the rush hour traffic. I spent most of the day thinking about my post-Camino life possibilities, and how awesome it would be to arrive in Santiago on my birthday, now only three days away.

When I attended Mass that Sunday evening, something stirred within. The service itself buzzed with an upbeat, positive energy, aided by a lively teenage youth group choir. Toward the end, as I sat surrounded by people and Spanish worship music, I felt a distinct nudge from God—like a tap on the shoulder—and an inner voice whisper: *"I want you to walk the entire next day with one thought in mind: My love for you. That's it. Just meditate on My love for you. Don't think or worry about anything else."*

I fell asleep that night wondering what the next day would bring.

Monday, October 9, 2017. The morning trek out of town had a similar feel to the previous few—cold, fog, mist, brown harvested corn fields, rolling green hills, and glorious nature all around. But instead of solitude, I had plenty of company. Groups of pilgrims were on the trail in front of and behind me—some in small packs, some solo. Rush hour. But despite the distractions, I focused and refocused my thoughts on God's love. As I did, many Day 1 messages came to mind:

"It doesn't matter what you do or don't do. My love for you will never change. It will never fade or weaken. It's like a fountain that never stops flowing."

"My love is always and forever. It does not depend on you. You can't earn it or deserve it."

"My love is always there for you. You can open yourself to it, or you can turn away from it—that's up to you. But it is always there for you."

Then, around 8:30 a.m., I entered a section where the trail was about twenty feet wide, half-covered with brown leaves, and bordered on both sides by towering trees that stood like ancient cathedral columns. The upper branches intertwined like raised interlocking arms, which created an arched hallway of peace and protection, sheltering me on the trail below. I had entered a holy cathedral, built by God's own hands. I stopped for a moment to feel the sacred space around me. Instead of the sounds of trekking poles, boots, and chatter from others, a hushed stillness filled the air. At that moment, I stood alone.

I resumed my walk forward and breathed in my surroundings. Birds sang in the branches above, and a soft breeze rustled the leaves. Peace and beauty embraced me. Then I felt a presence, as if Jesus himself walked alongside me.

"Do you feel this? This peace?"

"Yes, I do," I replied.

"This beauty?"

"Yes."

"My love and protection?"

"Without a doubt," I answered.

"This is like the trail that Annie walked at the end. I walked with her every single step of the way. She was never alone, not for a single second. I guided her on her trail home. I held her in my arms. She knew I was with her. She knew where she was going. She knew she was loved. She was at peace."

The words enveloped me like a peaceful wave as tears poured out. As I continued to walk and weep, I noticed a solitary walker about a hundred yards in front of me. As I got closer, I could see it was a woman. I slowed my pace to remain at a distance. We were the only two people on the trail, in this cathedral.

After around ten minutes of walking in synch with her, I watched as she approached the exit of the cathedral, where the tree canopy ended and gave way to a trail section bathed in bright morning light. The trail turned left and she disappeared from view. When I arrived at that spot a few minutes later, I saw what was around that turn: a large and beautiful house with white exterior walls and dark, painted window shutters. Someone's actual residence.

"In my Father's house there are many rooms. If it were not so, would I have told you that I go to prepare a place for you? And if I go and prepare a place for you, I will come back and take you to be with me that you also may be where I am." —John 14:2–3

The moment I made that same turn and saw that house, I stepped across a final threshold. Deep inside I had been holding onto the belief that God had abandoned Annie—not just with the brain cancer but in her final moments when she needed Him most—and left her to suffer. But God hadn't abandoned her. He guided and carried her safely home. And now I could fully let her go and release her into God's hands. Into her new heavenly home.

I too was released at that moment. My chains fell to the ground. The cave exit opened wide into the morning light. Nothing prevented me from walking into my new life, completely free. I had been given the gift of freedom. I didn't have to stay chained or stuck forever. It was time to exit the cave and step into a new life.

A sense of overwhelming gratitude, relief, and the wonder of "what now" filled me as my mind started to wander. *Wow, a whole new life! What would it look like? What would it feel like? Who would be in it? I could retire from my job. I could move to upstate New York or live there for a while—and mow lawns! Or I could work on a farm in Europe somewhere.* Possibilities buzzed inside my head like honeybees.

I walked the rest of the day on autopilot and couldn't stop thinking about what had happened. My Jesus encounter felt as real as the one with Jesús from Mexico on Day 1. I thought back to his words through the wind and rain: "You'll find what you're looking for."

By the time I finished the day's twenty-five kilometers and reached my hotel in Ribadaso, my tank was empty. All I wanted to do was get something to eat and be by myself. The hotel fit the bill perfectly—the window in my room faced westward, overlooking an endless landscape of trees and rolling hills.

After an early solo dinner at a nearby restaurant where I saw plenty of locals but not a single pilgrim, I returned to my room where I collapsed on my bed to soak it all in. I watched the wall and ceiling turn various shades of sunset orange as I listened to some of my favorite music. Eventually, darkness filled the space and exhaustion took over.

I can't believe this. Only forty-two kilometers left, just two more days. I'll arrive on my birthday—unless something goes wrong. But it won't. It can't. God is with me. He's led me this far. I can't believe what happened today. Jesús was right. A new life. My new life.

"*You cannot swim for new horizons until you have courage to lose sight of the shore.*"

—WILLIAM FAULKNER

CHAPTER 28

THE NEW SHORE

I started October 10 with an emotional and spiritual hangover from the previous day's mountaintop. My body felt heavy and flat-footed, and my spirit sagged under the emptiness of a letdown. *Why does a depressing low have to follow an awesome high? Why can't I remain in that incredible place?*

As I walked along the early morning trail, the reality of freedom started to sink in. *Where do I go from here? How do I start a whole new life? Where do I begin? Do I have what it takes?* Whatever direction my new life goes, it will be 100 percent up to me. It's all on me.

Like a faithful companion, the Camino knew exactly what I needed. Nature's beauty grounded me back into a peaceful place and slowed down my spinning mind. The warmth of the yellow-golden sun ascended over the eastern hills and literally burned away my gloom along with the morning haze. And the trail buzzed with energy from the many pilgrims as paths converged from some of the other routes to Santiago: the Camino del Norte, the Camino Primitivo, and my path, the Camino Francés.

Midmorning, I pulled alongside a young man (thirtyish) from Canada named Michael, whose slumped posture exuded sadness. Seconds after we greeted each other, he launched into his story, as if he couldn't wait to talk to someone. Earlier that morning, he had just said goodbye to a young woman from England who had to return home. They had fallen in love over the course of the Camino, and her departure tore them both to pieces. But their love connection had been established, and he told me they planned to reconnect soon, despite the distance.

"The two to three weeks we had together on the Camino felt like two to three years in real life," he said. "The Camino removes all pretense, and we immediately connected with each other on deep and intimate levels. We shared every aspect of our lives. It's so opposite from the real world. I miss her so much already. I feel like part of me is missing."

As we walked along, he groaned about his own return home. "I don't want to go back," he said. "I've always thought there was something unnatural about my routine life where I go to work Monday through Friday, take time off on weekends, and do it all over again. Week after week, month after month, year after year. What's the point? The Camino feels more like real life to me."

I nodded. "I've started to wonder the same thing. What if the 'real world' is like the *Matrix* movie—where we all buy into a system that isn't reality? The Camino is such a great break from the Matrix machine. Maybe this is the true reality."

Michael and I eventually parted ways, and I wished him well with his newfound love. I thought about what he said about intimacy and lack of pretense. We were complete strangers, yet he didn't hesitate to pour his heart out to me, just like I had done to so many along the way. The Camino pulled all of us together like trusted friends. Soul friends.

As the day progressed, each conversation reminded me that every one of us has a story, a journey, and a struggle—and we're all in it together, whether we recognize it or not. Yes, how I decide to live my new life is 100 percent up to me, but I wouldn't have to go it alone.

When I arrived in the town of Pedrouzo, it hit me that this would be my final overnight stop on the Camino. Tomorrow night I would sleep in Santiago—the end of my odyssey. My Camino passport, loaded on both sides with green, red, blue, black, and purple stamps from stops along the way, only had enough space for one or two more. A combination of sadness and relief swept over me. My magical mystery tour was coming to an end.

The next morning, I exited the B&B residence in the predawn darkness like I had many times before, but this time was different. This was my final day on the Camino—a relatively easy twenty-kilometer distance. A vibe of positive, calm, we're-almost-there energy filled every pilgrim I encountered on the busy trail, but I made a point to keep conversations short and return to solo mode. I wanted to feel every single step.

By midday, I arrived at Monte do Gozo, a hilltop park with a panoramic view of Santiago and St. James Cathedral, now only five kilometers away. I could see it in the distance, the equivalent of Dorothy's view of the Emerald City, sprawled out under a clear, blue sky. Several pilgrims lingered and rested at the park, but after I took a few photos, I jumped back on the trail for the final push. My mood shifted to that of a marathon runner who finally sees the long-awaited finish line—just get there. Could this really be the end? Nothing else mattered. No more time for reflection.

As I entered the outskirts of Santiago, I encountered all the elements I saw in Pamplona, Burgos, and León: cars, people, buildings, commotion, and noise. Big city life. But this was Santiago. My heart pounded faster and faster as I navigated my way through the crowded, narrow streets toward the domed cathedral, which I could spot over the city rooftops. At that point, I wasn't following arrows or other pilgrims—just a sense of direction based on my sightings. Soon enough, I found myself on the final approach: a narrow street packed with tourists, children, and locals—and a few backpacked, laser-focused pilgrims like me about to cross the finish line.

I heard the distinct sound of a bagpipe up ahead, in the path to the cathedral, which pulled me forward. I fumbled with my phone camera as I tried to capture my final steps as my hands trembled with excitement. Then I entered a large archway cut into a wall—a tunnel. A passage. An entrance.

When I stepped from the bright daylight into the darkened tunnel, the deafening sound of the bagpipe reverberated off the walls. This was it—the final few steps. An electric current of victory pulsed through every fiber of my body, like a victorious ballplayer in the final seconds of the championship game. My heart raced as I walked toward the sunlit exit. I stepped through and emerged into Saint James Square.

I made it! I finished! Oh, thank you, God!

The wide-open, stone-paved square—several football fields long and wide, bordered by the towering cathedral—buzzed with energy and emotion in the midafternoon sunshine. Some pilgrims lay flat on their backs, trekking poles and backpacks at their sides, soaking in their arrival. Others danced, embraced, and wept in joyful reunions. Groups of pilgrims who traveled together hugged and sat together to savor the moment. The scene resembled a combination between a graduation party and a post-marathon celebration.

Relief, exhaustion, and a sense of disbelief filled me as I roamed through the crowd. I had nothing left in my physical, emotional, and spiritual tanks. I exchanged congratulatory greetings with a few familiar faces but didn't have a reunion "moment"—until I saw Dora and San from the beer brigade. We hugged, laughed, and celebrated in the sun-soaked square. A few moments later, Joseph from India appeared, and we repeated the cycle. None of us could contain our smiles and laughter. I had only known them for a few weeks, but they had become part of me.

We walked up the concrete steps to St. James Cathedral and stepped inside. This was it—the famed cathedral that every yellow Camino arrow pointed toward. I had seen so many cathedrals along the way that nothing here grabbed my attention, except for one thing: the notion that this was the burial place of St. James. Dora pointed out where to sit during Mass to get a great view of the swinging incense pot, which I had seen in *The Way* movie.

After a short tour of the church and surrounding area, my body issued an executive order: REST. We all agreed to meet up later that evening for a night on the town, and I headed to my hotel.

As I walked through the streets of Santiago, it hit me that my Camino had come to an end. It was over. No more stages. No more arrows. No more destinations for the day. Could this also be the end of my grief journey? Is that even possible? Or maybe a transition to a new grief phase? Joy-sadness and relief-exhaustion filled me.

Many pilgrims I met along the way talked about one or two more destinations after Santiago. One was Cape Finisterre, the "end of the Earth," another ninety kilometers west of Santiago on the Atlantic coastline of Spain. The other was Muxía, another coastal town further north that contained a spiritual significance related to Saint James. I didn't feel compelled to go to either spot, except possibly Finisterre, and definitely not on foot. My Camino walk ended in Santiago. Any new destination would be done on modern transportation, not on my feet.

For my first two nights in Santiago, I decided to live large like I did in León and reserved a room at the luxurious San Francisco Hotel Monumento. After I checked in and collapsed on the bed, I read from the hotel literature that the original structure dated back to the year 1214, when Saint Francis himself walked the Camino. Many centuries later, the building complex was converted into a luxury hotel, which kept his name's reference and several elements of the religious convent.

After I rested for an hour, instead of a recharge, I felt a head-chest-sinus infection set in, which zapped my energy. But I had to get up and out. More than anything, I wanted my Compostela—my certificate of completion—to show the date of October 11, 2017. And I wanted to celebrate my sixty-first birthday with my dear friends.

I left the hotel and navigated my way to the Oficina de Acogida al Peregrino—The Pilgrim's Reception Office—and took my place at the back of an impossibly long line. During the two-hour wait in the late afternoon heat, a woman fainted fifty feet in front of me. Those nearby came to her aide, and she eventually recovered her strength. We were all accustomed to walking in the heat, but not standing in it.

When I finally got inside the building and stepped up to the service counter, I presented my fully stamped Camino passport to the seated woman. I recalled the moment in St.-Jean when my passport got its first stamp with the date of September 5. Every single stamp that followed represented a steppingstone on my way to the new shore. Each stamp held its own lesson and unique significance. Each stamp validated me and my path.

The friendly woman behind the counter reviewed and confirmed my Camino passport with a final stamp on top of the "Spirit of the Camino" text, the only spot available. Then she filled in my Compostela certificate and handed it to me with a smile. The diploma-like document, printed in Latin text alongside a colored-ink image of Saint James, contained my handwritten name and date: Robertum Ludovicus

McGuire, 11 Octobris 2017.

As I held the document in my hands, I saw it as a diploma of survival —not just for the Camino, but for the past eighteen months through the darkness. Through the fear. Through the cave. I walked out of the Pilgrim's Reception Office validated. Recognized. Proud. Grateful. Taller. Affirmed.

Less than an hour later, I joined Joseph, Dora, San, and Lucas (the beer brigade adoptee) in the jam-packed, bustling downtown area of Santiago. When we sat down at our table, Dora presented me with a birthday card and a present—a black T-shirt printed with white and yellow lettering—"Santiago Road." It showed four peregrinos crossing the road a la Beatles-style on the Abbey Road crosswalk. I pulled it on and wore it proudly, like the victorious golfer who puts on the famous green jacket at the Masters tournament ceremony.

The birthday card showed my favorite Camino symbol, the yellow arrow, and had these words written on the back: "Dear Bob, We wish you all the best in your life. We are really happy we met you. Thank you for being our friend. We love you. Happy B-Day. Dora, San, Lucas."

Despite my failing voice and near-zero energy, I wasn't going to miss a single moment of this night. We bar hopped from place to place, Spanish-style: beers, drinks, tapas, and the local specialty, octopus. As we talked, laughed, and celebrated, I realized there was no place on Earth I would rather be. This gathering felt like family to me. Eventually, exhausted, intoxicated, and full, we all agreed to meet the next morning at the square, and then dispersed into the city.

On my return walk to the hotel, I passed through St. James Square, which teemed with people and late-night energy. A Spanish musical troupe of six—complete with black and red capes, guitars, accordion, and booming voices—filled the air with lively music. The gathered crowd clapped their hands in rhythm and danced up and down. A woman from the crowd jumped into the middle of the group and danced as everyone cheered.

Farther on, at the tunnel entrance to the square where the bagpiper had ushered me in, a male soloist poured out soulful opera music in his tenor voice. The crowd watched in silence, mesmerized by his voice that echoed into the night air.

As I left the square and walked along the quiet street on the final approach to the hotel, I wondered if I would see any of my other friends in Santiago: Jesús, Hana, Dominique, Paulo, Daniel, Anne from England, or one of many others who walked alongside me and touched my life. Whether I saw them or not, they would all remain a part of me.

I fell asleep at the close of the most memorable of birthdays. I had made the crossing and now stood on a new shore. What awaited me? Whatever it was, I was ready. Or so I thought.

*"Every new beginning comes from
some other beginning's end."*

—Seneca

CHAPTER 29

THE END AND THE BEGINNING

I awoke on October 12, 2017, to a strange and uncomfortable reality: I had nowhere to go and nowhere to be. Nothing to follow.

The time had come for me to map out my own return home. I had two weeks before my return flight, which I had booked many months ago, so I had a blank travel canvas to fill. I knew my first destination had to be Finisterre, so I booked a bus trip for an overnight there, and then a return to Santiago for one final night. I had some ideas for the other days that began to percolate.

In the meantime, I attended Mass at St. James Cathedral and, thanks to Dora, positioned myself in a perfect spot to witness the incense spectacle—roughly a hundred feet away from the main altar.

Toward the end of Mass, a group of five men dressed in maroon-colored robes gathered on the altar of the church in front of the presiding priest. Each man grabbed onto a stranded tail-section of a thick rope that traveled up to a pulley system mounted to the cathedral ceiling more than 150 feet high. The rope came back down from the pulley to a huge, golden, smoking incense pot (about five feet tall, two feet in diameter) in front of the priest.

In one synchronized motion, accented by the soaring voice of a female soloist, the men thrust down on the ropes such that the incense pot launched into the air into a swinging arc. As the men continued to pull the rope in unison, the arc widened until it traveled about twenty feet directly over my head. Incense billowed out from the censer as it flew from one side of the church to the other, like a swinging trapeze.

We all stood in awe with our heads and hearts lifted for several minutes until the censer was lowered and the soloist's voice faded inside the
stunned and silent church.

I spent the afternoon at the nearby Peregrino Museum and strolled
around Santiago. That evening, I bumped into my friend Blake, and we
got caught up over a "proper" dinner.

The next day, when I stepped onto a full bus headed to Finisterre, I
thought for a second about feeling guilty for not walking the ninety
kilometers, and then quickly dismissed the notion. This was an add-on
destination to the Camino itself, and I didn't have the energy.

After the bus arrived at the coastal town and I checked into my
hotel, I grabbed my trekking poles and headed for the coast, the "end
of the Earth," a few kilometers away. But as I walked along, something
felt totally off—completely flat. As much as I wanted to get there, I
realized this wasn't one of the many stages of the Camino. It was just a
casual stroll. A jaunt. I had suddenly morphed from pilgrim to tourist.
I groaned inside.

Despite the beauty that surrounded me—the hillsides that sloped
into the sea, the green trees, the vast open ocean, and the glowing orange sunset later that day—nothing danced, spoke, or whispered to
me like it did on the Camino. That intimacy somehow vanished after
I arrived in Santiago, like the doors had closed behind me on a sacred
tunnel or chamber—and wouldn't reopen. The elements that made the
Camino my Camino were gone. Like Dorothy, I had awaken and found
myself back in Kansas.

Or maybe I had entered another phase of the Camino.

Another cold shot of reality hit me when I arrived back in Santiago the
next day. After a good night's sleep at a basic hotel, I entered the breakfast area the following morning. I sat by myself at a table, getting coffee
and a few bites to eat. As other hotel guests entered, I could literally
feel people's guards go up—the customary defenses, the stranger dan-
ger. No eye contact. No smiles. No greetings. No trust. Pretend like we
don't see each other. The complete opposite of the Camino.

I sat at my table and lamented the contrast. The Camino connected me with everyone, and the real world disconnected me. Lord, have

mercy. In less than four days, my soul already yearned for the Camino spirit and mourned its absence.

I realized what a rare gift I had been given: to connect on a deep and personal level with people from around the world—people I would have never met otherwise. But I also realized that the spirit of the Camino is located inside me. It's not "out there" somewhere. It lives in everyone. It just needs the opportunity, the conditions, and the permission to engage.

Later that day, right on cue, the Camino tapped me on the shoulder as I sat alone at a restaurant table for lunch. A young man in his thirties with ruffled blond hair and glasses walked up and asked if he could join me. At first, my "real world" reflex threw up a momentary hesitation, but then I caught myself and said, "Sure!"

"You have that peregrino look," he said as he sat down. "How was your Camino?"

For the next several hours, Alan from Utah and I talked about our Camino experience and how it felt to be in reentry mode. When I mentioned my idea for an educational foundation for addiction therapists, he proceeded to tell me that he had done that very thing in honor of his late mother, who died from issues related to Alzheimer's disease. He established a foundation to pay for the educational expenses of six health care workers who in turn dedicated three years helping people with Alzheimer's.

That evening, I met up with Mary Ellen from Australia, Ruth's good friend and walking partner. She was my age and married with two grown kids. We had traveled back from Finisterre together and decided to meet for dinner. What would be considered a date in the real world was just a get-together on the Camino. We enjoyed dinner and a bottle of wine, but more than anything, simple and open conversation. After dinner, we took a walk, ate some gelato, and then hugged and wished each other well. No stress. No romance. No drama. Just a simple and real connection.

Back in my hotel room, I reviewed my plan for the coming days: take a bus to Fatima, Portugal (a companion location to Lourdes), then another bus to Lisbon, then a flight to Rome to visit my twenty-three-year-old niece, Katie, who was there as part of her college's study-abroad program. Then a train to Zurich, Switzerland, to see my friend Nicholas from the beer brigade, and finally, a train to Paris to visit with Anne from France before my flight home.

Along the way, Hana texted me that she made it to Santiago after getting sidetracked by a flu bug. Then, in true Hana form, she hiked west to Finisterre, then north to Muxia.

I arrived in Fatima on the one hundred-year anniversary of the 1917 Marian apparitions to three Portuguese children and subsequent worldwide attention. A sprawling shrine complex, similar to Lourdes, was the focal point for visitors to participate in acts of prayer and devotion. As I walked through the grounds and basilica, I felt the same sense of detachment I did at Lourdes.

I sat on the edge of the immense central square in quiet reflection and noticed several people walking on their knees down a five-foot-wide pathway that ran the length of the square. I noticed one woman in her fifties or sixties who held a rosary in her hand as she crept forward on her knees. As I watched her perform this Catholic act of devotion and penance for nearly an hour with no sign of stopping, my heart ached. I imagined myself in her place and could visualize Jesus standing on the path right in front of me saying: "Bob, stop. You don't have to torture yourself anymore. I accept and love you just as you are, whether you do this or not."

When I arrived in Lisbon, the bustle and beauty of the city astounded me. I spent an entire evening at an international food court packed with every conceivable form of food and drink.

One evening after I arrived in Rome, I sat with my niece Katie at an outdoor table as we enjoyed a bottle of Prosecco and a classic Italian dinner.

"I don't want to pry, Uncle Bob," she said, "but are you dating anyone these days?"

"Kind of," I said. "I'm seeing someone now, but I'm not sure. I don't know. I've met several women through a matchmaker service, but no one has clicked yet. I'll just keep trying and see what happens."

"Well, whatever you do, Uncle Bob, don't settle."

"Don't worry, I won't."

The rest of my post-Camino tour took me to places I had only seen in photos or movies: Saint Peter's Square, the Basilica, the Sistine

Chapel, the Vatican Museum, the Coliseum, and as many ancient trea-sures of Rome as I could cover. My eyes and soul soaked up the awe and beauty of every sculpture, painting, building, and bridge.

I traveled through the northern Italian Alps via train into snow-capped, majestic Switzerland where Nicholas gave me a guided tour of Zurich and beyond. We video-called the other members of the beer brigade, all back in their home countries. Screams of joy erupted as each member appeared on screen.

When I arrived in Paris, Anne gave me an expert guided tour to as many sights as we could cover in two days—the medieval Sainte-Cha-pelle (residence of kings until the fourteenth century), the top of the Eiffel Tower, the Notre Dame Cathedral, a boat cruise down the Seine River, the Versailles Palace, the Arc de Triomphe and Champs-Élysées.

Every destination along the way sang its own tune and presented me with new sights, cultures, tastes, and experiences.

I spent the final day of my odyssey solo in Paris, starting with the Louvre Museum and ending with a quiet dinner of wine, bread, and cheese in the République Plaza area. The next morning, despite giving myself what I thought was ample time, I ran in a panic through the airport terminal to get to my gate on time. Heart pounding, breathless and grateful, I took my place at the tail end of the line as the final few passengers boarded.

The instant the plane touched down on the San Francisco airport run-way, I thought back to a time one week before I left for the Camino. I sat on the couch in Gregor's therapist office as I tried to work through my fear and anxiety about my leap into the unknown.

After I talked for a while, he led me in a guided meditation: "Picture yourself on your return flight home," he said. "The plane has just landed. You've just returned from your Camino. The plane taxis to the gate and comes to a stop. The ding sounds to unbuckle. Picture yourself standing up out of your seat and standing tall in the aisle. Take in the strength you're feeling. Feel it. You did it. You made it. Then walk off the plane into your new life."

The plane taxied to the gate and came to a stop. The overhead ding sounded. I unbuckled my seatbelt and stood up out of my seat and into the cramped aisle. I felt the solid strength in my legs, down through my knees, all the way to my feet inside my boots. I stood so tall I thought my head would pop through the ceiling. I felt a relaxed sense of victory in every step as I slowly walked off the plane. I did it. I made it. A new world waited for a new me.

I smiled at the customs agent and told him how great it felt to be home. It felt familiar, and it felt like home. But wait a minute. Was it really my home? What would it be like on the new shore that used to be my home? How would my friends respond to the post-Camino me? How would I navigate my new life with no arrows? What happens now?

PART 3

MY NEW LIFE

"Our brightest blazes of gladness are commonly kindled by unexpected sparks."

—SAMUEL JOHNSON

CHAPTER 30

SURPRISE

I gazed dumbfounded out the taxi window as the familiar scenery rolled past my jet-lagged eyes. Was I really back in the Bay Area? Had my Camino adventure come to an end?

Despite the familiar look of everything around me, a sense of dread wormed its way in as if to say: "Don't think you've come home. Maybe you've changed, but your reality here hasn't. It's right where you left it eight weeks ago, waiting for you. You didn't escape it. Welcome back."

Heaviness pushed me deeper into my seat. In less than two hours from my triumphant airplane exit, I already felt the pull of misery. I longed to be back on the Camino trail, where nothing looked familiar but somehow felt more like home. *Was my Camino odyssey for nothing? Why am I feeling this way?*

When I arrived at my house around 3:30 p.m. on Saturday, October 28, 2017, a bright and cheerful "Welcome Home, Bob" sign with balloons tied to the front porch greeted me. Some dear friends made sure I felt their love and support. I retrieved the house key buried at the bottom of my backpack, unlocked the front door, and stepped inside. For a split second, something deep inside felt like I had come home, like I had stepped back into the world I once knew. But like the silent pop of a soap bubble, that notion instantly vanished. As soon as I closed the door behind me, dead silence rushed in to capture me, like a fugitive who had been caught after an escape and thrown back into his cell. No sounds. No life. No home.

I shifted my thoughts to a diversion—I plunged into unpacking and prep mode for visitors. My friends who put up the balloons were due to arrive in a few hours for a welcome back party with pizza and beer. I needed their company now more than ever.

Around 6:00 p.m., the fun and joyful reunion commenced, filled with hugs, smiles, laughs, and stories. I joked about turning my house into an albergue. But after a few hours, everyone said their good-byes, and the diversion ended. They had their lives to go back to. I closed the front door and stood in the silence—right back where I started. *Did I just go in one gigantic circle?*

Exhausted, I collapsed into a deep sleep in my ridiculously comfortable bed at about 10:00 p.m., only to pop wide awake at 2:00 a.m. from the deafening silence. My heart pounded as waves of doubt, fear, and loneliness flooded in. *Had nothing changed?* I got out of bed, paced around the kitchen, and ate a bowl of cereal. I turned on soft music just for noise, but it didn't help. I squirmed and prayed for God's comfort as my confused brain tried to figure out what kind of life I had come back to.

Early the next morning, disoriented and weary eyed from minimal sleep, I started my laundry and sorted through eight weeks of U.S. mail. I tried to get settled but couldn't; I had nothing to settle into. I needed human contact, so I started to make phone calls. Friends, family, work colleagues, neighbors, anyone I could get in touch with. Each conversation boosted my strength—until I got Stephen's call from the Orange County Jail.

After I told him I had returned from the Camino, I didn't know what else to say. Since Annie's death, Stephen's life had been a dark and murky combination of jail sentences and unknown whereabouts.

"I hope to get out of here in late November," he said. "Maybe we can get together."

"Sounds good, Steve. Keep me posted. Love you, Steve."

"Love you, Dad," he said.

Later that day, I drove my car for the first time in months, which felt like a futuristic spaceship, to the 5:30 p.m. Mass at San Carlos church. Maybe something familiar and routine would help, like it did in Spain. As I sat on the hard wooden pew in the middle of the old familiar mission church, surrounded by a familiar congregation, I felt my body start to relax as the recognizable words of the service and music welcomed me back. Afterward I walked back to my car with the emotional and spiritual boost I needed to face my first week back.

I stayed asleep through the night, comforted by God's presence and words like I sensed on Day 1 of the Camino: *"I love you completely. Immerse yourself in My protecting love. All is well. Stay with Me. My love will never change. No matter what. I love you."*

I woke up Monday morning ready and eager to return to work. The daily routine grounded and settled me. I felt my anxiety disperse as my co-workers greeted me back: "Hey, Bob, it's great to see you!" "Welcome back!" "How was your trip?" "We missed you around here!"

And it wasn't just the work routine that helped. With each passing day of the week, the more I anticipated the upcoming Friday night when I would see Lauren again. The November 3 date had been on my calendar since Alice called me to arrange it in late August. Lauren would be visiting from Los Angeles, and this would be our first get together since we first met in March—a lifetime ago.

Even though no sparks flew on our initial meeting, and no contact had occurred since, I looked forward to seeing Lauren again. Back in March, I had no sparks to give. All I could think about then was how to get through the one-year anniversary of Annie's death. But that was March and this was November, and so much had changed with me.

After counting down the Friday workday hours, I jumped into my car and bolted out of the parking lot. I drove home, changed clothes, grabbed a bottle of red wine, and made a beeline to the gathering at Rob and Susan's house. Rob greeted me at the front door and escorted me into the kitchen, where the greetings erupted. "Welcome back, Bob!" Alice and Tim exclaimed as we all hugged each other.

After the greetings concluded, Susan said, "Hey, you have a new look!" referring to the facial hair I grew into a short beard, a post-Camino reminder that I decided to keep. I then turned to Lauren, and we hugged hello. She looked familiar but different, as if I were seeing her for the first time. She stood five-feet, four-inches tall, with blond hair down to her shoulders, and golden-brown eyes that twinkled when she smiled. She wore a maroon, off-the-shoulder top. She looked striking.

"What do you think?" I asked as I tried to play it cool, pointing to my whiskers. "Should I keep the new look?"

"It looks good!" she said, smiling.

After everyone's wine glass was poured, we toasted one another and then moved over to the living room for appetizers and conversation. Lauren and I sat next to each other on the couch, and within a few minutes, I realized how vastly different this meeting was from March. Not only did I not fail to notice her incredible attractiveness, but her engaging personality and sense of humor.

"I brought some pictures of the wedding," she said as she put some three-by-five color photographs on the coffee table.

"The wedding?" I asked, confused.

"Oh yeah, didn't you know? I got married!" she said joking, and then explained it was her oldest son Brendan's wedding from a few weeks earlier.

Relieved and amused, I settled into the couch. I couldn't wait to learn more about her. Our conversation flowed naturally, and after a few minutes, I didn't see or notice anything else around me but her. It felt like we were the only two people in the room.

"So, how was your Camino trip?" she asked.

"It was exactly what I needed. It helped me say good-bye and move forward." Then I looked at her and asked, "How did you manage to get through the loss of your husband? It's so difficult."

She looked at me with those beautiful eyes, then glanced down as her tears welled up. "My two sons, Brendan and Sean. My family and my friends. And my dog, Daisy," she said. "It's not easy."

I wanted to reach out and hug her, right then and there. I saw so much tenderness, love, and pain in those eyes. Instead, I nodded, and thanked her. We sat together in the silence for a moment. My heart immediately told me I sat next to an incredibly special woman.

We continued to connect in our private bubble until we heard the call to the dining table. As the dinner, laughter, and group conversation bounced along, I couldn't stop thinking about this intriguing woman who sat only inches away from me. I answered questions, told a few Camino stories, and fully participated in the conversations, but the back of my mind raced. *Who is this woman? What's happening here? I can feel her energy. I want to get to know her. How do I let her know? How did I miss this before? She lives in LA, but so what? How do I send a message to her? I have to do something!*

Finally, a crazy idea hit me. I pushed through every internal warning light and decided to take the plunge.

As the six of us kept the dinner conversation going, I took a deep breath and slowly placed my left hand on her right leg, just above the knee, underneath the table—my first ever attempt at such a maneuver. My heart pounded while I tried to smile and look normal. My intended message was simple and direct: *"I notice you and want to get to know you."*

I didn't know what to expect, but seconds felt like hours. What would she do? Push my hand away? Stand up and slap me? Politely excuse herself from the table? I held my breath.

After an eternity, I felt her warm hand softly land on top of mine. And gently squeeze. And stay! An Apollo rocket engine ignited under my seat and launched me out of my chair. I left my hand right where it was and heaved a sigh of relief and elation. My heart switched to a different beat. Message received, acknowledged, and returned!

For the next hour, our fingers communicated with each other under the table. If they could have talked, I imagined they would have said something like:

"I'm so sorry I didn't notice you before. I feel like such an idiot. How could I be so blind?"

"Don't worry about it. You had things you had to get through, and you did. What's important is we're here now."

"I can't believe you're holding my hand right now."

"I can't believe you made that move—but I'm glad you did."

I thought no one else around the table noticed my maneuver, but even if they did (and they did), it didn't matter. I had to act. Move. Go!

That moment, another barrier shattered. A brick wall fell. And what was on the other side? A beautiful woman who had endured her own grief cave. She got it. Here was someone who could relate to what I had been through and still had the willingness and courage to step out and say: *"I want to get to know you too."*

As the evening wound down to a close, my mind raced forward to figure out when I could see Lauren again. Would she want to see me? Was she just being polite under the table, to avoid a scene until I left? I asked if she would like to accompany me the next day on a drive to Carmel Valley and Monterey for wine tasting. She smiled and said, "Sure, I'd love to."

We all said our good-byes with hugs all around. I stepped out into the dark November night and climbed into my cold car seat, but a fire burned inside me that warmed me from head to toe. In less than six hours, my world had completely flipped right side up. I drove my hovercraft ten feet off the pavement as I replayed every moment of the evening over and over.

I went to bed that night with a thousand questions running through my head, and without a clue of any answers. But it didn't matter. Hope surged through my veins. I couldn't wait to see this incredible woman again in a few hours.

"It is a risk to love.
What if it doesn't work out?
Ah, but what if it does?"

—PETER McWILLIAMS

CHAPTER 31

WHO ARE YOU?

Not since my college days, more than forty years ago, had I looked forward to a date like I did the next morning. *Was last night with Lauren a fluke? A dream?*

I arrived back at Rob and Susan's house at 11:30 a.m. eager to find out. Lauren greeted me with a warm smile at the front door, ready to go. She looked so attractive in her sharp outfit, sparkling eyes, and warm smile. We drove off into the sunny autumn day and immediately the conversation started—and flowed like water. Within five minutes, I marveled at how easy and natural it felt to talk with her, like we somehow knew each other.

The day flew by as we enjoyed wine tasting, a casual lunch, a walk on Cannery Row, and a stop at my house where we sat together on the couch and watched the movie *P.S. I Love You*—a recommendation I heard on the Camino.

Aside from what we already knew about each other—that we were the same age and graduated high school in 1974 in the same southern California area—we discovered plenty of things in common: We both hung out at Newport Beach in the summertime. We each attended Calvary Chapel Church in the early 1970s when services were held in a huge outdoor tent. We both liked to travel and planned to retire from our jobs soon.

But it was the underlying ease of being with her that told me whatever this was, it had to be explored, no matter where she lived. When I dropped her off around 9:00 p.m., we exchanged phone numbers, hugged, and kissed good-bye. My heart sagged and jumped at the same time. I didn't want our time together to end but couldn't believe how good it had been. She had to return home to her dog, Daisy, and her third-grade students.

I drove away with a kaleidoscope of emotions turning inside: sad, happy, excited, shocked, curious, intrigued, confused, anxious, and reflective. In only twenty-four hours my world had been rocked in the best possible way. But who was this person, really? And what was going on here? Only one way to find out: I texted Lauren the next day to arrange a time for a phone call once she got home and settled. She texted back right away. A phone date was set for Sunday evening.

On that first call, we spoke for over an hour, with as much ease and comfort as we had in person. I suggested a question-answer game, where I would ask her a question but would answer it first. Then she would ask me a question and do the same.

"Are you involved in a relationship now with anyone?" No for both.

"Have you dated since you became a widow?" Yes for both.

"What's the most important thing to you in a relationship with someone?"

On and on it went—values, beliefs, family, childhood, etc. The more we talked, the more I wanted to know about her. Layer after layer after layer, everything just got more interesting. We finally decided to hang up and get some sleep before our early Monday morning work alarm clocks sounded. We said good-night and agreed to a phone date the next night—I'd call at 8:30 p.m.

On that first Monday night call, I relished the opportunity to call exactly at our agreed-upon time to prove to her how important this was to me. Night after night, our phone calls continued, with rarely a miss. I looked forward to each evening's phone date, which became the highlight of every day. We texted each other during the day, just enough to feel connected.

The pain of being alone in the empty house lessened as we talked. It wasn't just me anymore. Our talks got deep, like the joys and sorrows we experienced on the roads that brought us here, and our hopes and dreams for the road ahead. I told her everything about Stephen and his addiction, and how I struggled to know what to do and not to do. Like an X-ray image, the phone conversations revealed each other's inner thoughts and true selves, somehow beyond the level of face-to-face. With each call, trust between us grew. At the end of each call, I sat in silence and marveled at how we connected.

Over time, I saw how Lauren gave herself in loving service to others, starting with her family. She stood strong through the rough years of pain and struggle related to her late husband's (Kevin's) illness, an early onset of Parkinson's disease that rendered him disabled in his forties. Lauren cared for him and managed to raise their two sons on her own. She held everything together at home and work and endured what most people couldn't or wouldn't.

Lauren's joy came from her two boys, now in their thirties, her close friends, her family, her ten-year-old yellow lab, Daisy, and her third-grade students.

"You know what?" I said one evening. "You have a truly good heart. You are an amazing woman."

"I don't know about that," she said.

As the Thanksgiving holiday approached, a crazy idea surfaced on one of our calls. I would fly to Los Angeles, rent a car, and make two visits: one to see my family in Orange County, and one to see Lauren at her home in LA—and stay with her for a night or two. Way different than our first weekend. Way different than phone calls. It would be a bold first test, but the extra bedroom in her home and my brother John's place provided pressure-relief options if needed.

It was a huge leap for both of us. Yes, the first November weekend was amazing, the nightly phone calls were great, and we both felt so comfortable with each other—but an overnight stay at her home? Would everything suddenly get awkward? Or fall apart like a house of cards? Would the ideal image of Lauren I had built up in my mind prove to be just a mirage? Had I overexaggerated the potential of this and blown it out of proportion?

On a warm and sunny Thanksgiving Day at around 11 a.m., 2017, I disembarked the airplane at LAX and walked to pick up my rental car, with my black carry-on suitcase in tow. *What are you doing, Bob? Do you have any idea what you're doing?*

I climbed into the rental car and plugged Lauren's home address into my phone's GPS. My heartbeat picked up its pace. Lauren and

Daisy awaited my arrival. I didn't want to set myself up for disappointment, so I pushed away any thought of expectation or enthusiasm. *No, I have no idea what I'm doing, thank you very much. Just breathe. Stay calm.*

After a half-hour drive or so, the GPS told me I had arrived. I parked along the residential street across from a single-story home and took a deep breath. I retrieved my suitcase from the backseat, walked up the concrete driveway, and wondered if Lauren's neighbors spotted me. I stepped onto a curved red brick walkway that led to the front door. I took another deep breath and pressed the doorbell. *PLEASE be the same person I saw in early November and have talked with every night since. Please be the same!*

A deep-toned dog bark responded to my presence outside. A few seconds later, the door opened. Lauren's glow and warm welcome made my heart jump for joy and relief. A giant green "GO" light beamed inside me. *This IS the same person! That same smile!*

"You made it! Welcome!" she said, as Daisy sniffed at my shoes and pant legs. "Come in, come in," she said. "How was your trip?"

As Lauren gave me a brief tour of the front room, the kitchen, and the backyard, I barely heard a word she said or noticed anything around me. *Wow, I can't believe this. I've only known this woman for three weeks— so what am I doing inside her house?* Everything spun inside my head: the grief cave, the Camino, our whirlwind weekend, our nightly phone calls, and now this. It seemed too new to be real. Too good to be real. Too much to even process.

Lauren proceeded to cook up cheese omelets as I hovered in the galley-styled kitchen and entertained Daisy as she continued to welcome me. Everything flowed so naturally. The smells of home cooking on a stove-top and the feel of the warm kitchen resonated with me, reminding me of my parent's Tustin home.

As we sat at the dining room table and enjoyed our brunch, it struck me how normal and good this moment felt. It was an entirely new world for both of us, but like two kids on training bikes, we pedaled and rolled along. Despite the newness of it all, a sense of calm and peace prevailed. A sense that this was right.

Once we finished brunch and talked some more, the time had come for us to pause our maiden voyage to attend our own respective Thanksgiving get-togethers and reconvene later that evening. As I made the hourlong drive to my brother John's house along the once-familiar LA freeways, my mind raced with thoughts about Lauren. All during the Thanksgiving dinner with John, Pete, and their families, 80 percent of my brain focused on Lauren.

But when a phone call appeared from the familiar 866 number, my heart skipped a beat. Sure enough, Stephen was calling from jail. I accepted the call.

"Dad?" Stephen said.

"Hi, Steve."

"Great news. I'm getting released in the next day or two."

"Wow, that's great, Steve. I'm actually here at Uncle John's house for Thanksgiving."

"That's awesome!" Stephen said. "Can you pick me up when I'm released? I'll let you know the exact timing once I know."

"Sure, Steve. I'll be there. Let me know."

My head instantly started to spin in a new direction. My stomach tightened as my anxiety rose. I hadn't seen Stephen since the funeral, and couldn't say no. *Oh God, I can't believe this timing. Where will I take him? How much should I do for him? I need to tell him about Lauren. This throws everything off. But I need to see him.*

By the time I returned to Lauren's house later that evening, my head and heart were split in two: I wanted to focus on the time with Lauren, but Stephen's release was front and center. What could have been a romantic evening was anything but.

"I'm sorry," I said. "I'm not myself. I struggle with anything related to Stephen, and I'll be seeing him for the first time in a long time."

"That's OK," Lauren said. "I understand what family chaos is like. It's OK. Don't worry about it. Is there anything I can do?"

"You just did," I said. "You understand. That's all I need."

Stephen called several times over the weekend as his release date and time kept changing, eventually to Monday, which caused me to split time between Lauren's house and my brother's. I worked out a tentative plan with my brother John that Stephen and I would spend Monday night at his house, I would leave for LAX early Tuesday morning, and John would take Stephen wherever he needed to go.

Lauren and I relished every moment together on that long and fragmented weekend. Just time in each other's presence felt so energizing, like we had each discovered a buried treasure. She showed me the scenic highlights of the Palos Verdes Peninsula—the wide-open views of the ocean, the rocky cliffs and coastal hills, and the view of Catalina Island twenty-nine miles away—all under a clear blue sky, a warm sun, and a soft ocean breeze.

At one point we parked the car and walked along a wide public sidewalk in Redondo Beach known as the Strand. As her blond hair danced in the ocean breeze, I reached out my right arm and wrapped it around her waist. I felt her warm body underneath the smooth leather coat as I gently pulled her next to me. Then I felt her left arm wrap around my waist and hold me tight against her. Heaven. We walked along in total heaven.

Before I knew it, the time had come for me to leave to pick up Stephen. Two opposing forces pulled at me as my heart soared at the same time my stomach churned. What I needed to do overruled what I wanted to do. Lauren and I stood at her front door as we hugged and kissed goodbye. Already, I knew she was the woman for me. We still had so much to learn about each other, and so many questions to answer, but everything inside me shouted *yes!* I held my breath that she felt the same, but only time would tell. *One step at a time. Don't rush. Don't push. Let it unfold.*

I arrived at my brother John's house around 6:00 p.m. Monday to await the phone call that Stephen had been released from the Orange County Jail. As each hour passed without a call, the tighter my stomach twisted. Finally, at about nine o'clock, the call came.

"OK, Dad," Stephen said. "They told me I should be released in the next hour or so."

"OK, Steve. I'll be there."

I followed my phone's GPS through the dim-lit streets of downtown Santa Ana until I arrived at the multistory parking garage with signs for the men's jail, the women's jail, the central courthouse, the police department, the sheriff's department, the crime lab, and other buildings. My heart pounded in my chest when I realized where I was. Then it broke when I realized Stephen was imprisoned here and had been so many times before. I had entered into the edge of his dark world. *What had this place done to him? What will he be like?*

The dark, quiet, still night held an ominous air, a tension I didn't know or recognize. My body stiffened and my brain prepared for self-protection mode. Two or three shabbily dressed men loitered around the sidewalks next to the parking structure. I saw a bail bondsman car parked along the street and headed toward it as a reference for which building to enter.

When I walked into the large front lobby of the building, a line of people stood in front of an information desk, which sat behind a wall of steel and protective glass, occupied by two law enforcement agents. I took my place at the end of the line and looked around at the waiting area filled with blue-green plastic-vinyl chairs. Some women sat in random spots as their restless children hovered nearby. I also noticed a secured glass door with the words "Exit Only" and a poster next to it that read "Drug Use is Life Abuse."

When my turn came, I spoke through the glass opening and told the officer I was here to pick up Stephen McGuire. "Inmate number?" the officer asked. After I gave it to her, the officer looked up some information on the computer screen and said, "He should be out in twenty minutes or so. Take a seat. He'll exit the door on your left."

Thirty minutes later, we spotted each other the instant he emerged through the door. We walked up to each other and hugged. I didn't know the person I hugged, but I knew it was my son Stephen. His brown eyes and once-gentle face now had a battle-worn, hardened look. His oily, long brown hair was pulled back in a ponytail. His stocky build looked heavier but not in a healthy way. Inside, I recoiled from the smell and sense of him but tried to hide it.

"Hey, Dad, thanks for picking me up," he said as we walked to the car.

"You bet, Steve. So, what do you need?" I asked him.

"A cell phone. Some clothes. A bus pass," he said.

Over the next hour, we got all of them and tried to get caught up through the awkwardness. We played it safe in our conversation—he didn't talk about anything other than sports, and I didn't ask questions about his jail sentences or lifestyle. I didn't want to know. We stumbled along as we sat side by side in the car. Over the last eighteen months, the gap between our two worlds had only gotten wider. But I had to tell him about Lauren.

"Well, Steve," I said, "the main reason I'm here for Thanksgiving is because I met someone, and we're dating. Her name is Lauren, and we were introduced through Alice who lives next door to her sister. Lauren is also a widow, lives in LA, but comes up to Monterey to visit her mom and sister."

After a longer than expected silence, Stephen said, "That's great, Dad. I hope to meet her someday."

We drove through a fast-food place where Stephen ordered a double cheeseburger with fries and a milkshake. We arrived at John's house after 10:30 p.m., where he and his wife, Diane, welcomed Stephen with open arms. No questions. No judgments. Just acceptance. Eventually, we all said good-night and retreated—Stephen to the living room couch and me to the extra bedroom.

At six o'clock the next morning, I walked into the darkened living room, packed and ready to go. Stephen was awake with the TV on. Alone on the couch. Lost. What had his life become?

I broke the ice, and we talked briefly about his plan to stay with a friend in Fullerton.

"Thanks for picking me up, Dad," he said.

"Sure, Steve. Good luck with everything, and keep me posted."

We hugged each other good-bye.

"Love you, Steve."

"Love you, Dad."

I drove off into the cold, dark morning not knowing who Stephen was or where he was headed. I didn't know what to think or how to feel. All I could do was recite the Serenity Prayer, let it soak in, and focus on the task at hand, which was to get back to the airport.

"*The greatest gift you can give somebody is your own personal development. I used to say, 'If you take care of me, I'll take care of you.' Now I say, 'I will take care of me for you, if you will take care of you for me.'*"

—JIM ROHN

CHAPTER 32

WHO AM I?

The more Lauren and I got to know each other, the stronger our relationship became and the more convinced I became that we belonged together for the long haul. We connected on so many levels it shocked me. We were also at the same place in life, and ready to transition from work life to a new phase. What could be better than doing it together? We committed to each other and closed the door on dating other people.

One day while driving with her in southern California, I sent up a trial balloon: "Would you ever consider getting remarried?"

"Maybe," she said, "but I would have to know the person for at least a year before I would even consider it."

Noted. I also realized that if anyone had to relocate, it would be me. Lauren's life had to be near her two sons in southern California. My family resided there too, so it didn't make much sense to stay up north based solely on my job, house, and friends.

But as our relationship developed, something gnawed away at me inside: *The last time you started a long-term relationship, you were in your early twenties and barely knew yourself. Now you're in your sixties, and you're trying to restart your entire life. But who are you? Who are you now? You have to put some time and energy into you.*

One day after a GriefShare group, where I continued to volunteer each week, my friend and fellow volunteer, Chris, approached me. "Hey, Bob," he said, "I think the Breakthrough for Men program would be a great thing for you, and a good next step after all the grief work you've done. It's a self-development workshop geared toward men. I went through the program several years ago, and it made a huge difference in my life."

He went on to suggest I attend an introductory class and decide for myself, which I did. One evening after work, I walked into a fluorescent-lit, classroom-style room, with about thirty other men of various ages. I found and took an open seat in one of the five rows of side-by-side chairs. A speaker's podium stood at the front of the room, along with an instructional white board and a viewing screen that displayed a blue background with the word *Welcome*. A few feet to the right, a sign mounted to the wall read "3 MPH." I noticed several doorways that led to other rooms, like mini classrooms.

No one in the room seemed to know each other, so an awkward silence pervaded the room. Everyone kept their eyes to the front of the room and sat in their seats. The presenter, a tall, lean man named John with short, reddish-blond hair who appeared to be in his late sixties, stood up in front and welcomed everyone. We all remained attentive as he provided a rundown of the program.

"Breakthrough is divided into two parts, like two semesters," he said. "In a nutshell, Part 1 helps you redefine your relationship with yourself, the most important relationship you'll ever have. Part 2 helps you redefine your relationships with others. The program gives you life tools to strengthen your relationships, starting with yourself."

Sold. I needed a self-reconstruction project, like Humpty Dumpty. This was my opportunity to rebuild myself and my life within a structured program, along with other men. I wouldn't have to do it alone. I enrolled, and by mid-February, I had two relationships under construction: one with Lauren and one with myself.

Everything seemed to be going along fine until the anxiety truck blindsided me. Suddenly I felt overwhelmed, overpowered, and afraid, like a riptide had me in its grip. The more I struggled and fought against it, the further it pulled me into a turmoil. By mid-March I gulped for air. I was drowning in anxiety, fear, and panic. *This is too much. Too big. I can't do this. But this is supposed to be a happy time. A great time. A new lease on life. So why do I feel this way? What the hell is happening?*

I ran to God for help and comfort, but helplessness and a loss of my sense of self raged on. I ran to Gregor for therapist help, and he guided me back to my childhood years when I first felt powerless, vulnerable, and afraid. A frightened child quivered inside me and needed safety and protection. *But why? Why the fear? Protection from what?*

Each day, I struggled to stay afloat until the day I sat in the Breakthrough classroom and listened to the presenter talk about physical and emotional boundaries. "We are not born with boundaries," the presenter said, "so we have to learn them along the way, if we're lucky. For many, that never happens. The starting point is the awareness that each of us is a unique and separate individual. We are each our own person."

That sounded so simple yet so profound. Somehow, I never got that memo. In fact, I got the opposite: It was never about me and what I needed or wanted. I was raised to focus on everyone except me, which stuck throughout my life.

The presenter continued, "We can set and maintain boundaries for our own safety and sense of well-being. If you often feel overwhelmed, chances are you have weak or no boundaries. And believe it or not, you have a choice in the matter. You have a choice over what you think and feel. You are the sole owner of your thoughts, feelings, and experience. No one else. Just you."

It dawned on me that I had turned the prospect of my new life into a force that overwhelmed and overpowered me. Zero pressure came from Lauren; it was all self-created. How could I possibly leave my job, move to a new city, and start an entirely new life? How could I manage those kinds of seismic changes? Who would I be without all the familiar things I know?

My focus suddenly switched from external to internal. Not to God. Not to any form of rescue. Just me. Now I was being told that I had the power over my path instead of being overwhelmed by it. I had the power to choose how to respond to whatever came my way. Whether I realized it or not, I sat in my own driver's seat and created my own experience. An internal power source—untapped and dormant—waited patiently inside me, and I didn't even realize it.

The presenter read an excerpt of a book by Marianne Williamson: "Our deepest fear is not that we are inadequate. Our deepest fear is that we are powerful beyond measure. It is our light, not our darkness, that most frightens us.... We are all meant to shine, as children do. We were born to make manifest the glory of God that is within us."

For the first time in my life, I gave myself permission to focus on me and take charge of my own sense of self. I could set my own boundaries and create my own path. Week after week I learned new things about myself. One of the most surprising was my long-held beliefs that limited or restricted me. My core limiting beliefs.

I learned to identify and challenge those beliefs, one of which was powerlessness. I realized that for most of my life, I had forfeited my power to other people, places, events or outcomes – and didn't even know it. Through the workshop, I learned how to affirm and embrace my own power – loving and good power – a complete revelation for me.

No longer did I have to surrender to the force of an underwater current. I reached for the bottom and discovered it was only three-feet deep. I stood up. I stood in control of my life and could walk in the direction of my choice. No longer did things have unfettered control over me. Not life changes. Not people. Not places. Not outcomes. Not situations.

I now had a sense of control. A two-ton boulder lifted off my back. *Why did it take me so long to learn this stuff?*

So began the process to redefine my relationship with myself. Each week I learned a new life tool that opened me to things I missed along the way, like how to identify and breathe into feelings, how to accept myself, and how to love and affirm myself. I encountered myself in a way I never had before.

Through a guided meditation, I was taught how to get in touch with my inner child who still lived inside me. "Close your eyes and locate your little boy self in a place you knew well as a kid," the presenter said. "It could be in your room, up in a tree, or in a secret hiding place outside. See him there by himself. What's he doing? How is he feeling? Approach him and gently get his attention. Tell him that you are him all grown up and have come back to be with him in whatever way he needs. You will stand up for him and protect him no matter what."

The concept of my inner child was relatively new to me, but I plunged ahead with the exercise. I traveled back to my childhood home in upstate New York on a warm summer day in 1964, when I was seven years old. I stood at the front door of the house and looked through the glass pane into the empty hallway. I turned the brass knob and opened the heavy, white-painted front door and stepped inside. I stood in the wood-floor entry and recognized the pile of baseball gloves and bats, basketballs, badminton rackets, footballs, and lawn darts on the floor.

All was quiet in the house. I took a few steps down the hall and turned right into the front room and glanced at the familiar surroundings: the brown wooden floor, the wallpapered walls, the old double hung windows, and the old radiator heater underneath one of them.

There I saw seven-year-old Bobby lying on the wooden floor with an open coloring book and a box of Crayola crayons. I recognized that blond hair, blue jeans, and baseball T-shirt. He was busy coloring with the red crayon, focused on his work. I cleared my throat, and he looked up at me with a surprised but not startled look. He shifted into a seated position and continued to look at me.

"Who are you?" he asked.

I got down on my knees about ten feet away from him. "You won't believe this," I said, "but I am *you* all grown up."

He just continued to look at me as if it didn't register.

"I know that's hard to believe," I said, "but I'll prove it. The Detroit Tigers are your favorite baseball team, your best friend Vince lives down the street, and you have a marble collection in a wooden box with a sliding top—and a great baseball card collection. Your bedroom is the first door on the right at the top of the stairs. You love to play outside, climb trees, and ride your bike. But the first time you rode a two-wheeled bike you crashed into the pine tree at the bottom of the hill because you didn't know how to brake. Should I continue?"

"No," Bobby said. "That's OK. I don't get it, but that's OK. What are you doing here?"

"I came back for you," I said. "Just for you. I know there are a lot of things you don't understand, and I know how you often feel invisible and afraid, like you don't matter. But you do matter. And you're not invisible. And you don't have to be afraid. I am here to be your friend and to protect you."

Bobby sat and listened to every word. Then he said, "Do you want to go outside?"

"Sure," I said. "How about the tire swing at the oak tree? Or we could try to find our cat, Willie."

Bobby smiled and jumped onto his feet. "Let's go!" he shouted.

We both ran outside, across the driveway's hot black asphalt and down to the oak tree. The warm summer air caressed my face and body. I kicked off my shoes and pulled off my socks and felt the blades of soft green grass poke up in between my toes. Yellow flowers and white puffs of dandelions spotted the grass, and the melodious sound of cicadas filled the air.

We ran, explored, climbed trees, and played outside all afternoon. We drank water from the rubber garden hose, which came out hot and slowly cooled off and had a familiar, cold, plasticky taste. We played catch with an old, worn baseball and hit towering fly balls with a wooden bat.

Finally, exhausted, dirty, and sweaty, we sat on the warm grass in the late afternoon shade of a tall pine. I pressed the tips of my fingers together through the blackened sap and pulled them apart, which smelled like a Christmas tree.

I looked at seven-year-old Bobby and saw so many incredible things: His love of life. His innocence and trust. His sensitivity. His joy in simple things. How could I not completely love and accept this kid? Then it hit me: He was me. How could I not completely love and accept myself?

A sad look came over his face. "Do you have to go back now?" Bobby asked. "Do you have to leave?"

I reached out and held his little hand in mine, which stuck together from the dirty pine sap. I looked into his vulnerable blue eyes. "No," I said, "I'm never going to leave you. I'm always going to be with you. I'm here for you, no matter what. I will love and protect you forever."

He looked at me and said, "Really? You promise?"

"I promise," I said. "Cross my heart and hope to die."

He sat and thought about it for a moment, smiled, and said, "Let's go look at my baseball cards!"

Through that exercise, I had opened a door to myself that had been off-limits my entire life. I had always equated self-care to selfishness, which translated into "bad" and "wrong." But no more. The time had come to embrace myself in every way, even that little boy inside me, free from guilt or shame.

But as I developed this new relationship with myself, I wondered how it would all work with God in my life. How would my new sense of self merge with my sense of God? My spirituality?

I searched and found a book titled *The Missing Commandment: Love Yourself* by Jerry and Denise Basel, and another titled *God Loves Me and I Love Myself!* by Mark DeJesus. Both helped me pave the new road. Both sited a common Biblical reference with two tiny words ("as yourself") that often get ignored or overlooked.

"One of the teachers of the law came and heard them debating. Noticing that Jesus had given them a good answer, he asked him, 'Of all the commandments, which is the most important?'

'The most important one,' answered Jesus, 'is this: "Hear, O Israel: The Lord our God, the Lord is one. Love the Lord your God with all your heart and with all your soul and with all your mind and with all your strength." The second is this: "Love your neighbor *as yourself*." There is no commandment greater than these.'" —Mark 12:28–31.

Nothing could be more radical to me than a commandment to love me, myself, and I. It turned my belief about me upside down, exactly the direction it needed to go. I started the slow process to reprogram my lifelong habit of self-rejection and began to love myself.

Over time, I recognized that any element of my faith based on deficit, negativity, condemnation, judgment, punishment, or shame had to go. Any notion of me not being enough, not good enough, or not acceptable had to be thrown out.

I started to question any external thing that created a dependency in me to feel acceptable, or anything that contributed to a sense that I had no worth of my own, in and of myself. Activities like regular attendance to Mass, a prayer service, or a sacramental service did not make me acceptable to God. My acceptance isn't something I need to earn, demonstrate, or prove.

I received the same message from the Camino, and it made so much sense. Do I earn the air I breathe, the sun that shines on my face, or the life that I've been given? God's love is wrapped up in all of these, and so much more—and I don't need to punch an "earning ticket" to receive them.

The external dependencies never lasted anyway. I had to keep going back for more, like a spiritual orphan version of Oliver in a circular soup line. Someone or something had what I needed—it was always "out there," not "in here." I had always been the dependent one. The needy one.

No more.

It was my old system of faith that had to be thrown out, not God. My faith in God continued to grow and strengthen as I grew in self-love and acceptance. I still saw God as the Creator of life and the Eternal One who holds everything together. I still saw God as the highest of powers, but not one to micromanage my life.

The stronger I became within myself, the more I saw myself in a loving dance with God. He has his part and I have mine. As a human being created in God's image, that makes me a co-creator with God. We walk together, love together, and create together. Granted, on two different scales, but we each do a percentage of the work. Is it God 99 percent, me 1 percent? 98–2? 80–20? Whatever it is, what a difference my percentage makes. Like a catalyst added to a chemical solution, it changes everything. Instead of a dependent weakling who does nothing but follow and obey, I get to be an active participant with God. I get to be in partnership with God.

The year 2018 became a rebuild year for me in ways I couldn't have imagined. I started the year with an "I-can't-do-this" ALTERED life mindset—fearful, overpowered, weak, and dependent. But step by step, month by month, a "what-am-I-making-it" NEW life mindset emerged, along with an overriding sense of peace, loving power, and direction.

Just as I stood up and walked off the post-Camino airplane, I now stood up on solid ground and stepped into my future.

*"The shadows:
some hide, others reveal."*

—Antonio Porchia

CHAPTER 33

THE HIDDEN REVEALED

As my personal and spiritual growth spurt continued, the love between Lauren and me continued to strengthen and grow. The long-distance aspect of our relationship turned out to be an advantage—after each get-together, every two to three weeks, we had time and space away from each other to regroup, breathe, and think. Our nightly phone calls kept us connected, and then we'd take another step forward.

Each time I visited Lauren at her home, the possibility of a future move-in for me started to come into focus for both of us. But a thousand things needed to happen first, one of which was the expiration of Lauren's one-year timer. But I waited patiently—she was one in a million, and I couldn't imagine life without her.

In the meantime, we each started to be introduced to the other's world of family and friends, the panel of judges who had to weigh-in on this new person. One by one, I met Lauren's tribe in some form of social setting, usually at a restaurant. The meet-and-greets were light and fun, and numerous enough that I needed a scorecard to keep track of names and how they connected to Lauren.

Then came her immediate family, who represented a whole new level of scrutiny—the Supreme Court of evaluators. I had already passed the review of Lauren's sister Susan, but her brother, Brian, would be another story. Men are tougher on other men, especially when it comes to entering the protected and sacred circle of family. Anyone who got close to Lauren had better measure up—no ifs, ands, or buts.

Despite the anticipated pressure, I looked forward to meeting Brian, who worked as a commercial airline pilot and had served in the military as a Navy pilot. Over Easter Brunch at a restaurant in San Jose, I was introduced to Brian, his wife, Renee, and their two teenage sons. Their warm and welcoming demeanor told me I passed my initial inspection.

Then it came as a pleasant surprise when Lauren's eighty-nine-year-old mother, Dorothy, gave me a warm greeting at our initial meeting. She smiled at me from inside her brown recliner chair, surrounded by a soft multicolored blanket, looked at Lauren and said, "He's cute!"

But I was most nervous about meeting Lauren's two sons, Brendan (thirty-four years old) and Sean (thirty years old). The mother-son relationship is hallowed ground, so I expected to encounter full resistance from these tall young men with athletic builds. If my mom had introduced a new man in her life after my dad died, every protective instinct inside me would have been in battle-station mode.

I also knew I couldn't hide or fake anything related to Stephen. I had to confess the reality of his life as an addict and accept whatever reaction they had—good, bad, or whatever. Over the years, I had learned to deflect any question from anyone about Stephen with vague details such as "He's living in southern California, trying to figure things out." But I couldn't do that with Brendan and Sean. They needed to know the truth from the beginning.

The moment came one day over the 2017 Christmas holiday, on my second visit to Lauren's home. I fidgeted as I anticipated their response to my dark family secret. When they arrived, we greeted one another courteously, like opposing players who exchange pleasantries before the start of a game. No suspicious looks. No fisticuffs.

Lauren had laid out plates full of food that covered the kitchen table. An NBA basketball game played on the TV in the background, which provided a welcome diversion. As the conversation attempted to gain traction, my mind rehearsed what I would say about Stephen. While I talked with Sean and Brendan, a familiar recording played in my head—the same one I heard every time I saw or met a young man around Stephen's age: *Why can't Stephen be like this? Why can't he live a normal life?* As much as I hated it and beat myself up over it, I could never shake the shame and embarrassment I felt about Stephen. Then came the guilt and shame for feeling that way.

When the question "So you have a son?" was asked, a wave of heat rose in my body. My heartbeat doubled. My face flushed. They both looked at me with full attention. I braced myself for looks of disbelief, judgment, rejection, confusion, or all the above. "Yes, I have a son, Stephen, who's thirty-two years old," I said. "There's no easy way to say this, but he's an addict. He has struggled with drug addiction for years."

Sean looked at me with an expression of genuine concern and sadness and said, "I'm sorry to hear that. I know some people who have been in that situation." Brendan also listened with a look of concern on his face.

I couldn't believe my eyes and ears. No looks of disgust or judgment. My heartbeat and temperature started to return to normal. My lungs opened to allow air back in. I had just met these two young men and already felt a sense of acceptance for me and for Stephen. No rejection. No interrogation. Just acceptance. Wow.

Lauren's introductions to my family and friends were fewer in number and straightforward, except for Stephen. When the month of May 2018 rolled around, a less-than-ideal opportunity presented itself for the two of them to meet. Stephen had landed back in jail and asked me if I could visit him. It was one thing for me to go, but it was the last place on Earth I wanted to bring Lauren. I insisted she wait until sometime down the road after he got released, but she insisted back. "It's OK," she said, "I want to meet Stephen, and I want to go with you."

"I don't know," I said. "I have no idea what to expect, but I guarantee it won't be easy or pleasant. For the record, I want Brendan and Sean to know that I am *not* asking you to go. This is not my idea or my request."

"OK," Lauren said. "I understand. And I still want to go."

I coordinated the date and time with Stephen, and on a late Monday morning in early May, Lauren and I walked into the visitor wing of the Theo Lacy Facility jail in Orange, California. We had both read the visiting rules:

- Visitors may only possess identification and keys while inside the facility for their visit.

- No food, drinks, candy, gum, cigarettes, matches, lighters, pepper spray.

- Weapons or anything deemed inappropriate are not allowed in this facility.

- Cell phones, laptops, cameras, and other electronic devices are prohibited and not allowed on the facility.

- Clothing that is derogatory, offensive, revealing, or deemed inappropriate by the visiting staff will not be allowed.

- Visitors who are disruptive or under the influence of drugs or alcohol will not be allowed and are subject to arrest.

- Visitors shall proceed to their assigned seat and remain there until the inmate arrives.

A mixture of sunlight and florescent light filled the open, high-ceiling area as we took our place at the back of a line of ten to fifteen others, mostly women and children. Two uniformed officers occupied a protective glass check-in desk, and two or three officers stood guard at other locations. When our turn came, I stated Stephen's name and inmate number, and we showed our California driver's license ID's and answered questions that confirmed our adherence to the visitor rules. The officer directed us to the next step, a metal detector entrance that led to the visiting area.

Once through the metal detector, we were escorted by a female officer down a long hallway that led to an area connected to the visiting rooms. Each room was roughly fifteen feet wide and thirty feet long, with about twenty (ten on each side) individually numbered, three-foot-wide, blue partitioned booths, each with a phone handset and a single stainless-steel seat and shelf for the visitor. Thick glass panels faced the inmate side of the partition, a mirror image of the visitor side. The numbered partitions also had glass panels so the visitors could see one another to their left and right.

The officer led us to one of the rooms and said, "You're in slot number seventy-three. Take a seat there and wait for your inmate to arrive, which should be thirty minutes or so."

We entered the room, which felt cramped, cold, and stark—like it could be cleaned out with a fire hose. Everything was either concrete, glass, or steel. Bright florescent light reflected off the concrete floor and stainless-steel seats. We stood awkwardly at our booth and looked around. Eight to ten others were in the room, mostly women and kids, amid sounds of intermittent one-way conversations. Some waited for their inmate to arrive. Children fidgeted near their mothers. *What are we doing here? What is Lauren doing here? This isn't good. This isn't a good place to be. What if something happens?*

A sickening feeling came over me, like we were trapped. Could we leave? Yes. And no. We stood on the doorstep of a dark and dangerous place—the place where Stephen lived—separated by a pane of metal and glass.

A man and woman occupied a booth next to us, speaking Spanish to an eighteen- to twenty-year-old inmate we assumed to be their son. The woman held a tissue to wipe her tears as she spoke to him. She handed the phone to the father who stood alongside her, and continued to weep.

Thirty minutes went by. Then forty-five. I started to think there was a problem and wondered how long we should wait it out. I felt more restless by the minute, and so out of place. Lauren looked around in constant awareness of her surroundings. At one point she nudged me and whispered that an inmate on the opposite side flashed a hand-gesture gang sign to the young man who spoke to his parents. My body's muscles instantly tightened. *What the hell is a "gang sign" anyway?* I wanted to get Lauren out of there. I wanted to leave but couldn't.

Finally, Stephen walked into the inmate side, sat down across from us, and picked up his phone. I pulled the slick, grubby phone from the wall, attached by a short, stainless-steel cable. I held it lightly and put the mouthpiece far from my mouth like it came out of a dirty trash can. I swallowed hard. I had talked to him in jail before, but the sight of him made it real. And unreal. Here was my son, confined inside a dark world. A hopeless pit. Shame and sadness for him filled me.

His oily brown hair was pulled back in a ponytail, showing his receding hairline and some scars on his roughened forehead, face, and broadened nose. He wore the jail-issued orange shirt and pants. He looked overweight and pale. Lauren stood on my right side. *What must she be thinking?*

He looked at me through the glass. For a split second, I recognized the real and vulnerable Stephen in his brown eyes, which then flipped to a tough exterior, like a switch had been thrown.

"Hey, Dad," he said. "Thanks for coming." Then he looked up briefly at Lauren and said, "You must be Lauren. It's nice to meet you. Sorry about the circumstances."

I relayed the message to Lauren, and she smiled at him. "It's nice to meet you, Stephen," she said. "I've heard so much about you." I passed the message on to Stephen, and he managed a closed-lip smile.

We talked for several minutes, but about nothing in particular. It was always so awkward and foreign. Lauren came to the rescue. "I don't know if Bob told you," she said, "but I have two sons around your age, Brendan and Sean. They're huge basketball fans. They look forward to meeting you someday."

"That sounds great," Stephen said as he nodded and smiled.

After multiple attempts to keep the conversation going, it eventually ended, and we said our good-byes.

"Thanks again for the visit," Stephen said.

"You bet. Love you, Steve."

"Love you too."

After he hung up the phone, he waved good-bye to us and disappeared, back into a dark world we couldn't begin to comprehend.

Heavy sadness mixed with deep gratitude filled me as we walked away. Lauren didn't need this in her life, but she accepted it willingly. She could have turned and run in the opposite direction, and I wouldn't have blamed her a bit. But she didn't. She stayed, in full acceptance of me and of Stephen.

"Life is either a daring adventure or nothing."

—HELEN KELLER

CHAPTER 34

JUMP!

The rest of our first year together hummed along, as if we were meant for each other. Even in the realm of faith things seemed to work. Although Lauren wasn't raised in a particular religion, she believed in God and identified as a Christian. Her late husband, Kevin, had a Catholic upbringing like me, and they raised Brendan and Sean in the Catholic faith.

But the more our relationship deepened, the more I noticed how the Catholic faith took us in different directions. When we attended Mass together, the restriction that non-Catholics could not receive Communion meant she couldn't participate like I could. I started to see the hurt and separation it created; my Catholic status made me "acceptable" but not Lauren, which didn't make sense.

Despite that, as I looked ahead to a possible wedding down the road, I decided to write a letter to the Monterey Bishop requesting a priest for an outdoor ceremony. My request was denied based on a requirement that it be held inside a Catholic church. The inflexible rules, requirements, and separation pushed me further away from the Catholic religion, which both saddened and emboldened me.

As the sand inside Lauren's one-year sandglass trickled to the end, I planned accordingly. Instead of a ring, which I wanted Lauren to pick out if things went as I hoped, I worked with a local jeweler to make a custom necklace—two interlocking ovals, like a fancy number 8, both representing the long road we each traveled to meet. A yellow topaz stone for November occupied the intersection of the two roads, the month we started our journey together.

But before anything, I had to talk with Brendan and Sean. One week before Lauren's timer expired, I traveled south and asked if she could ask the two of them to go out to lunch with just me—as a way for the three of us to get better acquainted. They both agreed.

On a warm Saturday afternoon in late October, we sat together in the outdoor patio of one of their favorite Mexican restaurants in Redondo Beach. As the two of them focused on the disappearing tortilla chips, bowls of red salsa, tacos, burritos, and Cadillac margaritas, I focused on how I was going to break the news.

After twenty to thirty minutes of conversation, I saw an opening, took a quick breath, and dove in. "Well, guys, I have something to talk with you about," I said. The full-speed ingesting suddenly shifted into a slow-motion crawl. "Next Saturday will be the one-year mark that your mom and I have been seeing each other," I said, "and I plan on asking her to marry me. But before I do, I want to make sure you guys know, and see if you have any questions or concerns."

Full-stop on the Mexican feast. Both sets of blue eyes locked onto me—Brendan in his T-shirt, dark-brown hair, dark eyebrows, and stubby black whiskers, and Sean in his T-shirt, broad shoulders, shaved head, and clean-shaven face. A momentary but what felt like an hour-long silence hung over our table, accented by the low hum of nearby diners' conversations.

I braced for a cross-examination:

"What will we find out when we Google you? (Tell us now and save the embarrassment.)"

"How much money do you make?"

"Where do you plan to live? (There's only one correct answer: Here.)"

"How good is your retirement IRA?"

"What's your criminal history?"

"What are your health issues?"

"Where do you stand on the Lakers?"

Instead, Brendan broke the silence and said, "That's great news. Congratulations." *What? What did you say?* Sean stayed silent but didn't give any sign of disapproval. I sat in a pleasant state of shock as the consumption of food and beverage slowly resumed. After lunch, we took a short walk and chatted. When we eventually said our good-byes, I shook my head in gratitude that these two young men were in my life, hopefully to stay. But that would depend on Lauren's answer.

Finally, November 3, 2018, arrived, one year from that unforgettable evening. Lauren had traveled up to visit me, fully aware of a one-year anniversary dinner planned that night with Tim, Alice, Rob and Susan.

Earlier that afternoon, we went for a walk in Carmel Valley and took a seat on a wooden bench. The warm sunshine lit up Lauren's hair against her sleeveless black top. I took a deep breath and jumped. "Do you remember," I said, "when you told me you wouldn't even consider getting married unless you knew the person for a year?" She nodded. "Well, it's been one year—so, would you consider getting married? Will you marry me?"

Her curious expression turned into a look of shock. "Yes!" she said as her eyes and entire face twinkled with joy. I presented her the necklace. She opened the box, and I explained the meaning. "It's beautiful!" she said as she hugged me.

My heart jumped for joy as a wave of elation lifted me off the ground. We hugged, kissed, and couldn't stop smiling and laughing.

Later that night, we broke the news to the group. "We have some news," I said as we stood around the whirling margarita blender in the kitchen.

"You're pregnant!" someone joked.

"No, but we're engaged!"

Shouts and screams of joy erupted as we all jumped and danced around the room.

"Any transition serious enough to alter
your definition of self will require not just small
adjustments in your way of living and thinking
but a full-on metamorphosis."

—Martha N. Beck

CHAPTER 35

TRANSITIONS

Two weeks after our engagement, in mid-November 2018, Lauren and I pulled into the driveway of a single-story house in Tustin. It was a sober-living house, a group home where recovering addicts live in transition from a closely monitored rehab program to the real world. It looked the same as any other house on the block—clean, landscaped, and modern. We were there to pick up Stephen for a dinner outing with my brother and his family.

From the time of his release from jail in October, Stephen entered a drug-rehab program based in Santa Ana, a few miles away, and had successfully transitioned to the second stage.

We parked in the wide driveway, walked up to the front door and rang the doorbell. A tall, middle-aged man answered the door, introduced himself as the house manager and welcomed us inside. I had prearranged the pickup, so he knew we were coming.

"Steve!" he yelled toward the back of the house. "Your dad's here!" Then he turned to me and said, "For your outing tonight, obviously no drugs or alcohol. And have him back at a reasonable hour."

"No problem."

A minute later, Stephen entered the room. His thick, full-framed upper body filled out the XXL T-shirt, with tattoos visible on his elbows and lower biceps. His dark-brown hair, which receded two inches above his forehead, looked clean and trimmed. No ponytail. His face was clean-shaven except for a trimmed, black goatee on his chin and lower lip, and his brown eyes looked clear.

"Hey, Steve!" I said smiling.

"Hey, Dad."

We gave each other a quick hug, and then he turned to hug Lauren. "Hey, Lauren," he said. "This is much better than the first time we met."

Lauren smiled and said, "It sure is. So good to see you, Steve!"

As we walked out to the car, Stephen looked at both of us and said, "Hey, congratulations on your engagement." We both thanked him as we piled into the car.

On the drive, the conversation flowed easily between all three of us. Stephen spoke with energy in his voice, along with some enthusiasm and hope.

"So, how's it going, Steve?" I asked.

"Good," he said. "It's much better here, and the house manager is cool. The guys who live here are mostly younger than me, but they're OK—some get on my nerves. We all have jobs. I'm a security guard for an apartment complex. It's all right. We come back to the house for dinner and meetings. We each have our own room. If I do well, I could become a house manager at some point."

"Wow," I said, "that's great, Steve." I looked at Stephen in the back seat through my rearview mirror. His stoic face looked straight ahead, but I caught a glimpse of hope on his face.

"Steve," I said, "do you realize this is only a few blocks away from Grandma's house where I grew up?"

"That's crazy," he said.

Later that night, Lauren and I dropped off Stephen at the house and hugged him good-bye. The family dinner had gone perfectly. Everyone expressed a warm and welcoming acceptance of Stephen. He had a loving family, no doubt. He was clean and had been for well over a month. He had a job. And a vision for the future. As we drove away, Lauren and I both looked at each other with hope in our eyes.

Several weeks later, as I drove south on Highway 101 to Lauren's house, my phone rang. "Hello, Mr. McGuire?" the voice said.

"Yes," I said. I recognized the voice as the recovery center administrator I worked with to get Stephen into the program.

"I'm sorry to tell you this, but Stephen left the house yesterday and hasn't returned. We've tried but haven't been able to get in touch with him. I'm afraid he's back on the streets and can only assume he's back in his addiction. I'm really sorry to have to tell you this. We'll let you know if we hear from him or if he returns."

I didn't know what to say, but nausea immediately filled my stomach. That familiar heavy sadness arrived as my body sagged into the seat. I did the only thing I could: I focused on the road in front of me and breathed in cycles of the Serenity Prayer along with recovery principles. And continued to drive south to Lauren's house.

I am powerless over the addict. Detach with love. Release him to his higher power.

It didn't take long for Lauren and me to come up with a wedding date: Saturday, November 2, 2019. We were in no hurry and needed a long runway to allow time for the myriad of things that had to happen first—mainly my retirement and move south.

Mentally and emotionally, I was ready. The once-overwhelming prospect of transplanting my entire life was now an unfolding reality too good to be true—beyond my wildest dreams. How could this be happening? A long row of hurdles sat on the track in front of me, but every single one looked doable.

Lauren and I continued our nightly calls and biweekly visits, but they took on a whole new meaning. We talked about our future together. Our plans. Our hopes. Our dreams. I created a vision board that I kept in focus every day.

Before I drove to Lauren's house for the Christmas holiday, I moved a bunch of clothes from my closet to be put into the new closet we had cleared out for me.

When I saw Sean and Brendan on Christmas day, we gave each other big hugs. Lauren's friends greeted me with warm hugs and congratulations. Even some neighbors found out and came over to congratulate us. I put my handyman skills to work and started to fix things around Lauren's house, like broken light fixtures, loose door hinges, and anything computer or tech related.

When I returned to Seaside, I went to work on my transition plans: to leave my job at the county, my volunteer work at GriefShare and Breakthrough, my friends, and my house. I now looked at everything around me in a nostalgic light—the people, the landscapes, the roads, the restaurants, the neighborhoods, the parks, the coastline—and reflected on the past thirty-three years of life in the area. Sometimes sadness arrived. Sometimes tranquility. Sometimes anxiety. But gratitude remained at the core. I couldn't believe I had been given the opportunity to start a new life with a loving companion in a loving family.

One by one, I donated every item in the house: couches, chairs, tables, cabinets, lamps, bookshelves, end tables, nightstands, dressers, mirrors, plates, cups, silverware, serving dishes, pots, pans, and on, and on, and on. With every item I reminded myself: *Someone needs this. Someone can use this. Someone will benefit. Everything will get a new life.*

Many items required special handling, like Annie's acoustic guitar and upright piano. Her dear friend and fellow musician Cindy burst into tears when I offered her Annie's guitar, telling me she would treasure it forever. When I offered the piano to a music teacher who taught children piano lessons in her home, she looked at me in disbelief and wanted to know Annie's story. I emphasized how much Annie's piano teacher meant to her growing up, and how those music lessons became therapy sessions that shaped her life. She would love nothing more than to give it a chance to make a difference in other young lives.

As the house emptied out—item by item, room by room—rather than depression and sadness, a new and positive energy surged inside me. Clear the runway. Make space for the new. Prepare for a whole new life!

I used one room in the house to stack up boxes and the things I planned to take with me, about 10 percent of the total. It was a strange feeling to look at the entirety of my life's physical belongings on the floor in front of me.

In early February 2019 I submitted my retirement notice and picked Thursday, April 18, as my last day at work. I set a countdown retirement calculator in front of me on my desk.

I found an outdoor wedding venue at a Carmel Valley winery, among the vineyards, which Lauren loved at first sight. Then I connected with an Episcopal priest, Pastor Linda from the Church of the Good Shepherd, who had no restriction on an indoor versus outdoor ceremony. After our meeting, I let go of the idea of a Catholic priest's involvement and felt complete peace. Linda was a perfect fit for Lauren and me, and rejoiced at the message of joy, new life, and celebration.

Throughout March and early April, I met with various friends to say farewell. Everyone wished me well. My fellow employees threw a farewell barbecue luncheon for me on April 17. The next day, I turned in my work badge and keys, said my final good-byes, and drove away from work for the last time.

On my final evening in the house, I walked from empty room to empty room. The silence that once tortured me no longer held any power. A quiet peace filled the house. Every wall was blank. Every closet empty. I opened and closed every cabinet door and slid open every drawer—all empty. I opened the sliding glass door and stepped outside onto the back patio area. Everything was gone—the BBQ, the table, the chairs, and the windchimes. I walked down the side of the house and into the garage—all empty.

The endless checklist was completely done. Every single arrangement had been made. I ate some leftover lasagna from a farewell dinner at a friend's house the night before. I made my final long-distance call to Lauren and plopped onto an inflatable mattress at 10:30 p.m. A fully packed ten-foot U-Haul truck waited for me in the driveway.

At 5:30 a.m. on Friday, April 19, 2019, I walked out my front door for the last time. A bright full moon in a dark sky looked straight at me, surrounded by a thin layer of clouds that glowed with colors of diffused blue, purple, and white light. It was the darkness before the dawn of Good Friday and the first day of Passover.

I climbed into the truck's driver seat, started the engine, released the parking brake, and put it in Drive. As I headed out the driveway with every physical possession I owned, the enormity of it all came into focus. This wasn't a road trip or a quest. I wasn't coming back. This was a one-way journey, a permanent passage to a new home and a new life.

As the truck rumbled down the road, I expected an outflow of emotion, but a sense of tranquility and reflection entered in instead. Over the next hour, I watched the mystical process of transition unfold out the front windshield: The predawn darkness slowly transformed into the soft glow of a new day, followed by the emphatic brilliance of a clear sunrise. A new day had arrived.

The drive on Highway 101 South surrounded me with the calming elements of nature—green rows of manicured agricultural fields, endless rolling hills of new-growth vineyards, open green fields, and gentle hills—until I hit the multilane chaos of weaving sports cars and SUVs on the outskirts of Los Angeles. Thankfully familiar with southern California freeways, I shifted into LA mode and drove through the madness until I arrived at my new home in the early afternoon. By the time Lauren arrived home from work around 4:30, the truck had been unloaded and returned, and I was busy getting settled. Our new life together had begun.

Less than three weeks later, I couldn't believe my eyes. I sat across the table, face-to-face with Stephen. Not in a jail or a rehab center, but at a Rock & Brews restaurant in Buena Park. We arranged it over a couple phone calls, and it happened. Lauren and I talked about the rare opportunity for some one-on-one time, so I went solo.

When he walked up to me at the gas station in Anaheim where he asked me to pick him up, I gasped at the sight: He stood tall and looked healthy. His face was clean-shaven except for his black goatee on his chin and lower lip. His eyes looked clear and vibrant. He wore a clean, black-and-white zipped jacket over a black T-shirt and a black San Francisco Giants baseball cap, on backwards as was his custom. A positive and strong energy vibrated out from him.

He had a companion with him—a woman named Lola who appeared to be a few years older. After an introduction, they both got in the car, with Stephen in the front seat. As we drove to the restaurant, I learned they lived together in an apartment in Anaheim, and they both had jobs and seemed to be making it work. He even had a car. With insurance. A near miracle.

On the twenty-minute drive, Stephen's fun, quick-witted personality was on full display. Funny comments and quips flowed out of him like his old self. "Hey Dad," he said. "Check out the place on the left, Medieval Times. They have this whole thing with horses and jousting and shit, and you have dinner and get crazy. We should do that someday!"

Once we got to the restaurant, we sat in an open, noisy dining area filled with people and picnic-bench style tables. Loud rock music filled the room and TV sets mounted high on every wall were tuned to NBA playoff games.

"Hey, Dad," Stephen said, "I'm buying you dinner tonight. No arguments."

"OK, Steve, thanks. I won't argue!"

I sat in pleasant shock throughout the whole evening. He ordered orange soda with his dinner, not beer or alcohol. We talked, joked, and laughed back and forth about the NBA games and anything that came to mind. We posed for a few silly-faced photos. I tried to pretend this was our normal relationship, even though I knew it wasn't. But I got to see the real Stephen—the person trapped inside the addict—and savored every second of it.

At the end of the night, I drove them back to their apartment building. When they got out, Stephen said, "Thanks for coming, Dad. Oh, and I got something for you and Lauren." He handed me a greeting card envelope, something he rarely ever did, even for Annie. Then he handed me a small package, another rarity. "The card is for you, and the package is for Lauren."

"Wow, thank you, Steve. Hope to see you again soon."

"Me too," he said.

When I got home, I opened the card, which had a trophy image on the front cover. Inside, the printing read: "BADASSNESS UN-MATCHED! Congratulations on reaching a whole new level of amazing." Underneath, in his handwriting, I read: "I'm very happy for you that you made it to official retirement! You work harder than anyone I know and you deserve to do whatever you please from here on out! You really are my hero Dad and I hope you know that. I admire everything about you and I'm very blessed and grateful that you are my Dad. Love you man. Steve."

I stood with Lauren in the kitchen as tears filled my eyes. I handed her the small package, which she opened to reveal an ornate, pink high-heel shoe with Tinkerbell perched on top, a Disneyland memento.

I fell asleep that night overcome with shock and gratitude. Did that really just happen? Was it possible he's heading in the right direction? All I could do was whisper a huge "Thank you!" and hope for the best.

When his thirty-fourth birthday came three months later in August, I couldn't wait to take him out to dinner again, this time with Lauren. He asked us to pick him up after work in the parking lot of the security guard company's main office. We arrived at 5:30 p.m., eager with anticipation. We had a dinner reservation at a nearby Benihana Japanese steakhouse, one of Stephen's favorites, where the food is prepared in dramatic fashion on a large steel grill surrounded by a wraparound tabletop that seats eight to ten people. We had birthday present and a card ready, which Lauren had carefully prepared with her expert wrapping skills. But above everything, I relished the thought of some quality time with Stephen and Lauren.

"If this goes well," I said, "wouldn't it be great to arrange a time for Brendan, Sean, and Stephen to meet each other?"

"Absolutely," Lauren said. "I know the boys want to meet him, and think of how great for Stephen to form a connection with his new family."

From across the parking lot, I saw Stephen and waved him over to the car. He wore a black hooded sweatshirt, blue jeans, and black tennis shoes, and walked in a semislouched posture. I stepped out of the car to give him a hug and instantly noticed a ragged look and down energy about him. He barely hugged me back and felt thick, heavy, and hot. His dulled eyes avoided mine. He climbed into the backseat and sat still.

"Hi, Steve!" Lauren said as she turned to face him with a warm smile.

"Hey, Lauren," he said with his eyes cast down.

"How are you doing?" she asked.

"Good."

Conversation sputtered and stopped as we drove to the restaurant. Lauren tried to get a conversation started, but every attempt fell flat. I tried and got the same. Heaviness and confusion filled the car. Awkward silence lingered longer than spoken words. I wanted to reach for the noise of the radio but didn't. More silence. More confusion. More awkwardness. I couldn't see Stephen through the mirror because he sat right behind me, but I could feel the heaviness. The cloud. The darkness. I didn't need to look at Lauren to know she felt as awkward as me, probably worse. No one knew what to say. Tension hung in the air like a fourth passenger.

To break the silence, I started to narrate our way to the restaurant. "It looks like we have two and a half miles to go. Our next turn is a left a half-mile ahead. This area looks familiar. I think the airport is located that way. Have you been to this place before, Lauren?"

It was a pattern I knew well. Since his teenage years, Stephen could shift into his own shutdown mode and close up tight as a clamshell. No one could get in, no matter what. All I could do was endure it, try to make up my own conversation, and get through it.

When we arrived at the restaurant, I checked in with the hostess, who told us our table would be ready in fifteen minutes. We took a seat at a small round table in the bar-lounge area and ordered some specialty soft drinks. Thankfully, Stephen ordered a Japanese soda that doubled as a conversation piece, and I got as much mileage from it as I could.

Despite the cool, air-conditioned room, I noticed sweat covered Stephen's forehead, another familiar sign of his drug use. He was in another world, unreachable. I looked at Lauren who graciously rolled with it as if nothing were wrong. But everything was wrong.

When we got seated at our table, Stephen sat on the far-right side, closest to the chef. Lauren sat next to Stephen, then me, then an empty seat, and then a young family of four—a man, a woman, and two children under the age of seven.

Normally, a community-style meal at Benihana elicits friendly and fun conversation, even among total strangers. Lauren and I smiled and nodded hello at the young family. They smiled and nodded back, and then looked over at Stephen. The look in their eyes said everything. The contrast was so stark I wondered if they thought we had picked up a homeless person. They didn't say a word, looked away, and just kept to themselves.

I knew that look. It came over my face hundreds of times before. How do you respond to someone trapped in a black hole that sucks out all life and energy? It pulls and repulses at the same time, leaving the observer in a state of confusion where all they can do is turn away. The chef ignored Stephen and focused his attention on the two of us and the young family.

A wave of embarrassment and shame surged up from my queasy stomach into my flushed face. The noisy sounds of the restaurant softened, like I had earplugs. The smell of food directly in front of me faded like my nose was plugged. This was my son, my addict son, who can't even look at me or have a simple conversation. Who can't even give Lauren, the dearest and most important person in my life, the re-spect of common human courtesy despite her continued attempts at conversation.

I wanted us to hide or disappear but instead carried on a conversa-tion with Lauren and the chef, pretending everything was OK. I wanted to engage the young family in conversation but didn't dare, so I pretend-ed to ignore them.

The moment Stephen finished his dinner, he mumbled something about going outside for a smoke. I nodded acknowledgment, and he got up and left the table. As soon as he left, the elephant released its foot from my chest, and I could breathe, hear, and taste again. I looked over at Lauren, who had a look of bewilderment on her face. I just shook my head and whispered, "I don't know. I'm sorry. He's obviously using again."

The drive back to his apartment was equally silent and awkward. I couldn't wait for it to end. When I parked the car, Lauren reached back and handed Stephen a decorative gift bag with his birthday gifts. "We got you a few things for your birthday," she said.

"Thanks," he said.

He rifled through the paper into the presents—a beach towel, a T-shirt, and some gift cards. "We thought you could use the towel for a picnic at the beach or a park," Lauren said with a smile. "And who can't use gift cards?"

"Thanks," he said again. "And thanks for the dinner."

"You're welcome, Steve," I said.

"See you later," he said, and stepped out of the car, leaving all the wrapping behind in the back seat.

I got out and gave him an awkward hug. "See you, Steve," I said. "Love you, dude."

"Yeah," he said, "love you, Dad."

I climbed back inside the car, and we both watched as he walked away and disappeared in the darkness.

"Let there be spaces in your togetherness,
And let the winds of the heavens dance between you.
Love one another, but make not a bond of love:
Let it rather be a moving sea between the shores of your souls.
Fill each other's cup but drink not from one cup.
Give one another of your bread but eat not from the same loaf.
Sing and dance together and be joyous,
but let each one of you be alone,
Even as the strings of a lute are alone
though they quiver with the same music.
Give your hearts, but not into each other's keeping.
For only the hand of Life can contain your hearts.
And stand together yet not too near together:
For the pillars of the temple stand apart,
And the oak tree and the cypress
grow not in each other's shadow."

—Kahlil Gibran

CHAPTER 36

———◆———

NEW LIFE

Novewber 2, 2019.

I stood on top of the world, in between two oak wine barrels on thick green grass next to Pastor Linda, surrounded on three sides by lush green-yellow vineyards. The midafternoon sunshine drenched everything in warm yellow light out of a clear blue sky. Seated in rows in front of me sat about thirty family members from both sides of our families.

The song "Can't Help Falling in Love," sung by Haley Reinhart, started to play in the background, and I watched as Lauren slowly emerged from the vineyard walkway in her white wedding gown. Her beautiful face and blond hair glowed. She carried a bouquet of white- and maroon-colored roses in front of her. Sean and Brendan, dressed in classic men's suits, escorted her, arm in arm, one on either side.

Everyone's eyes locked on her as the three of them made the final approach up the center aisle. Lauren's eyes smiled at mine as she drew near until we were face to face. Brendan and Sean released her to me, and we turned to face Pastor Linda.

Twenty minutes later, everyone stood and cheered as we were announced husband and wife. A group of thirty friends joined the festivities shortly thereafter for a reception, dinner, dancing, and joy-filled celebration into the late-night hours. Not only was everyone there to celebrate us, but to honor the chance to love again and start a new life from the ashes. All through the day, I lifted my head in gratitude that any of it came to be.

Except for one thing: Stephen's absence. Months earlier, we had sent him an invitation along with everyone else, but never heard back. With no reliable means of contact, I let it go. If he couldn't respond, chances were that he was active in his addiction, and I couldn't allow the addict to attend—and probably ruin—our most special day.

But it still gnawed at me, and I dreaded our inevitable conversation. When he called me in early December and I told him we got married the previous month, he slammed the door in my face. Everything I said fell on angry and deaf ears. I was shut out. Only silence and stalemate remained. The call ended with a thud.

By the time the Covid-19 pandemic arrived in full bloom in March 2020, my mind raced with worrisome thoughts of Stephen. Would he become another statistic of the respiratory virus that killed its victims or left them attached to hospital respirators clinging to life?

Then my phone rang from an unknown number. I answered and heard Stephen's normal voice. He didn't mention the wedding but must have come to some form of forgiveness or resolution. He wanted to get together, but I told him that Lauren and I couldn't risk any exposure to the virus. We chose to comply with the state and county lockdown restrictions—stay home if possible—which kept us confined to our house. He didn't like it but respected my position. But we finally talked. Somehow, mercifully, the ice had broken.

Spring turned to summer. Summer turned to fall. Sporadic phone calls were the only contact I had with Stephen, usually from a different cell phone number. I wanted to rebuild a relationship with him but couldn't. Each time I heard from him, at least I knew he was alive. In between, to combat worry, sadness, frustration, and anxiety, I connected via an online video conferencing platform to a Saturday morning Nar-Anon meeting, which never failed to keep me grounded and centered. Every week I left the meeting with a dose of serenity, thanks to the experience, strength, and hope of other parents of addicts.

Lauren and I settled into our new life together, unexpectedly aided by the Covid-19 lockdowns. We quarantined in our home and adapted to the recommended practices of disinfecting everything, wearing facemasks, using hand sanitizer every five minutes, going to early morning senior hour at the grocery store where no one looked at or talked to anyone else, and staying connected to family and friends with video calls. But everything, no matter how crazy, just brought us closer together.

As our one-year anniversary approached and the pandemic restrictions loosened, we jumped at an opportunity to host a small family gathering with Sean, Brendan, and their wives, Monique and Sarah. Fall was in the air. Lauren decorated the house in a classic Halloween theme. Tree colors had shifted from green into yellow, red, and orange. The sun sat lower in the sky each day as the air grew colder. Pumpkins, scarecrows, and Halloween decorations accented front lawns throughout the neighborhood, along with an occasional whiff of smoke from a fireplace.

The six of us hadn't been together for months, so the family gathering took on an extra level of fun and grateful enthusiasm. The sounds of old-school '70s R&B music played as we all mingled and talked. Lauren and I were busy in the kitchen when Sarah walked in to join us. The others were outside on the back patio carving pumpkins. I noticed Sarah's Harry Potter T-shirt. "Hey, Sarah, that's a cool T-shirt with all the Harry Potter magic stuff."

"Thanks, and did you also notice what's at the bottom?"

"No," I said as I scanned images of a broomstick, a wand, a wizard hat, and the words "Magic in Progress."

"The little feet," Sarah said. At the words "little feet," Lauren stopped what she was doing and turned to look at Sarah. "The little baby feet," Sarah said, "right here. I'm pregnant!"

Lauren gasped out loud. "What?! You're pregnant?"

"Yes!" Sarah said with a huge smile on her face. Lauren half-screamed and half-cried as she ran to hug Sarah.

"Do you know if it's a boy or a girl?" Lauren said as she stood back.

"It's a girl!" Sarah said. Lauren's overjoyed screams filled the house, which brought everyone running into the kitchen. "Sarah and Brendan are pregnant!" Lauren said with tears in her eyes. Hugs, laughs, and congratulations filled our joy-bursting home.

Over the next few months, a smooth pregnancy turned into a difficult one, and then a scary one. Sarah was admitted to the hospital for continuous monitoring of a dangerous condition called preeclampsia. Brendan stayed by her side after the hospital granted them a rare exception to the "no contact" Covid restrictions. Day after day, hopes and prayers went out for mother and baby. *Would Sarah make it? Would the baby make it? Would they be OK?*

25 weeks. 26 weeks. 27 weeks. 28 weeks. 29 weeks. Every Friday became a day of minicelebration after another week had passed.

30 weeks. She would make it now.

31 weeks. 32 weeks. 34 weeks. 35 weeks.

Then, at the 36-week mark, in April 2021, little Fiona made her entrance into the world. Four weeks early, but perfect in every way. A brand-new life had arrived safe and sound. Tears of joy, gratitude, and thanksgiving abounded for the family's miracle baby.

Along with Fiona's arrival, life slowly evolved into a new normal amid the up-and-down Covid restrictions. The new parents couldn't take their adoring eyes off her. The new grandparents on both sides celebrated and made plans to visit and support the young family. We couldn't wait to see her. Eventually, we did.

When Lauren held tiny Fiona in her arms for the first time, tears of unsurpassed joy poured out. "My baby's baby," she sobbed through tears as Brendan sat next to them on the couch.

As Fiona grew day by day, life rolled on.

Then, on a warm Saturday afternoon in early August 2021, my phone rang. Lauren and I were driving along the LA freeway to a friend's wedding. I answered.

"Hey, Dad, it's me," Stephen said.

"Hi, Steve!" I said. "Lauren and I are in the car on our way to a wedding."

"Hi, Steve," Lauren said.

"Hey, Lauren, how's it going?"

"Great, Steve!" Lauren said. "We have a granddaughter, Fiona. Brendan and Sarah are the proud parents."

"That's awesome. Hey, Dad, sorry I missed your call on my birthday."

"No problem, Steve," I said. "But happy thirty-sixth birthday! Wow—thirty-six years old!"

"Yeah, thanks, Dad. Things are going good. I bought myself a new PlayStation for my birthday. It's awesome. I can play the new games and the old classics."

"That's great, Steve," I said. "What was the one you always kicked my butt on? Well, all of them, but which one had the jet skis on a water racetrack?"

"*Jet Moto!* I still love that game! And get this, Lola and I have opened a tattoo parlor. She does the actual tattoo work, and I help with getting the word out. She's still learning, but she's pretty good."

"I guess I won't be coming to your place for my first tattoo, then," I said.

"Yeah, probably not. But I can take photos of awesome tattoos from magazines and tell people she did them."

"Careful, Steve," I said laughing, "you don't want to piss off some six-foot-eight Harley Davidson dude."

Stephen chuckled and then started a whole new thread of conversation about sports. I glanced over at Lauren with a look of amazement on my face. He rattled off player's names, which colleges they went to, and how teams were doing. He sounded like the old Stephen. We talked back and forth—back and forth in the most natural way.

A surge of joy lifted me out of my seat. Stephen was happy. He had a companion. He had involvement in a new business endeavor. He had his sense of humor, his intelligence, his uniqueness—all still intact. And he had reopened to me. Maybe we really could start over again.

After twenty minutes or so, we said our good-byes. "Well, Steve, enjoy the PlayStation," I said, "and good luck on the new tattoo business. Keep me posted on how it's going."

"OK, Dad. Have fun at the wedding. I hope to meet Fiona someday."

"Me too," I said. "Love you, Steve."

"Love you, Dad."

For the rest of the weekend, I kept saying to Lauren: "That was the best phone call I can remember with him in forever. He sounded so good. So happy. So much like the real Stephen! I can't believe it. I can't believe it."

I couldn't stop smiling.

And hoping.

"For everything there is a season,
and a time for every matter under heaven:
a time to be born, and a time to die."

—ECCLESIASTES 3:1–2

CHAPTER 37

THE CIRCLE

One week later I sat at home on Saturday morning about to attend the 11:00 a.m. Nar-Anon virtual meeting when the front door-bell rang. I opened the door and saw two middle-aged men dressed in business attire.

"Hello," one of them said, "are you Robert McGuire?"

"Yes."

"Are you the father of Stephen McGuire?"

"Yes."

My head started to spin. A few hours earlier, after I woke up and checked my phone, I had two frantic voice mails from Lola saying that Stephen had been in an accident and had been checked into the UC Irvine Trauma Center. I called her back immediately—no answer. I called Stephen's phone number from last Saturday's call—no answer. I called the UCI Trauma Center and they couldn't find any record of Stephen. My mind and heart raced, but I had seen him endure so many close calls before, I assumed they released him.

Since his teenage years, Stephen had been in multiple car accidents and hospitals, and always made it through. He had nine lives. Not only car accidents, but he survived homelessness, infections from needles, one in his neck, near overdoses and multiple stints in jail. He survived physical fights, one in which he was ambushed by a group of fellow high school classmates over a drug incident gone bad. On a freezing cold winter night in Pennsylvania, he crashed a car into a telephone pole on a deserted rural road and somehow survived. He was the ultimate survivor. Indestructible.

"I'm Detective Smith from the Anaheim Police Department," he said, "and this is Detective Jones. Are you aware your son was in an accident early this morning?"

"Yes, I got voice mails from his girlfriend, but when I called the trauma center, they had no information on him, so I assumed he had been released."

"No," he said. "That's not the case. I'm sorry, but your son didn't make it. He's deceased. He died this morning at 1:15. I'm sorry."

My body folded in half. I couldn't feel the ground. I couldn't breathe and started to choke. I couldn't think. I couldn't talk. Tears flooded my eyes. My insides fell away. I stumbled over to a short brick wall on our front lawn and sat down for support. I held my head in my unsteady hands and tried to breathe. *He always survived. He always made it. Always. He can't be gone. He can't be. Impossible. How could he be gone? How? How?*

The sudden void sucked the life out of me like a vacuum. A void where there was a life—a vibrant life only a week ago. A void that always lurked in the background, but I never expected to feel.

The detective started to explain the details. "I'm sorry," I said, "I have to go inside...to tell my wife."

Lauren took one look at me and grabbed me in her arms, sobbing with me. I sputtered out some words. Weak and empty, I sat down on a living room chair. The detectives took a seat across from us on the couch.

For the next twenty minutes they explained how Stephen was killed, run over by a pickup truck in a parking lot. Targeted. Driven by someone Stephen knew. Over a money dispute.

None of the details mattered. Stephen was gone. How?

Gone. Impossible.

At 1:00 p.m. on a Thursday in early November 2021, I stood with Lauren underneath a red-tiled gazebo in front of an outdoor cremation niche wall. A handful of family and friends, along with the cemetery director, stood with us. No priest. No formal service.

But God was present. And like he always does, Jesus walked alongside. I had no doubt that he guided Stephen home in his final moments, like he did for Annie. It didn't matter that Stephen didn't attend church or follow a prescribed religious path. Stephen is as much a child of God as anyone else. He's loved by God as much as anyone else. It didn't matter that Stephen struggled with addiction his entire adult life. God never abandoned him, no matter how dark or troubled his path. God's light glowed inside Stephen and always had. And God's love, which transcends all, remains inside Stephen and holds him with an everlasting embrace.

The early afternoon sunlight warmed the back of our necks, and white noise from a nearby water fountain could be heard in the background. No one spoke.

The twelve-inch-square, brown-speckled granite niche front had been removed and set on a table draped with an emerald-green cloth on my right side. The top line of large black-engraved letters read "Mc-Guire," the second line read "Annie," and the third "Woman of Faith." Underneath an engraved crucifix were the dates "1956–2016." Underneath that read "Stephen," then "Rest in Peace" followed by "1985–2021."

Surrounding the niche cover sat multiple photos of Stephen as a child: One fast asleep in his crib surrounded by stuffed animals when he was about one year old. One of him dressed in a yellow bedtime onesie, wrapped in Annie's arms as she sat in front of the fireplace, with me alongside her. One at five years old with a glowing smile and sparkling eyes in the late afternoon sunlight in the backyard. One in a posed photograph with me when he was eight years old—I'm lying on my stomach, propped up by my elbows holding an NFL football in my hands. Stephen has me in a headlock-hug, grinning from ear to ear.

Next to the photos sat a Little League baseball inside a plastic cube box, one of his home-run balls. The local league had a tradition in which any kid who hits a homer gets to keep the ball. In between the red stitches, the worn leather cover had the date and the final score of the game written in faded black ink. Eventually he had so many that they were stacked up in pyramid formation on top of his chest of drawers. Those Little League days were among his happiest and our best times as a family.

I remember the first time he hit a home run over the fence at a Little League field. Before the season started, the two of us went over to a nearby field on a Saturday morning with a small bucket of baseballs and Stephen's black aluminum bat to work on his swing. The ting-ting-ting of his bat sounded as he hit line drives, some grounders, and some fly balls. But then he dialed it in and clobbered one of my pitches. At that moment, an older kid Stephen knew rode by on his bike, saw the deep fly ball clear the left-field fence, and shouted: "Hey, that's a home run!" Stephen instantly grew a foot taller inside the batter's box.

When the small service began, I passed the photos one by one down the line and talked about Stephen as a little boy. He glowed with life, light, and happiness. He had an infectious laugh and a clever sense of humor. He loved getting cozy on the couch and watching movies with Mom and Dad before we stopped being cool. He loved life in every single way.

And now, like that little boy, he's free. Free from pain. Free from addiction. Free from struggle. In total peace. And together with his loving mom. I hold onto that boyhood image of Stephen for dear life, which keeps me from sinking into despair. Addiction took so many things away from us as a family, but nothing more precious than Stephen's essence, his beautiful soul, which I grieved over for so many years.

But like an ember buried deep under a pile of ashes, his loving soul still glowed, as I discovered when I uncovered a letter he wrote to his mother, sent from jail mere weeks before she died. His words tell of his admiration of her strength and determination, his yearning for the happy family we once were, his regret over the pain he caused, and the shame he felt as an addict. Stephen ended the letter by referring to a book that Annie used to read to him as a little boy, entitled "Love You Forever" by Robert Munsch. "The book showed the mother taking care of her boy until he was a man," Stephen wrote, "and then her son taking care of her. I wish I could do more for you Mom. I do pray for you every day, and I do love you forever."

On the one-year anniversary of his death, I sat overlooking the ocean shore in the early morning hours. The gray sky blended with the blue-gray water as sea gulls floated among the soft sounds of the surf that rumbled ashore. A few surfers waited on their boards for the right wave to come along. A lone walker tossed a tennis ball that his dog eagerly fetched along the wet sand and white foam.

Several minutes later, just beyond the surf line, I spotted a small pod of dolphins with their telltale dorsal fins that gracefully appeared and disappeared along the surface of the water. Suddenly one dolphin jumped completely out of the water, as if relaying a message from Stephen: "Hi, Dad! I'm OK. I'm happy. And I'm not alone."

On a warm and sunny spring day with Lauren, I held one-year-old Fiona in my right arm against my chest as the three of us meandered through the front yard. The sunshine lit up Fiona's softly curled light-brown hair, blue eyes, and long black eyelashes. She examined every flower, every bud, and every leaf like the wondrous miracles they are. I thought back to the nature discovery walks I had with Stephen at that age.

I looked at Fiona, who beamed back a smile that told me, "It's OK, Grandpa Bob. Everything's OK."

I smiled at Fiona, then looked at Lauren.

"It certainly is, Fiona. It certainly is."

Notes from the Author

The personal journeys I have recounted in this book have been a labor of love over the past five-plus years. The decision to publish is a scary proposition for a private person like me, but it will be worth it if the message of hope and new life through loss comes through on these pages, if only slightly.

I used the words "surviving the grief cave" in the title because they convey what it felt like for me to go through the process of grief, which I describe in Part I. Not only did I survive, I learned many things inside the cave and emerged a much stronger person. My sincere hope is that others, especially men in grief, draw strength from what I went through. It's often a lonely road that we as men travel, but it doesn't have to be.

Part II covers much of what I learned and experienced on the Camino, but the reality is I didn't want to go. I got pushed out of my old life, like a fledgling getting pushed out of a nest. The shove came from a deep fear that if I didn't budge from my existing life pattern, I would shrivel up and die a slow death, one year at a time. So, as painful and uncomfortable as it was, I made the decision to jump into the unknown, one of the best decisions of my life.

Part III recounts the period that began when Lauren entered my life, which has continued to unfold in ways I never could have imagined. The year 2024 marked our fifth year of marriage, and I consider myself blessed beyond belief. Did the blessings and joy I have experienced occur because of everything I went through? Or because of the loving and caring people in my life? Or because of the personal growth I experienced on the Camino, in the Breakthrough program, and along the way? Or because of divine timing, luck, fate, or destiny? Yes.

But life also demands that two opposing realities be held at the same time. On the one hand, love, joy, and new life. On the other, pain, loss, and suffering. Yet love and life prevail.

I mention in this book a nonprofit foundation that has yet to be established but hopefully will be someday. It would be in Annie's and Stephen's names and would go toward the work of addiction recovery support services. Whether funding educational scholarships or existing services, or a combination of the two, it would exist to make a positive difference in the lives of those struggling with addiction.

Regarding the young man who killed Stephen, he was arrested, pleaded guilty in court, and is serving a prison sentence.

If there's one final message I could pass on to those who have lost a loved one and are trying to find their way forward, it would be this: It's OK to seek a new life. It's OK to find a new way forward. This honors your loved one more than anything. I believe they would want us to live our lives with as much love and happiness as possible.

For additional information and resources, please visit my website at https://survivingthegriefcave.com.

RESOURCES

Below is a list of resources in the order I experienced them:

+ **NarAnon** – A 12-Step Program for Family and Friends of Drug Addicts **www.nar-anon.org**

NarAnon provided me with the tools and support I needed to navigate the alternate world of drug addiction, where up is down, right is left, and what seems like the most commonsense thing to do can be the worst thing.

My experience with NarAnon, one of many 12-Step recovery programs that have their roots in AA (Alcoholics Anonymous, founded in 1935), was a life changer. I am forever grateful for everything I learned and the loving souls with whom I shared this treasure.

+ **GriefShare** – A Christian faith-based grief recovery program. **www.griefshare.org**

GriefShare gave me the tools I needed to start making forward progress in the grief cave. The Christian faith aspect of the program resonated with me, but the practical tools I learned are what made the biggest difference.

+ **Camino Guides** – Website for Camino guidebooks and resources with an emphasis on the inner journey. **www.caminoguides.com**

The guidebook I used on the Camino, *A Pilgrim's Guide to the Camino de Santiago (Camino Francés): St. Jean Pied de Port • Santiago de Compostela* written by John Brierley, was indispensable. It simplified the entire journey into a manageable daily plan, while encouraging flexibility, discovery, and inner reflection.

The website provides multiple guidebooks based on the route chosen, and plenty of resources on how to prepare.

+ **Breakthrough for Men** – A nonprofit organization, unaffiliated with any religion, that provides workshops, seminars, and a community of personal growth and support for men. **www.breakthroughformen.org**

My involvement with Breakthrough gave me the tools and support I needed to work my way into a whole new life when I had to start completely over. The emphasis of the workshop's first half focused on my relationship with myself, and the second half on my relationship with others—both in the most loving and empowering of ways.

+ **Labyrinth Meditation Walk** – I didn't realize the value or application of a labyrinth until I entered my grief journey. I don't even remember why I started researching the topic online, but I'll never forget the first time I walked one, which happened to be located nearby. As I traversed the semi-circular, winding pattern laid out on the ground, I experienced a calming awareness that my life's journey is not linear or predictable. If I simply trust and surrender to the path in front of me it will lead me where I need to go.

ABOUT THE AUTHOR

Through his insightful writing, Bob McGuire takes the reader on his pilgrimage from intense grief into new life, love, and faith—from the physical world to the inner emotional dimension, and to the often camouflaged spiritual realm.

Born in Pennsylvania in 1956, he lived in Michigan and New York before his family moved to California in 1968. He graduated from a California university in 1980 and went on to careers in the fields of energy production and information technology.

Since childhood, he felt a connection with nature and the outdoors, so when grief invaded his life at 60 years old, he had a calling, a pull, to walk the Camino de Santiago—a pilgrimage that served as one of the vital aspects of a multifaceted healing process.

Writing had always come naturally to Bob, but only as a personal and therapeutic hobby—journaling to process his thoughts and feelings. However, the extreme pressures of his grief experience cracked open this lifelong practice into a more focused endeavor that resulted in this book. In doing so, he hopes that his own story will be helpful to those who find themselves faced with a similar struggle.

But writing something personal for others to read presented an internal conflict. At a young age he learned from his father to keep his feelings inside and to never "wear them on your sleeve." However, it was also his father who raved about a short school essay Bob wrote when he was 12 years old, in which he expressed his heartbreak at leaving his childhood home in upstate New York when the family moved cross-country to the San Francisco Bay Area. Over the years that followed, his father would bring up the essay and how it touched him.

The spiritual foundation of Bob's life led him to seek out guidance and direction within his Christian faith, which in turn brought him face-to-face with a crisis of faith when he questioned everything he believed. How could drug addiction and life-threatening illness be allowed to enter and destroy a happy family life, despite all the prayer and devotion that were supposed to protect them? How could God be so absent?

Perseverance and a sense of openness provided the compass that directed him in unexpected ways, leading to a new season of spiritual growth.

Bob's self-motivation and dedication to lifelong learning and personal development, spanning multiple facets of his life—work and career, and mental, physical, and spiritual health—equipped him with a determination to work through his grief and learn everything he could from it. Ultimately, this led to his personal growth, one of the most profound aspects of his healing process.

He and his wife live in Southern California where they enjoy family, friends, and living life, grateful for the blessing of every single day.